HANDFULS ON PURPOSE

SERIES I

BY

Pastor JAMES SMITH

Author of "A Survey of the Wondrous Cross,"
"Spiritual Patterns," etc.

WM. B. EERDMANS PUBLISHING COMPANY

Grand Rapids   Michigan

American Edition

———

Published in 1947, by

WM. B. EERDMANS PUBLISHING CO.
by
Special Arrangement with

PICKERING & INGLIS, LTD.
14 Paternoster Row, London, E.C.4
229 Bothwell St., Glasgow, C.2
Manchester—Newcastle—Liverpool—Edinburgh

PHOTOLITHOPRINTED BY CUSHING - MALLOY, INC.
ANN ARBOR, MICHIGAN, UNITED STATES OF AMERICA
1963

Guide to Series 1 to 12

PREFACE

THESE *Handfuls* have been sent out after much prayerful study of the Word in the hope that they might be helpful to some busy workers for the Master who may not have much leisure for study.

In these days when there is so much to tempt us away from the simplicity of the Truth it is needful for us to have our own minds and hearts well fortified with the deep and powerful thoughts of God. Other facts and things may interest and amuse, but we must have the "sincere milk of the Word" if we are to GROW. Everything that awakens and increases our appreciation of the Word of God is of immense value to our spiritual life, but our love for and delight in the Word will only be in proportion as we go on to *experience* its mighty power in our lives. We are convinced that the way to stir up and deepen the desires of others after Christ and the Scriptures is to present those God-given truths which meet the needs of an individual soul in all its various states and conditions. No book in all the world comes within a thousand miles of the Bible in this great and glorious mission, "PREACH THE WORD."

That there should be a growing demand from an ever-widening circle of interested workers for such plain spiritual teaching is hopeful and gratifying. "Points" and "Outlines" are but for the aid of the memory, and should be reckoned only of secondary importance.

In preparing these notes we have earnestly endeavoured to get into the heart-thoughts of the Word, so that weary workers might find food for the strengthening of their tired and hungry hearts.

We count it a great privilege and honour to be in this way a co-worker with any toiler in the Master's vineyard. If we can but help to sharpen another worker's weapons for the fight, or carry a cup of cold water to those who are bearing the burden and heat of the day, we will rejoice, and do rejoice.   JAMES SMITH

INDEX OF SUBJECTS.

INDEX OF TEXTS.

Handfuls on Purpose

SPIRITUAL PATTERNS.
NOTES ON THE TABERNACLE.

THE SETTING UP.

Exodus 25. 1-9; 30. 11-16; Hebrews 9.

IN seeking to give an exposition of the Tabernacle we do not wish to dogmatise, but humbly to follow the method of Paul as seen in his letter to the Hebrews. In referring there to the Tabernacle and the Priesthood he reveals his method of interpretation by such keynote sentences as the following: "The shadow of heavenly things" (Heb. 8. 5), "The patterns of things in the heavens" (Heb. 9. 23), "The figures of the true" (Heb. 9. 24), "A shadow of good things to come" (Heb. 10. 1). Seeing that these things were shadows, patterns, and figures of heavenly or spiritual things yet to come, I think we have sufficient warrant for taking all the spiritual teaching out of them we possibly can. The question is not, Does the Tabernacle *teach* this or that New Testament truth? but, Do you not *see* this or that spiritual truth prefigured in it?

All have not the same eye, because all have not the same light and experience. The deeper our Christian

experience is the more deeply will our eyes penetrate
into these dim shadows, and the more shall we praise the
God who showed Moses the pattern on the Mount.

Let us come to these types, then, as Simeon came to
the Temple "seeking Jesus." And unless our eyes are
holden, as were those of the disciples on the way
to Emmaus, we shall surely see Him, and our heart
shall rejoice.

I. **The Divine Request.** "Let them make Me a
sanctuary, that I may dwell among them" (Exod. 25. 8).
Who? Those who had been *redeemed* from bondage and
separated for Himself. God can *dwell* only with a separated
people. But notice that this proposal originated with
God Himself. He so loves those whom He hath saved
that He desires to dwell among them. This is but a
fresh manifestation of a long-standing purpose in the
heart of God. The great craving of the divine heart is
to get an abode with man. He dwelt with man in the
Garden, then in the Tabernacle, then in the Temple, then
in the Person of His Son, now in believers. "Know ye
not that ye are the Temple of God, and that God dwelleth
in you?" (1 Cor. 3. 16).

II. **The Pattern.** "Look that thou make them after
the pattern which was showed thee on the Mount" (Exod.
25. 40). It was because these things had a spiritual
meaning that they were to be made according to a heavenly
pattern. The plan of the Tabernacle, like the plan of
salvation, was all of God. Man's opinions and reasonings
were entirely excluded by the "Thus saith the Lord."
The whole thing was a *Revelation*. Rationalism could
add nothing to what was revealed on the Mount. The
scheme of redemption has been showed us on the Mount of
Calvary. There you and I may see Him, who is the Pattern
for our lives.

III. The Materials. Where did these pilgrims dwelling in a desert get all the rich and rare materials necessary for such a costly structure? "The Lord knew that they would need these things, so He gave them all they required before they left Egypt" (Exod. 12. 36). When the Lord's people are put into the possession of riches it is because the Lord hath need of them. They "offered willingly." Love is always liberal. If every redeemed one was offering to God what they have there would be no lack, no need of Church bazaars, or such questionable make-shifts (Acts 4. 34). Their liberality was so great that Moses had to restrain them (Exod. 36. 6). Instead of the people of God being restrained in these days, every art and dodge is being used to constrain them even to give a little.

IV. The Principal Workman. "See, I have called Bezaleel, and have filled him with the Spirit of God" (Exod. 31. 1, 2). Bezaleel means "In the shadow of God." How suggestive his character—in the shadow of God. His work—in the Spirit of God—filled with wisdom and understanding in *all manner of workmanship*, that is, all the workmanship needed to accomplish the mind and will of God. What a beautiful type of the Holy Spirit, the great Overseer, in this present dispensation during the building of the greater spiritual Temple, "an habitation of God" (Eph. 2. 22). Bezaleel, like the Holy Spirit, gave to "every man his work," and not only that, but also imparted to each workman the wisdom needed to make his work acceptable to God. Only that which we do under the guidance of God's Spirit will be pleasing unto Him, and fit for a place in the great Temple. Bezaleel alone had the right to devise (Exod. 35. 32). The Holy Spirit of God is sovereign in His work. We cannot limit the Holy One to old ruts and forms. "The wind bloweth where it listeth" (John 3. 8). The work of the Tabernacle, like

Christian work, had many different phases, but was all done for the glory of God under one guiding Spirit.

V. The Foundation. Seeing that this house was to be typical of heavenly and eternal things, we may be sure that something very special will be seen about the *foundation*.

In Exodus 30 we see that every man had to give half a shekel as an *atonement* for his soul. In Exodus 38 we find that this "atonement money," the price of souls, was to be made into sockets, in which the boards of the Tabernacle were to rest. The sockets formed the foundation, so that the Tabernacle literally stood upon "Atonement." Peter perhaps had this fact in view when he said, "Ye were not redeemed with corruptible things, as silver and gold,.. but with the precious blood of Christ" (1 Peter 1. 18-19). The Tabernacle had no standing apart from the atoning price of souls; neither has the Church of Christ, the House of God, any foundation at all apart from the *atoning*, precious blood. To deny the redeeming power of Christ's death is to deny the only foundation laid by God upon which it is possible to build true worship and acceptable service. "Other foundation can no man lay" (1 Cor. 3. 11). "All other ground is sinking sand."

VI. The Boards. As we have seen the foundation represents the atoning work of Christ. The boards resting on and fixed in the foundation we may take to typify the believer's relationship to Christ and to one another. Each board was fifteen feet long and twenty-seven inches broad, furnished with a tenon by which it laid hold of the silver socket (Hebrew for tenon means *hand*). The history of these boards may serve to illustrate the experience of many a soul. See them—

1. CUT DOWN. Saul had this experience while on his way to Damascus, severed from his old ways and works.

2. Dried Up. The old sap of selfishness and carnality must be dried up before much good work can be wrought on us or in us. David knew about this when he cried, "Thy hand was heavy upon me. My moisture is turned into the drought of summer" (Psa. 32. 4).

3. Cleansed. It is not enough to be cut off from the old life, everything about us that would hinder us from filling a place in the House of God.

4. Clothed. These boards were not only cleansed, but *covered* with gold. A new beauty was put upon them; so when the sinner has been cleansed he is clothed upon with the beauty of the Lord. "The righteousness of God, which is unto all and *upon* all them that believe" (Rom. 3. 22).

5. Fitly Framed Together. When planted in the foundation they were closely joined one to another. On the foundation alone could they be united together. True spiritual union can only come through our being joined together in Christ. There is a great cry for union in these days. Many of the boards want the union without the foundation. "All one IN Christ." Every board resting on the sockets of atonement had a point of contact and fellowship one with the other. Why should it not be so with every believer in Christ?

VII. The Bars. These strong bars encircled the golden boards like the arms of the Almighty, keeping them straight on the foundation and close to one another. What a picture of God's care over those who rest upon the atoning work of Christ! Kept by the power of God! Every board had three rings, through which the bars ran. Each believer has a threefold connection with the keeping power of God: Faith, Hope, Love—three golden rings clasping the threefold sufficiency of the three-one God, viz., "The *grace* of the Lord Jesus Christ, the *love* of God, and the *communion* of the Holy Ghost" (2 Cor. 13. 14).

VIII. **The Setting Up**. "On the first day of the first month thou shalt set up the Tabernacle" (Exod. 40. 2). So you see the Tabernacle was set up on "New Year's Day." It was a new beginning for them, because there was now to be a new order of things. Everything had to be set up and put in order before the God of Glory could come and make His abode with them. So is it still. All we are and have must be set up before God if we would have the mighty filling of His Holy Spirit. One vessel unconsecrated would hinder the divine indwelling.

But when all was given up to God, and everything set in order before Him, He did fulfil His Word and manifest His sanctifying presence. It is always a new start when God comes by His Spirit and possesses the Temple of our body. When the glory of His presence filled the Tabernacle every vessel, curtain, board, and pin were sanctified and made holy. His Holy Spirit *in* us sanctifies and makes holy every gift, faculty, and member we possess.

The ten days' experience of the disciples in the upper room also correspond to the setting up of the Tabernacle, in that there followed the powerful purifying presence of God. A new beginning was then made, a new order of things established, of which all believers have been made partakers.

IX. **The Purpose**. The Tabernacle was not set up as an ornament nor as an exhibition of human skill, but as a sanctuary, a holy place for God. It was "God's House." Every Christian is to be "God's House." "Ye are the Temple of God" (1 Cor. 3. 16). We have been set up upon the sure foundation, not that we might be saved only, but that we might become the *habitation* of God. The Tabernacle had three courts—the outer, the holy, and the most holy. There are three parts in man—the body, soul, and spirit. It is in the inmost court that the Spirit of God dwells. If He has possession of our spirit, then all else will be yielded up to Him. But this tent in the wilderness was also to be a witness. It is called " The Tabernacle of Witness." Like the Church of God, it was a witness in the wilderness to the reality, power, mercy, and holiness of God. But what constituted it a witness? The presence of God. Until God possessed it it was no witness for Him. Here we have the secret of true witness-bearing. We can only be witnesses for God in proportion as we are filled with God. It is not you the world needs, it is the God that's in you. "Greater is He that is in you than he that is in the world" (1 John 4. 4). If the Holy Ghost is not filling us our testimony is but empty prattle. "*Ye* (not your tongues) are My witnesses" (Isa. 43. 10). "Ye are the light of the world" (Matt. 5. 14).

THE COVERINGS.
Exodus 25. 1-5; 26. 1-14.

THE coverings of the Tabernacle were four in number, each one different from the other, and may represent four different views or aspects of the character and work of Him whose name is Wonderful, just as we have in the Gospels four independent records of the one Person, Christ. Each Gospel, like each curtain, is complete in itself, but all are needed to give us a full-toned testimony of Himself. In the "*badger's skin*" covering we see in Matthew's Gospel Christ as a King in disguise; in the covering of "*rams' skins*" dyed red we have in Mark's Gospel Christ as the suffering Servant. In the third covering of "*goats' hair*" (white) we may see in the Gospel of Luke Christ as the Son of Man, pure and holy, obedient and pleasing to God. In the innermost covering of "fine-twined linen" we recognise in the Gospel of John Christ the Son of God, and the image of the Invisible One. Let us look at these separately, and as we look may the Holy Spirit take the things which are Christ's, and show them to us.

I. **The Covering of Fine-twined Linen.** This gorgeous covering of blue, scarlet, and purple, with its cherubim interwoven, was in ten pieces, perhaps having reference to the ten commandments, and was laid over the golden boards and formed the roof of the house, or, as it is called, the "covering of the Tabernacle." Christ is here exhibited in all the perfection of His glorious character. Note the colours—

1. It was BLUE. This points our eyes to the heavens. How calm and impressive is the deep blue of Heaven. Clouds may obscure it, but nothing can pollute it. It is high above all. No human eye can pierce it. It is illimitable, unchangeable, and eternal. How like the divine nature of the Son of Man, how like Him who was with the Father before the world was! In Christ we see this uncreated yet visible glory, the deep blue of unfathomable divinity.

2. It was SCARLET. This colour constrains us to look downward and think of the "red earth" from which man at first was made. If the blue tells of Christ's divinity, then the scarlet proclaims Him human. The one points to Him as the Son of God, the other as the Son of Man. The hunger, weariness, and tears of our blessed Lord tell how truly human He was.

3. It was PURPLE. Where shall we look for this? This is a new colour formed by mixing together the blue and the scarlet. The union of these two colours forms a third and distinct one. How beautiful! Christ is divine, Christ is human, and Christ is both in one distinct Person! In the purple, then, we behold our Lord in His mediatorial glory, the Mediator between God and men, the Man Christ Jesus.

4. It was INWROUGHT WITH CHERUBIM. Perhaps this may signify that He is Lord also over the angels, or, as

I am more inclined to think, they represent His own redeemed people, so closely united to Him that they become
part of Himself, "bone of His bone" (Gen. 2. 23). The
Church was interwoven with the character of Christ in the
purpose of God before the world was, "He was the Lamb
slain from before the foundation of the world" (Rev. 13. 8).
Wonderful thought! Oh, the unsearchable riches of His
grace, "Chosen in Him before the foundation of the world"
(Eph. 1. 4).

II. **The Covering of Goats' Hair.** This covering was
pure white, and was laid over and rested on the first one
of fine-twined linen.

May we not see here the spotless holiness of the Man
Christ Jesus, one fit to come into contact with and even to
rest on the awful holiness and righteousness of God. But
this curtain may also suggest to us the character and
privilege of the believer. Made *white* through the blood
of the Lamb, and resting in fellowship with Him, who is
both God and Man in one Person for ever, in heavenly
places with Christ Jesus, even now beholding His glory.
Purity only can have communion with divinity; the pure
in heart shall see God. Who shall ascend into this holy
hill of privilege? Who shall stand in this holy place?
He that hath clean hands and a pure heart (Psa. 24. 3, 4).
The divinity of Christ is a holy, devouring fire. Who shall
dwell with it? These are they which have washed their
robes and made them *white* in the blood of the Lamb.
Therefore are they before the throne of God (Rev. 7. 14, 15).

III. **The Covering of Rams' Skins.** Fine linen or
goats' hair does not imply suffering, but *skins* cannot be
got without sacrifice. "Rams' skins dyed red" suggest
both death and transformation. Jesus is before us here as
the "Man of Sorrows," with dyed garments, as the Lamb of
God which taketh away the sin of the world. Let us put

the shoes off our feet as we enter Gethsemane, and see there the skin of the Sacrifice being dyed red with the blood of agony.   In this covering we have Christ on the Cross; in the "goats' hair," Christ in the Resurrection; in the "fine linen," Christ in the Glory.

But these "rams' skins dyed red" speak to us as Christians. We are indebted to the transforming power of the atoning blood for our fitness to dwell in His holy presence. The white curtain was *under* the red one.   Purity in the sight of God can only be enjoyed "under the blood." We must be crucified with Christ before we can enter into resurrection life.   Are we willing to die to self that we might be made alive unto God?   As the white covering was kept clean by the crimson covering, so may we be kept clean by a constant trust in the ever-cleansing blood.

IV. **The Covering of Badger Skins.**   Some think that for "badgers' skins" we should read seal skins.   It was evidently meant for a waterproof, not for beauty, but for protection.

This covering may typify Christ in His rejection, "When we shall see Him, there is no beauty that we should desire Him" (Isa. 53. 2) without comeliness.   It had to bear the heat of the day, and was exposed to the storm and the tempest.   Think of our loving, gracious Lord, how He was misunderstood while being made a curse for us.   He was strong to bear.   Thank God, He was proof against it all. He answered not a word.   The Devil came, but found nothing in Him.   If to the world there was no beauty in Him, to the Father He was all-glorious.   "I delight to do Thy will, O My God" (Psa. 40. 8).   "This is My beloved Son, in whom I am well pleased" (Matt. 3. 17). Those who only saw the "badger skins" saw nothing of the hidden glory within.   Christ may still be to the world "a root out of a dry ground" (Isa. 53. 2), but to the Christian who has access within the veil He is the altogether lovely. Oh, that our hearts may be like the heart of the Tabernacle, the habitation of God, or like the King's daughter, "all glorious within." Although our faces may have the uncomely badger's skin appearance, yet in heart we may have the beauty of the Lord our God upon us.

These four coverings may also represent the **different divisions** in connection with the Tabernacle.

1. The Holy of Holies, by the "fine-twined linen."
2. The Holy Place, by the pure goats' hair.
3. The Court of Sacrifice, by the rams' skins DYED RED.
4. The wilderness without, by the "badgers' skins."

They also teach us, as we may have already noticed, **a fourfold experience** the Christian has of Jesus Christ as Saviour and Lord.

1. In our natural state we could only see the blessed Redeemer as the "badger skin" covering—no beauty, no attractiveness, because we had no sense of our guilt or need.

2. In the "rams' skins dyed red" we have been cleansed and changed by the power of His atoning blood through faith.

3. In the "goats' hair" covering we experience what it is to be made clean, delivered from the power of sin, hid in God, and kept by His almighty, overshadowing power.

4. In the innermost curtain of "fine-twined linen" we are walking in the light, as He is in the light, beholding His glory, and filled with all the fulness of God. Is this our experience? Do you know what it is to live within the Holy of Holies, in sweet, unbroken fellowship with the Holy One? This is your privilege in Christ Jesus.

THE PILLAR OF CLOUD.
Numbers 9. 15-21; Exodus 40. 33-38.

1. What it Signified. The origin and formation of the Pillar of Cloud is a mystery. It is a type of the incarnation of the Son of God. God was in the pillar; God was in Christ (2 Cor. 5. 19). In both we see the union of weakness and power, as weak as a "cloud," as strong as a "pillar." The Man *Christ Jesus*. Great is the mystery of godliness. God manifest *in the flesh*. To those outside the pillar may seem only a column of smoke, but to those who through the atoning blood had witnessed the glory within, it was the visible presence of the Eternal God. To some Christ was "without form or comeliness;" to others He was "the Christ, the Son of the Living God" (Matt. 16. 16).

God in the pillar may also be a foreshadowing of Christ in the Scriptures. "They are they which testify of Me" (John 5. 39). Sceptics may sneer at the cloudy pillar, and say, "The first desert storm will tear it to pieces, and melt it in the air." But they know not that God is in the pillar. All the storms of criticism cannot hinder the steady and stately march of the Scriptures of Truth. There is a living divine personality abiding and breathing through this holy pillar—"His Name is called THE WORD OF GOD" (Rev. 19. 13). May we with holy reverence bow before it, and with obedient hearts follow on.

II. What it was to the Israelite. It was to them the evidence of—

1. A PERSONAL GOD. The cloudy pillar was the visible evidence of the invisible God. "God is in the midst of her; she shall not be moved" (Psa. 46. 5). Jesus Christ is to us what the pillar was to Israel, the visible expression of the invisible God (Heb. 1. 3). "I and My Father are one" (John 10. 30). The glory was hid until the veil was rent—the veil of His flesh—then the glory shone forth in the coming of the Holy Ghost.

2. OF DIVINE FELLOWSHIP. "God spoke to them out of the cloud" (Deut. 5. 22). He was a sojourner with them. Wonderful condenscension! "Lo, I am with you alway"

(Matt. 28. 20). Out of the pillar of His Word God still speaks to His people. The Holy Spirit is now the "Urim and Thummim" of every individual believer. He takes the things of Christ, and shows them to us. Our fellowship is with the Father, with the Son, and with the Holy Ghost.

3. THE PILLAR WAS ALSO THE GUARANTEE OF ABUNDANT SUPPLY. While abiding with the pillar all their wants were met. Here the manna fell daily from Heaven. The waters also from the smitten rock followed the guiding pillar. "They drank of the rock that followed them, and that rock was Christ" (1 Cor. 10. 4). All the promises of God are in Him. Abide in Him, and the fulness of God will abide in you. Oh, follow Him, for lameness will bring leanness!

4. THE PRESENCE OF THE PILLAR ALSO MEANT PRO-TECTION. At the Red Sea the pillar came *between* the Israelites and the Egyptians (Exod. 14), delivering the one and destroying the other. How significant are the words, "The Lord looked *through the pillar*, and troubled the host of the Egyptians" (Exod. 14. 24). The Lord looked through Christ, and saved us. He still looks through Him to protect and keep us. He will also one day look through Him in judgment upon the ungodly. "He will judge the world *by that Man* whom He hath ordained" (Acts 17. 31). The coming of Christ to the Cross was the coming of the pillar between us and our great enemy sin. He came between that He might overcome the foe, and save all them that believe.

5. THE PILLAR WAS A SHELTER TO ISRAEL. It was, in fact, a huge umbrella overshadowing the whole camp, with its shaft resting in the midst, upon the mercy-seat. They could truly sing, "The Lord thy shade" (Psa. 121.5). The presence of Christ with the believer has a wonderful shading and comforting effect when the hot, fierce rays

of adversity are falling upon us. "In the day of adversity consider" (Eccles. 7. 14), consider that the Lord thee keeps. The Lord is thy shade. He shelters from sin and wrath by His blood, from sadness and sorrow by His comforting Spirit. Abide under His shadow and you will have great delight.

6. THE PILLAR WAS THEIR SOURCE OF LIGHT. It was a pillar of cloud by day and a pillar of *fire* by night. They had no.light of their own. Apart from the indwelt cloud, they had no light to lighten their darkness. Christ is the Light of the world. He that followeth Me, He says, shall not walk in darkness, but shall have the light of life. What is this light? The light of the pillar was the life in the pillar. "The LIFE was the light" (John 1. 4). To be filled with life is to be filled with light. There is no spiritual light but from the personal life-giving One. If we are the *light* of the world it is because we have the *life* of God abiding in us. If we would shine for God, then we must live for Him.

7. THE PILLAR WAS THEIR GUIDE (Num. 9. 18). When it moved they moved; when it rested they rested, whether it was for a day, or a month, or a year. To go without the pillar was to go without God. That meant without light, shelter, protection, or provision—without a promise. Let us ponder this. Without Christ we are out of touch with the person, the preciousness, and fulness of God. There is as much danger of losing His fellowship through lagging behind as running before. If we do not grow in grace, grace will not grow from us. Many Christians have ceased to be glad and useful because they have allowed the pillar to go out of their sight. Christ does not now fill the vision of their soul. To walk in the light is to keep in personal touch with the living God. This guide was *infallible*, because it was God *in* the pillar who guided.

The Word of God is a guiding "lamp to our feet," "a sure word," wherein we do well to take heed. In this "sure word" there is the "still, small voice" of the infallible God. The books that move men as they ought to be moved are the books of the Bible. The truth here taught move men ought of darkness into light, out of death into life. Oh, thou life-giving, soul-leading pillar of power move on!

Before we speak of the court itself, let us take a look at the **"pins and cords"** which kept the coverings in their place, binding them to the Tabernacle and to the earth. These pins were of brass, speaking of that which is able to endure (Exod. 27. 16-19). The earth symbolises the place of death. The pins were partly in the earth and partly out. The cords were fastened, of course, to that part which was above the earth, but the ability of the pin to bear the weight of the house depended on its connection with the earth. You see the parable. It signifies death and resurrection. On the resurrection of Christ hangs all the glory of the Church as the habitation of God. But what would have been the value of His life if He had not been driven into the place of death. He died for our sins, and rose again for our justification. The risen Christ is mighty, but because of His connection with the earth and its curse is He mighty to SAVE.

The cords were supposed to be of the same material as the veil, and the innermost covering of glory and beauty, blue, purple, and scarlet. This would represent the power of Christ in His mediatorial office to preserve His own House, or Church, on the earth. Men talk of preserving the earthly Zion, they forget that it takes the power of a glorified Christ to do that. The Tabernacle, like the Church of God, was in the world, but not of it. Its strength to resist lay not in itself, but in the threefold cord of Jehovah's love and grace and power. A threefold cord is not easily broken. How safe the blood-washed ones are!

"Kept by the power of God" (1 Peter 1. 5). "I will fear
no evil, for THOU art with me" (Psa. 23. 4).

The Court of the Tabernacle was a hundred and fifty
feet long, seventy-five feet broad, and was enclosed by a
wall, or hangings of "fine-twined linen," seven and a half
feet high. At the east end was the gate through which the
worshippers entered to the altar of burntoffering. From
the gate we may learn many precious lessons. Let us give
thanks to God that—

1. THERE IS A GATE. What a dark world this would
have been had there been no way of entrance into the
knowledge of and into fellowship with God! "Behold, I
set before you an open door" (Rev. 3. 8). But note that—

2. THERE WAS BUT ONE GATE. The Gate said, "I am the
Way" (John 14. 6). The wall of curtains said, "There is
none other name under Heaven whereby ye must be saved"
(Acts 4. 12). These hangings were suspended from "rods
of silver" made from "redemption money"—"hanging
on atonement." How suggestive. They seem to occupy
the place and do the work of the evangelist. They were
made of "fine linen"—this means the righteousness of
saints. They depended entirely upon the *price of souls*
(rods of silver) for their support (Exod. 30. 12-16). They
bore a united testimony that the only way to God was by
the altar of sacrifice, the Cross of Christ.

3. THIS WAS A WIDE GATE. It was the same size cubi-
cally as the door or the veil. What it lacked in height it
had in width. *Height* means greater or a more enlarged
spiritual experience; breadth indicates great liberty of
access. *Whosoever* will may come. The gate of atonement is as wide as the world (1 John 2. 2). The way of
substitution is as straight as the new birth. If few find it,
it is because few there be that seek it (Matt. 7. 7). The

way into life is straight in this sense, that it is the only
way, and that all who enter must have only one purpose
in their heart, and that is to trust all to Him who died for
sin—open for all, yet only for those who seek atonement at
the altar.

4. THIS WAS A STRONGLY-SUPPORTED GATE. It hung
on four pillars. The Gospel of Jesus Christ is supported
by four infallible pillars. Each holds up a different
aspect of Him who is "The Way, the Truth, and the
Life" (John 14. 6). Their names are Matthew, Mark,
Luke, John.

5. THIS GATE WAS OF THE SAME MATERIAL AS THE VAIL.
"Fine-twined linen, blue, purple, and scarlet." The
Son of God, the sinless Man, in one Person meets us at
the gate of life. A whole Christ to begin with is God's
provision. All was needed to open up the way. All is
needed to meet the need of man.

6. THIS GATE WAS THE WAY INTO LIFE. Immediately
in front of the gate stood the altar of sacrifice. It was
impossible to pass in without coming within sight of God's
provision for the sinner. Passing through the gate meant
the acceptance of God's way of salvation. What do we
learn from this? This one thing certainly, that the
moment the sinner trusts the Lord Jesus Christ as the way
to the Father, that moment he comes into personal contact
with the atoning blood of the Lamb, and may read his
title clear in the light of the Cross. Although two steps
may be indicated here between the gate and the altar, yet
in Christ there is but one. He is both Gate and
Altar. Experimentally we *decide* at the gate; we are
justified at the altar. The one act is ours, the other
is God's. "All that believe are justified from all
things" (Acts 13. 39). Precious faith ! Precious blood !
Precious promise !

THE BRAZEN ALTAR.

Exodus 26. 1-8; 28. 1-5; Leviticus 6. 7-13.

THE word "altar" means simply "high place," or that
which *lifts up*. The altar, with its sacrifice, is profoundly
significant of Christ on the Cross (John 3. 14). Through
the altar Israel was *lifted up* into fellowship with God.
The Cross of Christ is a ladder reaching unto Heaven.
Like the ladder Jacob saw, it is the way of God—to God—
set up on the earth. It lifts us up into communion with
the Father. To come into contact with the altar was to
come into touch with the claims and character of a
Holy God through sacrifice. At the Cross the sinner
comes into contact with the goodness and the severity of
God—condemnation of the sin, but mercy for the sinner.
This altar of burntoffering *lifted up* all that was laid
upon it. The sacrifice was lifted up in the form of smoke
by the consuming fire that burned continually thereon.
Heart-searching truth! Are we willing that our bodies
should be turned into smoke for the glory of God? Have
I been *lifted* up, crucified with Christ? Is the fire of the
Holy Ghost feeding upon my life? Am I wholly yielded
up to Him? and is He causing my whole being to *ascend*
as a sweet savour unto God? The sacrifice, being dead,
was unconscious of its own virtue. Moses wist not that his
face shone. Oh, for such a blessed state of unconscious-
ness! As He prayed, the fashion of His countenance
was changed.

But let us note further—

I. **The Purpose of It.** This brazen altar, standing
at the gate of entrance, represented the *claims of God*.
As a holy and righteous God He has claims that must be
satisfied before He can, in mercy, meet with man and bless
him. The altar must be filled before man can approach
God in peace. The altar was filled, and all the demands

of a holy God fully met when Christ cried on the Cross, "It is finished" (John 19. 30). The great purpose of the altar was to burn sacrifices. Here the sin-offering was slain, then carried without the camp, but its blood was poured out at the "bottom of the altar." The value of the sin-offering lay in the blood. "The blood is the life," or, "The life is in the blood." This was left at the foot of the altar, laid down before God. Here we see Christ as the sinner's Substitute, pouring out His soul unto death. "They overcame by the blood of the Lamb" (Rev. 12. 11).

The burntoffering, representing Christ as *the wholly-devoted One*, was entirely consumed upon the altar. Only the skin was saved; this was given to the priest for a covering —covered through sacrifice. Adam and Eve were naked, though clothed with leaves, till God made for them coats of skin. We are all naked till covered with the righteousness of God, which is unto all and upon all that·believe.

II. **The Position of It.** It stood right in front of the gate. This reminds us that atonement is the first necessity in our approach to God. The *first* blessing our gracious God desires to give us is the forgiveness of our sins, but "without shedding of blood is no remission" (Heb. 9. 22). When the sense of sin is brought home to the heart, how eagerly, like Job, we long for a "daysman" to come between us and lay his hand upon both. Those who refuse "Christ and Him crucified" as their sin-atoning Substitute have no *liberty* of access to God. To approach God disregarding the altar meant death. Cain tried it; he ignored the blood, and brought the curse of God upon himself. "A sin-offering *lieth* at the door" (Gen. 4. 7). God hath laid it there; it is there for us. It has a voice, "Look unto Me, and be ye saved, . . . for I am God" (Isa. 45. 22). Do not trample on it.

III. **The Materials of It.** Singularly enough, it was
composed of two different materials, "Shittim wood and
brass," two distinct elements in one altar. Man would
never have thought of putting *wood* in an altar had it not
been revealed to Moses on the mount. The altar, like
Christ, the Son of Man, must have a twofold nature. The
type is perfect; the wood speaks of the truly *human* sympathy of Jesus, while the brass reveals the strong, enduring
character of the *Divine* One—these two elements in One,
and that for the salvation of man. That the human
nature of Christ was not consumed in coming into such
close relationship with the divine is a mystery as great,
perhaps, as that the wood in the altar was not consumed.
The divine fire was in the human bush, yet the bush was
not consumed. Although the altar was partly wood, it
was never called the *wooden altar*, but the *brazen altar*,
one that was strong and mighty, so that when the sacrifice
was laid upon it, it was indeed "help laid on One that was
mighty."

IV. **The Size of It.** It would seem that by comparing
the measurements given of the other vessels with that of
the altar it had capacity enough to contain them all.
This is very suggestive. All spiritual blessings flow out
of the atoning death of Christ. "Delivered Him up for
us all, how shall He not *with Him* also freely give us all
things" (Rom. 8. 32). All the other vessels were sprinkled
with the blood of sacrifice, and so connected with the
altar (Heb. 9. 21, 22). It is a precious truth that when
we trust in Christ as a Sacrifice for us we may enter into all
the blessings of His resurrection and life. This we can
only do as we by *faith* are able to apprehend and appro-
priate. "Lord, increase our faith" (Luke 17. 5).

V. **The Horns.** This altar was four-square; it stood
solid and stable. At each corner was a horn. The horn

is the symbol of power. They pointed in every direction, and spoke of power sufficient for the whole world. The sacrifices were bound to the horns of the altar before being slain (Psa. 118. 27). What bound our Great Sacrifice to the altar of the Cross? Not the nails, but the cords of a love that was stronger than death. "No man taketh it from Me, but I lay it down of Myself. I have power to lay it down, and I have power to take it again" (John 10. 18). These are His own words. As the horns of the altar looked every way, so the power of the Cross of Christ looks over this whole sin-benighted, sin-smitten world. The value of this Sacrifice is sufficient to meet the dying need of all men.

VI. The Grate. Right in the middle of the altar was a grate, on which the fuel and the offerings were laid. The ashes fell through the grate into pans underneath. It is most significant to notice that the grate, although half-way down in the altar, was still as high as the mercy-seat (one and a half cubits). Who would have thought of this? Yet how could we think of an atoning scarifice *below* the lever of the mercy-seat of a Holy God. The mercy-seat was the throne of God, the sacrifice must be *equal* to it. Glorious truth! Marvellous grace! The Cross of the crucified Son of God is on a level with the righteous throne of God. The life and death of Jesus Christ are equal to the demands of the holy law, and of the just claims of a righteous God; and all this on our behalf as sinners before Him. Oh, self-righteous one, except your righteousness is equal to and on a level with the righteousness of God you have no hope! To offend, or come short in one point, is to be guilty of all. In the death of Jesus there is enough to satisfy God. Is there not enough to satisfy you?

VII. The Ashes. What about them? Cast them outside, anywhere, and let the winds scatter them abroad.

Yes, if human wisdom is to decide. But everything is
sacred here; nothing is to be lightly esteemed. The ashes
are a precious morsel in the priest's eyes, because of the
value attached to them by Jehovah. The ashes speak of
a sacrifice made, and more especially of a sacrifice accepted
by God through the consuming fire. The ashes were the
evidence that "It was finished," that the offering was
accepted in the sinner's stead. It was the last thing they
saw of the sacrifice. The last word heard from Christ on
the Cross was, "It is finished;" the work of suffering and
death was done; atonement was accomplished. The dead
body of the Son of God (the ashes) declared that all was
done that could be done.

But what was to be done with the ashes? They were to
be "carried out" and laid in a "clean place." The carrying
forth of the ashes was in the sight of Israel a solemn funeral.
They were precious, because they were to be used for the
"sprinkling of the unclean." In them lay the *merit* of the
sacrifice. This was applied to the cleansing of the leprous.
How suggestive! The body of Jesus was carried forth and
laid in a clean place, "a new tomb, wherein never man
before was laid" (Luke 23. 53). Now the merit of His
death and resurrection is for the sprinkling of the unclean,
the cleansing away of sin. The sprinkling process was a
very personal one. The value of the ashes does not lie in
what we think of them, but in the high estimate set upon
them by God Himself. Let us ponder this and praise Him.

VIII. **The Blood.** The blood of the offering was poured
out at the bottom of the altar. "The life is in the blood"
(Lev. 17. 11); thus the life of the devoted one was symbolically poured out before God. "All that a man hath
will he give for his life" (Job 2. 4). But when a man gives
his *life* he gives all that he hath. Our blessed Lord gave
His life, poured it out before God, and in giving His life

He gave all that He had. How much was that? "Though
He was rich, yet for your sakes He became poor, that ye
through His poverty might be rich" (2 Cor. 8. 9). Oh,
how poor He became! Oh, how rich we may become!
The blood, the life of the sacrifice, was for God; the ashes,
the fruit of the sacrifice, were for man. The death of Christ
had a double aspect; it had to make atonement to a Holy
God and cleanse a guilty man. The Hebrew word for
"atonement" is used in three different aspects: (1) *To
cleanse* (Lev. 16); (2) *to cover* (Gen. 6. 14); (3) *to appease*
(Gen. 32. 20). It has an *appeasing* power towards the
righteous Jehovah. "This is My beloved Son, *in whom*
I am well pleased" (Matt. 3. 17). As a holy and just
God no man can come before Him *empty-handed*. As
sinners we must have our hands filled with His offering
and our hearts cleansed by His blood. The atoning death
not only appeases God, but also cleanses and covers the
believing man. "Blessed is he whose transgression is
forgiven, whose sin is covered" (Psa. 32. 1). Think much
of the blood, the precious blood; the *mercy* of God is only
through the blood.

IX. **The Fire.** The fire on the altar was to "burn *continually*;" it "was *never* to go out." Where did this eternal
fire come from? From Leviticus 9. 24 we may believe that
it came directly from God Himself, from the Shekinah
Glory, or visible presence, which rested upon the mercy-
seat within the vail. It came from God; it was the symbol
of the holiness of God, and the visible token on the altar of
His presence with them. "Our God is a consuming fire"
(Heb. 12. 29). This fire is an awful element in an awful
place. Let those who deny that God demands atonement
for sin meditate upon it. Abraham went up the mount
to offer a sacrifice with the *knife* and the *fire* in his hand
(Gen. 22. 6). Every burntoffering had to come into con-

tact with the knife of the priest and the fire of God. Here
the sinner's Substitute must face, not the mercy or love,
but the FIRE of God. The fire must be satisfied on the
offering before the "ashes of sprinkling" could be taken or
used. The justice of God must first be fully met before
the mercy of God can freely flow.

The *continual* fire on the altar taught the Israelite that
God was *always* ready to receive them through sacrifice.
There was no other way. Christ, our Sacrifice, has been
offered once for all. Through Him God is *always ready*
to accept and forgive all who come (Heb. 7. 25). The fire
that was *never* to go out also proclaimed emphatically that
the *demands* of God, as the Holy One, would never be
lowered or changed. The continual burning demanded a
continual sacrifice. Let us give thanks unto God that this
incessant and inexorable claim has been, and is now, being
fully met in Jesus Christ, who died, and is now in Heaven
with the marks of the altar (the Cross) in His hands and
feet; whose blood constantly speaks, and who maketh
continual intercession for us. The fire of God's holiness is
receiving eternal satisfaction through the glorified Son of
Man at His own right hand.

There was no other altar for Israel. Private altars were
of no value, there was no God-given fire on them. "There
is none other name *under Heaven* given among men,
whereby we must be saved" (Acts 4. 12).

THE LAVER.

Exodus 30. 17-21; 38. 8; Titus 3. 4-6, R.V., margin.

THE laver stood between the altar and the door of the
Tabernacle, and right in line with the mercy-seat and the
altar of incense, signifying that the privileges and blessing
connected with it lay in the way of our *approach* to God.
In the altar we have Christ dying for our sins; in the

laver the ministry of the Holy Spirit. The laver comes after the altar. "The Holy Ghost was not yet given, because that Jesus was not yet glorified" (John 7. 30). First the Cross, then Pentecost; first justified by His grace, then sanctified through the truth. The laver was filled with water, the water is a type of the Word; the laver, of the Spirit. The great truth here is the ministry of the Word in the power of the Holy Ghost. This, of course, can only come after we have been justified from all things through the blood of His Cross. If you do not know your sins forgiven at the altar, the truth taught here will not likely profit you. Trust Jesus Christ now, and enter with us into the inheritance revealed. in type by the laver. We shall notice first—

I. **Its Origin.** In Exodus 38. 8 we learn that the laver was to be made of brazen "looking-glasses," which belonged to the women who assembled at the door of the Tabernacle. There are two ways in which we might see ourselves—in the light of our own polished mirror, or in the light of the Lord as we stand before Him.

When, like these women, we stand at the door of the Tabernacle, and see ourselves in the light of the presence of a holy and sin-hating God, we get so disgusted with ourselves that we don't wish to look at our own proud persons, and so willingly part with our looking-glasses that we might get that which will give us inward beauty and adorning. The choice has still to be made, even by redeemed ones, as to whether they will walk in the light of their own eyes or in the truth as revealed and applied by the Holy Spirit. These who live according to their own standard are simply seeing themselves in their own looking-glass. All the light such have comes from the sparks of their own kindling.

The law of God is a looking-glass to show us our need of

the laver of regeneration. When Nicodemus, a man
familiar with the looking-glass, came to Jesus He pointed
him at once to the laver of an inward change to be wrought
by the Holy Ghost. "Born of *water* and of the *Spirit*"
(John.3. 5).

II. Its Purpose. The chief end of the laver was,
of course, "to cleanse," "to wash withal." Judicial
righteousness was to be followed with personal
righteousness. Inward cleansing was to accompany the
act of justification.

Perhaps the polished brass of the laver helped to reveal
the uncleanness, while the water would cleanse it away.
This is, at least, the work of the Spirit, to convince of sin,
and to apply the cleansing Word.. The water of the laver
was only for redeemed ones. "Tarry ye in the city of
Jerusalem until ye be endued with power from on high"
(Luke 24. 49). The ministry of the Spirit gives fitness for
service. The priests must wash here lest they die. Unless
we are kept in constant touch with the Holy Laver our
testimony for God will die; we will become as withered
branches. Instead of having power with God and men, we
shall be trodden under foot of men, like savourless salt.

The fact that these two vessels (laver and altar) were
separated the one from the other, may also teach us that
the receiving of the Holy Spirit is to be a definite and personal experience (Acts 19. 2).

The blessings of the laver could only be enjoyed by
those who wished to serve in the holy place. Alas, is it
not true of many that they take the blessing of salvation
at the altar, and then turn away satisfied? They don't
press on to holy service in the presence of God, so they
know nothing of the special ministry of the laver, and little
of the joy of fellowship with God. Christ was crucified to
save us. He was glorified to sanctify us (John 7. 39). If

we have been saved by His blood, so may we be taught by and filled with His Spirit.

III. Its Form. When Moses received instructions to make "the laver and its foot," no mention at all is made of size or shape. At first sight one wonders at this. Is it an overlook? God can make no mistake. Every omission with Him is as emphatic as a declaration. It is surely significant that the vessel which represents the work of the Holy Spirit should not be limited to any particular form or size. "The wind (Spirit) bloweth where it listeth; thou hearest the sound thereof, but canst not tell whence it cometh and whither it goeth" (John 3. 8). Why was the laver not made of wood and brass like the altar? The answer seems clear and unmistakable. Christ had two natures—divine and human. The Holy Spirit is one Person. Let us adore the wisdom of God. Those who study and understand the types have no difficulty about the inspiration of the Scriptures.

The other vessels of the Tabernacle had staves or shafts by which they were to be carried. The laver had none. This may also confirm the inference that we have here not only a work represented, but a Divine Person. We are saved by the work of Jesus Christ for us; we are sanctified by the presence of the Holy Ghost within us.

IV. Its Connection with the Altar. Like all the other vessels, there was a blood connection between it and the altar of burntoffering. It was sprinkled with the blood of atonement. The laver could not be used till after the blood had been shed. The Spirit did not come till after the work on the Cross had been finished. The sprinkling of the laver with the blood was symbolically the consecrating and imparting of divine authority for its work. When Christ entered into Heaven by His own blood, He sent the Holy Spirit. The Holy Ghost received

His authority from the Son of God on the ground of His own atoning death. There is a very vital connection between Calvary and Pentecost. Would that it were so in the experience of every Christian.

The laver was to be filled with water—water, doubtless, from the smitten rock. Is this not wonderful? "That Rock was Christ" (1 Cor. 10. 4). The laver could be filled, and men could be cleansed, because the rock had been smitten. At the altar we see the blood of atonement; at the laver we see the water of cleansing. Both are needed. Both come to us through our Divine Redeemer. You remember that when they had pierced His side, "forthwith came there out blood and water" (John 19. 34)—the blood first, then the water.

The water, or ministry of the Spirit, always comes by way of the altar (Ezek. 47. 1-12). "He shall take the things of Christ, and show them unto you" (John 16. 13-15). Ye believe in the forgiveness of sin; believe also in the indwelling Spirit. Trust Him to apply the cleansing Word, and to impart fitness for service.

The water was in the laver. The two were very closely connected, but not more closely than the Spirit and the Word. If we would be mighty in the Spirit we must be mighty in the Word. It was when Ezekiel had eaten the book that the Spirit lifted him up and took him away (Ezek. 3. 1-14). The Spirit always lifts up and takes away those in whom the Word of Christ dwells richly.

V. Other Important Lessons. From the teaching of this vessel we further learn—

1. THAT THEY MUST BE CLEAN WHO WOULD STAND BEFORE GOD. Every time the priest entered into the holy place he must wash. Purity of heart is a necessity for seeing God. Without holiness no man shall see the Lord.

It is not so much a change of place we need to see God as a change of state. Believe, and thou shalt see.

2. THAT THERE WAS BUT ONE MEANS OF CLEANSING. There was but one laver; no other was needed. This was God's provision. They might wash themselves elsewhere, but that would not make them "clean before the Lord." Hear Job's testimony, "If I wash myself, . . . and make my hands never so clean; yet shalt Thou plunge me in the ditch" (Job 9. 30, 31). The snow-waters of earth and self-will never avail while the " Fountain opened for sin and uncleanness" (Zech. 13. 1) is neglected and despised.

3. THAT ONE LITTLE ACT MAY UNFIT FOR SERVICE. If the priest should refuse but once to wash at the laver, this one act of disobedience would unfit him for his priestly work. Our secret sins may not affect our lives before men for a while, but our relationship to God is affected at once. The flickering light tells of a crack in the lantern. An unsteady testimony speaks of failure somewhere. One fly will spoil the ointment. "If I regard iniquity in my heart, the Lord will not hear" (Isa. 52. 11). They must be clean that bear the vessels of the Lord.

4. THAT TO WASH WAS A MATTER OF NECESSITY, NOT OF OPINION. The priest, guided by his own carnal wisdom, might say, "Oh, I washed in the morning. I don't see the need of washing again in the evening. Besides, as far as I can judge, there is no uncleanness to wash." You see it was not "What saith the priest?" but "What saith the Lord?" "Wash, that ye die not." "If we say that we have no sin, we deceive ourselves" (1 John 1-8). While we are "clean through the Word," yet the feet need washing, and that continually. The feet represent our relationship as Christians to the world. It is most frequently in our connection with the ungodly and the things of this pre-

sent world that the defilement comes. It may come in
the form of hard, unkind thoughts about the unsaved, lack
of compassion, failing to embrace the opportunity of
witnessing for Christ, impatience, covetousness. "Cleanse
Thou me from secret faults" (Psa. 19. 12).

THE DOOR.

Exodus 26. 36, 37; John 10. 9.

WHY should there be a door between the ministry of the
laver and the service and fellowship of the holy place?
Perhaps to teach us that the work of the one was just to
fit us for the enjoyment and privilege of the other. To
grow in grace means receiving to the ·full the blessings
offered us in Christ Jesus. Those who walk in the light
they have shall receive more light "The path of the
just is as the shining light that shineth more and more"
(Prov. 4. 18). In the experience of the Christian there
is always more to follow.

The hangings which formed the door, like the gate
outside and the vail inside, were made of "fine linen—
blue, purple, and scarlet." Here, again, we have Jesus
as the Son of God, the Son of Man, and the Mediator between God and men. It must be Jesus in His threefold
character all the way with the believer. We live by faith
on the Son of God. The door had five pillars, made of
shittim wood overlaid with gold, the wood and gold again
pointing to the human and divine nature of Christ. He
Himself said, "I am the Door" (John 10. 9). The five
pillars may represent His fivefold name as given in Isaiah
9. 6, "Thou shalt call His Name JESUS." He is the (1)
King, (2) Eternal, (3) Immortal, (4) Invisible, (5) the
only wise God (1 Tim. 1. 17). If at the altar we have to
do with the work of Jesus Christ, here it is Himself in all
the riches of His glorious character that is presented

before us. The truth about the "fuller" or "higher Christian life" so freely taught in these days is here in type before us at the door. It is a definite acceptance of or entering into all the fulness of Jesus Christ, purchased for us by His atoning blood, offered to us in His Word, and accomplished in us by faith through the Holy Spirit. Having come under the power of the laver cleansing, we may now behold and enjoy the unsearchable riches of Christ. The Door was—

1. THE WAY INTO ACCEPTABLE PRAYER. Through the door, right in front, stood the golden altar of incense, the type of intercession. When Christ Himself becomes the chiefest among ten thousand to our hearts, then prayer will become a delight. Being now filled with His love and Word, we ask and receive (John 15. 7). The ministry of the Holy Ghost (laver) is needed to fit us for this holy and blessed privilege (Rom. 8. 26, 27). This is also—

2. THE WAY INTO CONTINUAL LIGHT. Within the door was the ever-burning candlestick, the light that was "never to go out." When the door is entered, or when Christ is received in all the fulness of His grace and power, then the soul enters into the sweet experience of walking in the "light of the Lord." Many Christians know nothing of this continual shining. Christ is seen by them only at the altar of atonement. They know their sins forgiven, but they don't know what it is to be "filled with all the fulness of God" (Eph. 3. 16-20). The teaching of the laver is neglected. O that men would believe in the Holy Spirit and submit to His power and teaching, then would Christ be glorified in them, then would they walk in newness of life.

3. THE WAY INTO ABIDING FELLOWSHIP. When the priest went through the door he also came into the presence

of the "table of shewbread." The table speaks of "fellowship." Here we have fellowship with God in His Son, who
is the "Bread of Life." This fellowship with Christ at
the table of bread is a fellowship which strengthens and
satisfies. This precious blessing, too, comes after the
sanctifying influence of the Holy Spirit, represented in the
laver. Every unclean thing must be put away if we
would abide in the soul-satisfying friendship of the holy
Son of God. How can two walk together except they be
agreed. This privilege does not come to us every now and
then like the ordinance of the "Supper." There is no
necessity why we should ever go down from this holy
mount. ABIDE IN ME.

4. THE WAY INTO NEARNESS TO GOD. In passing through
the door the priest must have been conscious that he had
approached nearer to God. Now there was only the vail
between him and the glory which rested on the mercy-seat
within.

This is the solemn experience of those who, through
the power of the Holy Ghost, walk in the light of the
fellowship of Christ. Only the vail between, only this
vail of flesh between us and the immediate vision of the
glory of God. "Absent from the body, . . . present with
the Lord" (2 Cor. 5. 8). When we think of our own sinfulness, well may we, like Ahab, "walk softly" (1 Kings
21. 27). When we think of the grace of God by which we
have been brought into this privilege, well may we rejoice
and adore. Let us fall down and worship.

5. THE WAY INTO THE CALM OF DIVINE SAFETY. No
matter how stormy the day might be, within the door there
was always calm and quiet. Here the worshipper had the
conscious assurance that he was specially sheltered under
the wings of Jehovah's presence. General protection was
promised to all who abode under the cloudy pillar. This

was a special blessing enjoyed only by the priests, the hidden ones; those only who had to do continually with the work of the laver, the ministry of the Holy Spirit. The importance of this truth is the only excuse for repeating it so frequently. We may be Christians living under the pillar of promise, and enjoying pardon through the altar of His Cross, yet all the while utter strangers to the calm and quiet of those who live and serve in the holy place. Here we are "hidden," hidden from the strife of tongues (Psa. 31. 20), from trouble (Psa. 27. 5). Here we are strengthened with "hidden manna," taught with "hidden wisdom" (1 Cor. 2. 7), and satisfied with "hidden riches" (Isa. 45. 3). Your life is hid with Christ in God. How calm, how quiet, how safe, how full, how holy, how happy, how thankful, how praiseful we should be! Through the door was also—

6. THE WAY INTO THE SPHERE OF HOLY SERVICE. Here, by priestly hands, the incense was put upon the coals of the altar, the lamps were trimmed, and the bread renewed. Holy work indeed—praying, testifying, teaching. Praying unto God; offering up, not cold, formal petitions, but desires, like incense from the burning coals of a holy, self-consuming zeal. The incense sent up no sweet perfume till it came into contact with the burning coals. The coals of our affection must be burning if our prayers are to ascend. Here the lamp of our spiritual life is kept regularly replenished and constantly shining, so that a steady, God-pleasing testimony is borne. Here the bread of His presence, ever fresh, is given and received. If we would minister to others in holy things, we must know what it is to minister "before God." This fitness for holy service, let me repeat it, comes through personally participating in the power and grace of the Holy Ghost. Yield yourselves unto God.

There was no floor in the holy place. The bare feet of
the priest still walked on the sandy desert. He was reminded that, although he was in the place of holiness
enjoying heavenly things, he was still on the earth. The
lesson here is obvious. These great spiritual blessings and
privileges are for us now in our present earthly state.
Many Christians relegate their possessions to Heaven instead of entering into the enjoyment of them now. "I am
the Door; by Me if any man enter, he shall be SAVED, and
shall go in and out, and find pasture"—*strength* for SERVICE
(John 10. 9). "Behold, I have set before thee an open
Door" (Rev. 3. 8).

These Studies are continued in Series II.

PROVE YOUR OWN SELVES.
2 Cor. 13. 5.

THIS is a needful work. Beware of the deceitfulness of
the heart. This self-proving should be done—

1. Instantly. The secret of our failure should be
searched out at once.

2. Willingly. Are you prepared to know yourself?—
ready to have a sight of hidden sin?

3. Carefully. Let no beloved sin deceive you. Judge
each by their fruits. Don't label things harmless that
are unholy.

4. Fearlessly. With the lamp of God's searching
Word (Heb. 4. 12).

5. Mercilessly. Spare no Agag. Make confession.
Acknowledge the sin (Psa. 51. 3).

6. Honestly. Be severe on the sin, but approve what
is good. Distinguish between sins and infirmities.

7. Prayerfully. Remember, the Lord alone can
search the heart. "Search me, O God; try my heart."

OLD TESTAMENT STUDIES.

CREATION.

Genesis 1.

"In the beginning God." Regeneration, like the work of creation, has its beginning in God (John 3. 5). The new creation, like the old, begins with the "*Word* of God" and the *moving* of the Spirit. Compare the order here with the experience of a soul passing from death into life. Observe—

I. **The State of Disorder (v. 2).** The threefold condition of man's state by nature is here very forcibly suggested:

1. Confusion. "The earth was without form." No order; nothing in harmony with the ultimate purpose of God. No perfect thing. The carnal mind is enmity against God. Spiritual things foolishness.

2. Emptiness. "Void." Utterly unable of itself to produce any good. Life and fruitfulness are the gifts of God. "In me, that is, in my flesh, dwelleth no good thing" (Rom. 7. 18). Man is utterly void apart from the moving Spirit. "Who can bring a clean thing out of an unclean?" (Job 14. 4).

3. Darkness. "Darkness was upon the face of the deep." There can be nothing but darkness till the light is sent forth. We would have been in darkness until now had not God *commanded* the light to shine forth (2 Cor. 4. 6). To be under sin is to be under the power of darkness. Satan is the Prince of Darkness.

II. **The Work of the Spirit.** "The Spirit moved." The earth may move, but its own motion could not mend

it. It must be moved *upon*. Regeneration is not the outcome of the movements of the natural heart. Not evolu-
tion, but creation (2 Cor. 5. 17). Born, not of the *will* of
man, but of God; born from above (John 6. 63).

III. The Power of God's Word. "God said, and there
was." He spake, and it was done. The Word of God is
quick and powerful. This Word, this mighty, moving,
re-creating energy is in the Gospel of Christ. It is the
power of God unto salvation. "Lazarus, come forth"
(John 11. 43). His Word was with power.

IV. The Divine Separation. "God divided the light
from the darkness" (vv. 4, 5). The Word of God, by the
power of the Holy Spirit working in the "new man,"
divides between soul and spirit, and separates the spiritual
and the carnal. "What communion hath light with
darkness?" (2 Cor. 6. 14-18).

V. The Manner of Fruitbearing. "Yielding fruit
after his kind, whose seed is in itself" (v. 11). Fruitbearing is the outcome of the light and the moving Spirit.
The result of a *condition*, not an effort; of what we *are*, not
of what we *do*. The fruit of Christ in us will be Christ-
likeness—fruit after His kind, and with the seed in itself.
Reproductive.

VI. The Position of the Lights. "In the firmament
to give light upon the earth" (v. 15). The light must be
above the earth if they are to shine *on* it. "Ye are the light
of the world." Not of it—lifted above it. Seated in the
heavenlies to shine *upon* it" (John 17).

VII. The Image of God. "God created man in His
own image." The climax of His creative power results in
His own likeness. It is so in the new creation, "After the
image of Him that created him" (Col. 3. 10). The great

work of the Holy Spirit is to renew the soul after the image of God. Both God and man will be satisfied when we are perfected in His likeness.

VIII. **The Crown of Honour.** "God gave him dominion." Power and authority come when we have been made like Him. In the Kingdom we shall reign with Him (Rev. 20. 6).

THE CREATOR'S SABBATH.
Genesis 2.

ONLY when God had *finished* the heavens and the earth did He rest. He found no rest until He had ended all His work. The Sabbath, or rest of God, means perfect satisfaction in that which has been accomplished. He alone was the worker. His alone was the rest. Let us notice:

I. **The Sabbath Ordained.** The seventh day was fixed and settled by God to be a time of rest and joy to Himself and to all creation.

1. IT IS A DAY OF REST. No more work to be done. He rested, not because He was weary, but because every good thing had been done that could be done.

2. IT WAS A DAY OF BLESSING. "God blessed it." The special favour and delight of God was in it—truthfulness and satisfaction.

3. IT WAS A SEPARATED DAY. "God sanctified it." Set it apart as His own possession and inheritance because it manifested the results of His own wisdom, power, and goodness. But note more particularly that—

4. IT WAS THE DAY OF GRACE FOR MAN. God made man on the sixth day, so that the first day that dawned upon Adam was the Sabbath of God, that is, man immediately entered into the enjoyment of the rest of his Creator. God finished the work; man enters with Him into the rest and

enjoyment of all that God had made. O the grace of God, to delight in bringing man into such a possession!

II. The Sabbath Destroyed. It would seem that man did not long enjoy the rest of God. The tempter came, man failed, the rest was broken, Adam fled from God. Sin ruined man for the enjoyment of God's rest. In the ages that follow man seems to have *forgotten* that the Sabbath was "made for man," so when the law was given (Exod. 22) the word "*Remember*" was significantly prefixed to the Second Commandment. The Sabbath of divine rest, which was a *gift* to man, now comes back to him in the form of *law*; but still it reminds him of God's rest. "No manna fell" on the Sabbath day. To enjoy rest now they have to gather double on the sixth day—not of grace now, but of works.

III. The Sabbath Restored. Through Jesus Christ man can be brought back to the enjoyment of God's rest.

1. THROUGH HIM ANOTHER WORK HAS BEEN FINISHED. "I have finished the work" (John 17. 4). He put away sin, the work of atonement is ended, and God has pronounced all very good.

2. ANOTHER REST IS ENJOYED. As God rested upon the mercy-seat on the Holy of Holies, so doth He now rest satisfied in the work of His beloved Son.

3. ANOTHER DAY OF GRACE IS PROCLAIMED. "Come unto Me, and I will give you rest" (Matt. 11. 28). As Adam entered into God's rest, so may we now through faith in Jesus. "There remained a rest (Sabbath) for the people of God" (Heb. 4. 1-9); "Enter into HIS rest." This rest means to us all that it meant to Adam: 1, A ceasing from works; 2, continual fellowship with God; 3, to bear His holy image; 4, to find our all in His possession; 5, to rejoice in God. "They could not enter in because of unbelief" (Heb. 3. 19).

THE GARDEN OF EDEN.

Genesis 2. 8-19.

THE garden in Eden speaks of grace upon grace. The man God made was invited to enter into and enjoy all the fulness of God. The garden may be regarded as a type of the provision God has made for man in Christ Jesus.

I. God's Gracious Provision. There is something in the fact that—

1. IT WAS A GARDEN. This suggests a *special* enclosure, a place prepared for a prepared man. We are reminded of the Covenant made with Christ before the world was. He was the Lamb slain from before the foundation of the world (Eph. 1. 4).

2. IT WAS PLANTED BY THE LORD. Man had no hand in the making of this inheritance. This, like the scheme of salvation, was the work of God: "Salvation is of the Lord" (Jonah 2. 9). Both the "plant" and the planting were His alone (John 3. 16).

3. IT WAS PLANTED FOR MAN. God had the good of man before Him in the planting of every tree. He considered all man's need, and made ample provision for his complete satisfaction. All the eternal forethought of God in our behalf is seen in the *fulness* that dwells in Christ. In Christ is God's provision for needy man. Look at some of these tree blessings:

(1) *The Tree of Life.* This stood in *the midst* of the garden (v. 9). LIFE is man's first need: "I am come that ye might have life" (John 10. 10). This was the tree of *eternal life* to Adam. The Cross of Christ in the midst is the tree of life for fallen man. Before Adam could die he had to be driven from the tree of life. To be without Christ is to be without hope.

(2) *Every Tree that was Pleasant.* Here also Adam found his pleasure. In God's provision for us in Christ there is life and every pleasant thing, every pleasure worth having—"Wisdom's ways."

(3) *Every Tree that was Good for Food.* There are many pleasures which don't satisfy; these are good for food. They build up and strengthen. Every promise of God is.a fruit tree; the garden of the Lord is full of them.

(4) *There was the "Tree of Knowledge of Good and Evil."* Would it have been better without this? Here is a deep truth. We cannot know *good* and *evil*, in a real sense, till we have been planted into Christ. Sin and grace are well known there.

(5) *There was a River of Water* (v. 10). A river watered the garden. "There is a river, the streams whereof shall make glad the city of God" (Psa. 46. 4). The blessings in Christ are all made fruitful by the power of the Holy Ghost. Surely in Christ we have a goodly heritage.

II. Man's Wondrous Privilege.

1. HE WAS PUT IN BY GOD. "The Lord put the man into the garden" (v. 15). Adam was not made in the garden. Our engrafting into Christ is a divine act. The provision is much, but that is not enough. The soul of man, by the Holy Ghost, must be brought into touch with it.

2. HE WAS PUT IN TO ENJOY THE WORK OF GOD. What grace! We are blessed with all spiritual blessings in Christ Jesus.

3. HE WAS PUT IN TO WORK AND WATCH—dress it and keep it (v. 15). The Christian life, though a life of faith, is not a life of idleness.

4. HE WAS PUT IN WITH A DIVINE LIBERTY AND WARNING (vv. 16, 17). Shall we sin that grace may abound. God forbid! Sin may not cut off sonship, but it will destroy fellowship.

THE FIRST MARRIAGE.

Genesis 2. 18; 21-25.

GOD said, "Let *Us* make man in *Our image*." This first man we may regard as a type of the Second Man, the Lord from Heaven, who is the *image* of the Invisible God. Eve may represent the relationship of the redeemed to Christ: "This is a great mystery, but I speak concerning Christ and the Church" (Eph. 5. 32).

I. **The Declaration.** God said, "It is not good that man should be alone" (v. 18). God considers this man's highest need, and thinks that *loneness* is not for his greatest good. Think of God away back in eternity saying this regarding the Son of His love! Not good for Him to be alone, the only Son, bearing the image and reflecting the glory of the Father! He will bring many sons into glory.

II. **The New Creation.** "I will make him an help meet for him" (v. 18). Eve was the workmanship of God, and His gift to the man in His own image. We are His workmanship, created anew in Christ Jesus. The Church is an help meet for Christ, is made by Him, and is the gift of the Father to the Son. "All that the Father hath *given Me* shall come to Me" (John 6. 37). "Them which Thou hast given Me" (John 17. 9).

III. **The Operation.** "The Lord caused a deep sleep to fall upon Adam" (v. 21). Sleep is the figure of death. While Adam was in this state the wonder-working hands of the Divine Operator brought forth a helper after His own likeness. It was a deep sleep the Lord God caused to fall upon the Second Adam when He bowed His head and gave up the ghost. "It pleased the Lord to bruise" (Isa. 53. 10). God took a rib from the first man, but nothing less than the blood of the Second Man would suffice if a helpmate is to be given Him. His Church had to be bought with His own blood.

IV. **The Presentation.** "The Lord brought her to the man" (v. 23). Every *Godlike* man may have his wife from the Lord. "The Lord brought her to the man." What for? To share his love, to enjoy his fellowship, to be a partaker of the blessings freely given him by God, and to be a joy and a comfort and a help to him. Thus the Holy Spirit brings us to Christ, that we may receive of His, and be workers together with Him. Every Christian is to be a helpmate to Christ.

V. **The Acceptance.** "Adam said, This is now bone of my bones" (v. 23). He acknowledged Eve, the gift of God, as a part of himself. "They shall be *one* flesh." He never thought of refusing her. "Him that cometh unto Me I will in no wise cast out" (John 6. 37). How close the union! We are members of His body, of His flesh, and of His bones. Yes, "He will receive you unto Himself."

VI. **The Result.** "Therefore shall a man leave his father and his mother, and shall cleave unto his wife" (v. 24). Every relationship that would hinder us from cleaving to Christ and serving Him must be broken. The whole heart and life are to be yielded if we would be faithful. Christ left His Father when He came to earth. He left His mother when He died on the Cross. He cleaves to His wife and His redeemed people. Leave all, and cleave to Him (Matt. 16. 24).

THE FALL OF MAN.
Genesis 3.

THE first sin was like Elijah's cloud, it was little at the beginning, but it blackened the whole heavens. By one man sin entered, and death came upon all. By Man (Christ) came also resurrection and life (1 Cor. 15. 21, 22). We have here the revelation of some root principles. There are:

I. Satanic Teaching. "Ye shall not surely die." The personality of the devil is clearly implied. He does not say "There is no God," but suggests that God does not mean what He says, or if He does He is not a God of mercy. His great purpose is ever to mar the design of God toward man. Wiles of the devil.

II. Carnal Reasoning (v. 6). She *saw*, because she looked, and, judging by appearance, she *desired*, and when the *desire* was nourished it grew into a deliberate act, she *took*. Then, not satisfied with taking for herself, she *gave*. The process may have been something like this: 1, *Giving* heed to the tempter; 2, *forgetting* God's mercies; 3, *looking* at the forbidden thing; 4, *wishing* God had not forbidden it; 5, *doubting* the Word of God; 6, *believing* Satan's lie; 7, *yielding* to taste.

III. Presumptuous Working. "They sewed fig leaves together and made themselves aprons" (v. 7). Their eyes were opened. Sin opens the eyes of the saints to see their own weakness, while it blinds the eyes of the ungodly. This is a vain attempt to cover sinful self. "He that covereth his sins shall not prosper" (Prov. 28. 13). Why not confess and receive forgiveness (1 John 1. 9).

IV. Guilty Concealing. "They hid themselves" (v. 8). Hid among the trees of the garden, among the very blessings God had given them. Many still hide *behind* the gifts of God while they live in sin. The "voice of the Lord" is always a terror to evil-doers. It is in vain for man to hide anywhere away from God. "I flee to Thee to hide me." Sin always separates from God.

V. Divine Seeking. "Where art thou?" (v. 9). This is the call of Grace. God is always the first *seeker*. When would Adam have sought God? This divine question (1) *Reveals great compassion*; this is the Good Shepherd seeking the lost sheep. (2) *It awakens conviction* by leading to deep heart-searching. (3) *It demands confession*; yield, and unburden all to God. (4) *It suggests judgment*, "Where art thou?" There is no escape from Him.

VI. Vain Excusing. "The woman *Thou* gavest, she gave me" (v. 12). His mouth has not yet been stopped (Rom. 3. 19). God justifies the believer, not the boaster. If men don't now lay the blame of sin on God, they go as near as possible when they blame circumstances. There is no excuse for doubting God.

VII. Merciful Covering. "God made coats of skin and clothed them" (v. 21). Man's best will never cover his nakedness in the sight of God. These coats of *skin* suggest sacrifice. It is significant to remember that *atonement* means covering. Adam's covering was the covering of another, substitution. It was of God's *making* and *giving*, the righteousness of God, which is unto all and *upon* all them that believe.

CAIN AND ABEL.
Genesis 4. 1-16.

OF Cain and Abel it may be said: "Two men went up to worship, the one was a Pharisee, the other was a publican" (Luke 18. 10). Although both enjoyed the same privileges and opportunities, they were far from being alike. Christian *privileges* will not in themselves make a Christian. We have here—

I. Self-will Rejected. "Unto Cain and his offering" God had not respect (v. 5). Cain must be acceptable first *himself* before his offering can be. His offering was rejected, because he himself was guilty. Christ was without spot when He offered Himself. The way of Cain was *his own way* (Jude 11). Man's own way is to seek acceptance with God without confessing guilt. There is no road this way; both the offerer and the offering are rejected.

II. Faith Accepted. "The Lord hath respect unto Abel and his offering" (v. 4). "By *faith* Abel offered up a more acceptable sacrifice than Cain" (Heb. 11. 4). The offering and the offerer stand or fall together. When by faith we lay hold upon Christ there is no possibility of rejection, for this offering has been accepted by God, and every believing offerer is accepted in Him All that believe are justified from all things. Faith in Christ is always acceptable faith.

III. Enmity Manifested. "Cain was wroth" (v. 5). He was religious in appearance, but in heart he was at enmity with God. He had the *form* of godliness, but he was a stranger to its power. Many there are in these days who have gone the way of Cain, content with the mere ceremony, while the living substance has never been touched or tasted.

IV. Mercy Revealed. "God said, Why art thou wroth? a sin-offering lieth at thy door" (vv. 6, 7). God in mercy points out to Cain that the only way of acceptance as a sinner is through a sin-offering. Christ bore our sins in His own body on the tree. This sin-offering lies at the door of every sinner. What a mercy that the atoning price is so near!

V. Righteousness Hated. "Cain slew his brother" (v. 8). And wherefore slew he him? (see 1 John 3. 12). He hated the righteousness of God as seen in his brother. The carnal mind of man would rather quench the divine

light in bloodshed than acknowledge sin. Christ was the
Righteousness of God, and men cried, "Away with this
Man" (Luke 23. 18). They loved darkness rather than the
light, because their deeds were evil.

VI. Wickedness Judged. "Now art thou cursed"
(v. 11). The counsel of God with regard to the sin-offering
was rejected; now the curse comes. What a striking fulfilment of John 3. 18. Rejecting Christ as the sin-offering
means no escape from the wrath and curse of God. What
think ye of Christ?

VII. Justice Vindicated. "Cain said, Mine iniquity
is greater than that it may be forgiven" (v. 13, margin).
He acknowledges the justice of his condemnation, yet so
hardened is he that he begs not for mercy. "There is mercy
at the eleventh hour," say many; but what if your heart
becomes so hard that you will not even yield to seek mercy.
The heart is desperately wicked; don't trust it. False
worshippers, remember the doom of Cain.

NOAH SAVED FROM WRATH.
Genesis 6. 7.

IN these chapters we have a dark, dismal picture of man.
After about two thousand years' trial he is here only as a
total failure. When man has altogether failed God comes
in sovereign *grace* and manifests His saving power. It is
always so. Grace comes when man is utterly lost and helpless. The coming forth of Noah and his family from the
ark may be a foreshadowing of the coming of Christ and His
saints to bless a new earth, purged by the judgment of
God. Look at the

I. Divine Verdict. "God said, The end of all flesh is
come before ME" (chap. 6. 13). What a poor end this was!
"Evil, only evil, continually." Mark, this is the end of

all flesh. Evolutionists predict a different end, but the divine verdict has already gone forth—"Only evil." "That which is born of the flesh is flesh" (John 3. 6). "They that are in the flesh cannot please God" (Rom. 8. 8). Unregenerate man, this is the end of your supposed good life, as seen by a righteous and holy God.

II. Divine Plan. "God said to Noah, Make an ark." Noah and his family could never have escaped the flood had not God been pleased to reveal this way of deliverance. It is not in man (1 Cor. 2. 10, 11). Salvation is of the Lord. What a revelation of grace has come to us through Jesus Christ! God laid on Him the iniquity of us all.

III. Divine Warning. "Behold, I, even I, will bring a flood" (v. 17). How gracious our God is in providing a Refuge for us in Christ, and in so plainly warning us of the coming wrath (Luke 3. 7). There is no escape for those who neglect His merciful provision (Heb. 2. 3). "Remember Lot's wife" (Luke 17. 32).

IV. Divine Invitation. "Come thou, and all thy house, into the ark" (chap. 7. 1). He who made the provision sends forth the invitation (Matt. 22. 2, 3). He who gave His Son up to the death for us invites us to "hear Him." The pleading of Jesus is the pleading of God in Him (Matt. 9. 28). God's gracious purpose is to save both you and your household (Acts 16. 31).

V. Divine Security. "The Lord shut him in" (v. 16). They are safely kept whom God shuts up. When He shuts, no man can open. If any man *enter in* he shall be saved (John 10. 9), kept (1 Peter 1. 5), and comforted (John 14. 16). To be shut in by God is to be shut out from the world—from its pleasures, its sins, and its doom. If your life is *hid* with Christ in God, seek those things which are above.

VI. Divine Carefulness. "God remembered Noah." Those who hide know where to seek. Those hidden by God are ever remembered by Him. All who are shut up in Jesus Christ, like Noah, are shut up to faith. It is a blessed privilege to be where we cannot be touched by judgment, and cannot be forgotten of God.

VII. Divine Commission. "God said unto Noah, Go forth" (chap. 8. 16). We go *in* for salvation, and go *forth* for testimony. We are first taken out of the world before we are sent into it (John 17). Those who go *in* and *out* will find pasture. To the unsaved God's word is, "Come in;" to the saved His word is, "Go forth." Blessed coming and going!

THE ALTAR AND THE BOW; OR, DEATH AND RESURRECTION GLORY.

Genesis 8. 20-21; 9. 12-16.

THERE is a very close connection between the altar and the bow. The same connection exists between the death and resurrection of Christ. The altar speaks of sacrifice, the bow of promise and assurance. Christ died for our sins, and rose again for our justification.

I. The Altar. It was an altar builded unto the Lord. It was both a witness and a confession that God had holy and righteous claims that must be acknowledged and met. The first thing that Noah did in coming forth was to recognise that God's place was the *first* place. "In the beginning God."

1. THE NEED OF AN OFFERING. A new beginning was now to be made. If the life is to be a blessed and fruitful one the favour of God must be secured. In the fulness of time the Son of God stepped forth. A new order of things was about to begin. He made peace by the blood of His Cross. By His offering we are reconciled to God. This is a good start.

2. THE NATURE OF THE OFFERING. "*Every clean beast.*" Every clean beast means the combination of every creature excellency. A perfect offering. When Christ offered Himself a sacrifice unto God it was an offering without spot or blemish. Although the first man failed, God found in the second every heart-satisfying virtue.

3. THE RESULT OF THE OFFERING. God found in it: 1, *A savour of rest* (v. 21, margin). Precious thought! Every desire of God's heart fully· met in the sweet savour of Christ's offering (Eph. 5. 2). 2, *An assurance of safety.* No more curse. There is, therefore, now no judgment. Never come into condemnation. 3, *The promise of unceasing blessing* (v. 22). Every spiritual blessing is ours in Christ Jesus (Eph. 1. 3).

II. **The Bow.** The bow of promise comes after the altar of sacrifice. As all the colours of nature are in the bow, so all the promises of God are in Christ. Every divine perfection is manifested in the resurrection glory of Jesus. Christ as our Sacrifice is seen on the altar of the Cross ; Christ as our Intercessor is seen in the bow of His mediatorial glory. The bow is—

1. A TOKEN OF GOD'S GOODNESS. How kind of God to give such a visible expression of His love and favour, such an assurance of heart. If Christ is not risen we are of all men most miserable. But now is Christ risen (1 Cor. 15. 17-20).

2. A TOKEN OF GOD'S FULNESS. There is fulness of colour and beauty in the bow, a fulness that is in sweetest harmony. Think of the fulness of the Godhead in Jesus

Christ, in Him for us, and all in perfect harmony with a just and holy God. O the riches of His glorious grace!

3. A Token of God's Faithfulness. "I do set My bow for a covenant" (chap. 9. 13). The setting of Christ at God's right hand is to us who believe a token of eternal security. He is faithful who hath promised. "Dost thou believe on the Son of God?" (John 9. 35).

THE TOWER OF BABEL.
Genesis 11. 1-9.

There are seven interesting points of contrast between this scene and the one recorded in Acts 1. The gift of new tongues by the Holy Spirit is the divine remedy for the pride that results in the strife of tongues. We have here—

I. A Revelation of Human Ambition. "Out of the heart are the issues of life" (Prov. 4. 23). A straw may indicate which way the wind blows. Observe—

1. The Object in View. "Let us make us a *name*." The natural man seeks a name for himself, and one of his own making. Name-making is a very common and popular business, although it never pays well in the end. See the failure of three name-makers in Numbers 16. It is possible to be doing Christian work with the same end in view.

2. The Method Employed. "Let us *build* a city and a tower." This purpose of theirs betrays a felt need of protection, abiding fellowship, and future prospect. Every man needs a city of safety and a tower of hope. The self-righteous seek to build them for themselves. "Going about to establish their own righteousness" (Rom. 10. 3). Thank God, Jesus Christ has built such a city and tower, where all may have salvation and hope.

3. THE MEANS USED. "Let us *make brick*." Those who would save themselves by their own works have much to do. They have not only the building, but the very bricks to make. Not only to do good works, but they have the very desires to manufacture (a hard task), and, after all is done, it is only brick at the best. In Luke 18. 11, 12 we see one of these brick-makers busy at work.

II. A Manifestation of Divine Displeasure. What will all our building do for us if it does not please God? It is only wood, hay, stubble—fit for the fire.

1. THE DIVINE INSPECTION. "The Lord came down to see what they had built." Every man's work will be tried. This is a very solemn truth. The eyes of Jehovah will scan every brick or jewel. Every motive and act alike must be tested. "Without *faith* it is impossible to please God" (Heb. 11. 6).

2. THE SUDDEN CONFUSION. "The Lord did there confound, so they left off to build." What a change when God comes! When the Spirit of God comes upon the self-righteous He makes them leave off their vain and presumptuous works. Think of it. The presence of God means confusion to the religious self-seeker. What may be very pleasing in the eyes of men may be suddenly turned into Babel at the approach of God. "He that BELIEVETH on Him shall not be confounded" (1 Peter 2. 6).

3. COMPLETE DISPERSION. "From thence did the Lord scatter them abroad." The very thing they were labouring to prevent was the thing that came upon them. Proud men labour to save themselves from being cast out by God at last, and their faithless works are securing for them the doom they strive to avoid. The city of God, seek ye it (Heb. 11. 10). The *name* of the Lord is a strong tower; flee unto it (Prov. 18. 10).

THE CALL OF ABRAHAM.

Genesis 12. 1-4.

THE life of Abraham, like the course of a river, had many windings, but it seemed to deepen and gather in strength as it went on. No Old Testament saint figures more prominently in the New Testament. A life of faith in God will always be fragrant for good.

I. **When the Call Came.** It came while he was living in ignorance and idolatry (Rom. 4. 10). He was not called because he was better than his countrymen. The grace of God seeks for no worthiness. Christ came not to call the righteous, but sinners. While we were yet sinners, Christ died for us.

II. **How the Call Came.** Whether he heard an audible voice, or whether the Spirit of God whispered the message into his heart by working in him an irresistible desire we know not. At anyrate, the call was very *personal*. He alone could answer it. The calling of God brings individual responsibility. God calls us not that we may be better than our neighbours, but better than ourselves. God's saving call comes to us through the Gospel.

III. **What this Call Involves.**

1. AN ENTIRE SEPARATION. "Get thee out." His country, kindred, or father's house must not hinder. Every connection and friendship that stood between him and the divine call must be broken and left behind. If a man is not willing to forsake his sins he is not willing to be saved (Isa. 55. 7).

2. A NEW LIFE. This life is a life of faith in God and fellowship with God—a blessed life. All who obey God live by faith. It is the transplanting by the Spirit out of the barren soil of self into the fat, fruitful soil of infinite grace.

IV. What Accompanies this Call.

1. THE PROMISE OF A POSSESSION. "A land that I will show thee." Many linger when God calls, thinking of what might have to be given up, forgetful of what God offers. The Prodigal had, of course, to give up his rags when he got the best robe.

2. THE PROMISE OF BEING MADE A BLESSING. "I will bless thee, and thou shalt be a blessing." All the families of the earth are being and will yet be blessed through Abraham's seed (Christ). We can only be a blessing for God after we have been blessed by God. This is God's order. We are saved to serve. It is out of those who come to Jesus and drink that the living water flows (John 7. 37, 38).

V. How the Call was Received. It would seem from chapter 11. 31 that Abraham was led by his father instead of the command of God. Under his leadership he only got to Haran. After his father's death Abram fully obeyed (v. 4). Worldly wisdom will never help us in the life of faith. There is no rest or blessing for those who stop short of Christ, no matter how far they may have gone. Not far from the kingdom is still outside. Almost saved means lost. "God is calling yet. O hear Him ! "

ABRAHAM IN CANAAN.
Genesis 12. 4-9.

PERHAPS Terah, the father of Abraham, was seeking only his own comfort when he called a halt at Haran. In such a spirit the Land of Promise can never be possessed. There must be a crossing of the river (Euphrates) and a passing into the desert if Canaan is to be enjoyed. Half-and-half Christians who abide on the border never inherit the fulness of the land (Joshua 1. 3).

I. A Prosperous Journey. "They *went forth* to go to Canaan, and into Canaan *they came*." The life of faith is always a life of *going forth*. "A going on still" (v. 9).

1. THE START. "They went forth." *What from?* From all the past sins and failures, from worldly pleasures, from self-ease, and self-seeking. *What on?* On the sure word of God's unfailing promise, not leaning on their own feelings, wisdom, or understanding. "He went out, not knowing whither he went."

2. THE JOURNEY. The way lay through the Syrian desert. The *passage* into the place of blessing may be extremely trying to flesh and blood, the *way* to the Cross may be sorrowful, but the burden rolls off when there. The entrance into the *fulness* of the blessing is always through the barren desert of self-despair.

3. THE END. "Into Canaan they came." Those who go out in the expectation of faith will not stick in the mud of disappointment. There are two great and common causes of failure in the Christian life. First, *stopping short* of the purpose and promise of God; second, going *without* the divine promise. Going forth in the energy of the flesh, having no special call of God to lean on. So when the heat of temptation comes they wither, having no root.

II. A Continual Difficulty. "The Canaanite was then in the land" (v. 6). Canaan is not a type of Heaven, for there will be no enemy there. It is typical of the new relationships into which believers enter after having trusted God, and gone forth in His Name. Here we have trial and warfare, and as pilgrims and strangers have need of continual faith. Being in the place of *warfare*, we are in the place where God has promised to bless. Abraham got no blessing while among *his own* kindred (v. 1). It is in the *high places* of promise that we wrestle against principalities and powers (Eph. 6. 12).

III. An Unfailing Assurance. "The Lord appeared unto Abram, and said, "Unto thy seed will I give this land" (v. 7). The assuring promise was given when Abram had got right into the *centre* of the land. When by faith we take our stand right upon His Word, then shall we find it sweetly fulfilled in our experience. The *centre* of God's promises is in Christ. We shall come short until we are found in Him. "All the promises of God are in Him" (2 Cor. 1. 20). Go forth, believer, into the heart and centre of all God's purposes in Christ. You will find grace sufficient there. The anxious soul must get to this centre before the *assurance* of salvation will be given. The sealing comes upon believing (Eph. 1. 13).

IV. A Powerful Testimony. "He pitched his tent, and builded an altar unto the Lord" (v. 8). Abram's great mission in Canaan was that of a *witness* for God. His altar was a public testimony. To this end is every Christian called. "Ye shall be witnesses unto Me" (Acts 1. 8). By his tent he declared himself a pilgrim and a stranger, looking for a city; by His altar he testified to

1. His FAITH IN THE REALITY OF GOD. While the Canaanite looked on he must have been convinced that Abram believed in a living, personal, prayer-hearing God.

2. His BELIEF IN THE HOLINESS OF GOD. The altar speaks of sacrifice. God is holy, and can only be approached through atoning blood. Does *our* lives bear this much-needed testimony? Do we by our acts condemn the world? (Heb. 11. 7).

3. His CONFIDENCE IN THE FAITHFULNESS OF GOD. He was not ashamed to lift up his altar in the presence of the heathen, declaring thereby his expectation of the fulfilment of the divine promise. How often are we afraid to venture much for God, lest He should fail and our confidence stagger.

4. HIS SURRENDER TO THE CLAIMS OF GOD. All who
really know the need and meaning of the altar will gladly
yield up all to Him. May our lives be lived in the light
of that awful altar and sacrifice lifted up on Calvary.
Yield yourselves unto God.

ABRAHAM IN EGYPT.

Genesis 20. 10-20; 13. 1-4.

IN the spiritual world of our Christian experience, as well
as in the natural world, changes may come very suddenly.
Who would have thought that a man with Abraham's
faith would turn aside at the first temptation. At our
best and strongest moment we are in danger of falling, if
not kept by the power of God *through faith*.

I. **The Trial.** "There was a famine in the land." It
is always a great trial to experience drought and lack of
pasture *in the Land of Promise*. But if faith is to triumph
and grow it must be tested. "The trial of your faith is
precious" (1 Peter 1. 7). Well-watered plains please the
eye. Faith must lay hold on the things which are unseen.
It is often in the place of blessing where the keenest pangs
of thirst are felt. Trials make the promise sweet; there is
no discipline of soul without them.

II. **The Failure.** "He went down into Egypt" (v. 10).
Why? Had GOD failed? Ah, no! But it seems to have
happened to Abraham as it often turns out in our own experience. He had been trusting more to the land than to
the God of promise; looking more to the blessing than the
Blesser. This God will not permit. Our faith must not
rest on His gifts, but on Himself. Note what this downward step led to.

1. IT LED TO FEAR (v. 12). He was now afraid they
would take his life. His courage for God is gone. None

are so weak and silly as Christians when turned aside from the life of faith.

2. IT LED TO SELFISHNESS (vv. 11 and 12). He is more concerned about his own safety than the honour and chastity of his wife. When a man turns away from God his interest is sure to become centred in himself.

3. IT LED TO HYPOCRISY (v. 13). He pretended to be what he was not, only the *brother of* Sarai. This was a deliberate misrepresentation. This is the next step of the backslider, pretending not to be what he really is.

4. IT LED TO OPEN REBUKE. Pharaoh said to him, "What is this that thou hast done?" (v. 18). It is sad when the child of God has to be warned and corrected by the man of the world.

5. IT LED TO TROUBLE UPON OTHERS. "The Lord plagued Pharaoh because of Abraham's wife" (v. 17). The plague of divine judgment will doubtless need to fall upon many because of the unfaithfulness of many of God's believing people. May our light so shine that they will be led to glorify our Father in Heaven.

III. The Restoration. "Abraham went up out of Egypt, and came unto the *place of the altar* which he had made *at the first*" (chap. 13. 1-4). It has been said that "the man of God makes but a poor worldling." Abraham built no altar in Egypt. There is no fellowship with God while we walk by sight and not by faith. The only remedy for backsliding is to come again to the place of the altar, the Cross of Christ. This is the place of sacrifice, forgiveness communion, and consecration. There was no happiness nor restoration for the prodigal until he came back to the place from whence he had wandered away (Luke 15). "Ye have forsaken ME," saith the Lord. "Return unto ME, and I will heal your backslidings."

ABRAHAM, THE SEPARATED ONE.
Genesis 13. 5-18.

ABRAHAM and Lot are types of two classes of Christians. Lot was a righteous man, but, living by sight and sense, he sought only his own pleasure and profit. He is the type of an unconsecrated Christian. Abraham lives by faith on the promise of God. He may fail, but not like Lot, who never could do anything to help Abraham. Lot builded no altar. The unconsecrated life can live without worship. The well-watered plains have more attraction for the worldly believer. The "higher Christian life" just means higher motives in living.

I. **The Impossible Relationship.** "The land was not able to bear them" (v. 6). The conditions of the country would not permit of Abram and Lot dwelling *together*. Even the Land of Promise is not able to sustain such an unequal yoke as the life of faith in God and the life of sense and worldly wisdom. This is a strife that often takes place in the heart of the believer, a conflict between the fleshly life and the spiritual. As long as the *strife* goes on the Land of Promise seems to yield no blessing (see Rom. 7). Worldly Christians, like Lot, set no value on the promises of God.

II. **The Generosity of Faith.** "Abram said to Lot, The whole land is before thee; separate thyself" (vv. 8 and 9). The friend of God can easily afford to let others have the first choice. Either hand will do for the man of God. The servant of God must not strive. We can show our trust in God by standing back from the strife of tongues, and by allowing others to occupy the chief seats. Let us stand up for God, and God will stand up for our rights. All our rights are in Him.

III. **The Selfishness of the Worldly-Minded.** "Lot

lifted up his eyes" (vv. 10-13). He looked for the best, and chose it, and never said "Thank you." He separated himself from the man of faith with a light heart. Worldly Christians do not set much value on the *fellowship* of a holy man. His mind was set on earthly prosperity, not on heavenly things. How much did he gain by it? He pitched his tent (no altar) toward Sodom, and was burned out of it himself, saved as by fire.

IV. **The Privilege of the Separated.** "The Lord said unto Abram, *after* Lot was separated from him, Lift up *now thine eyes*" (v. 14). After the separation comes the message of comfort, "Come out from among them, . . . and I will receive you" (2 Cor. 6. 17). Greed and covetousness constrained Lot to lift up his eyes. Abram lifted up his eyes at the invitation of the Lord. Herein lies the great distinction between the worldly Christian and the faithful one. The one is moved by self-interest, the other by the Word of God. "Looking up" is the abiding attitude of every separated one. Lot goes leaning on his own understanding. Abram goes leaning on the promise of God (see Gal. 2. 20).

V. **The Altar of Testimony.** "Abram came to the plain of Mamre and built there an altar unto the Lord" (v. 18). Lot pitched his tent toward Sodom; Abram pitched his toward God. The self-seeking Christian bears no testimony for God. When he does attempt it, it looks like mockery (Gen. 19. 14). The just shall live by *faith*. Live to the will of God (1 Peter 4. 1, 2).

ABRAHAM, THE MAN OF FAITH.
Genesis 14. 18-24.

GOD called Abram, and he went out, not knowing whither he went. Lot went *with him*. Lot followed Abram, and

Abram followed God. Lot is soon found *dwelling* in Sodom. Now we see him as a *captive*. Worldliness is sure to lead to spiritual bondage. Abram's character shines out here as—

I. A Man of Sympathy. "They came and told Abram that his brother was taken captive" (vv. 13 and 14). Think of what he might have said: "He has himself to blame. Serve him right; he should not have gone *into* Sodom." Just the wages of worldliness. But not so. He at once bestirs himself to seek his deliverance. Those who walk in fellowship with God cannot remain indifferent to the sufferings and sorrows of their brethren.

II. A Man of Courage (vv. 14 and 15). With his handful of servants he goes forth against the four kings. The man of faith attempts great things. He knows that God can use weak things to confound the mighty. Abram's faith worked by love. He loved his brother Lot, and dared to do this great deed. Great faith constrains to attempt what seems impossible. Think of Nehemiah, of Moses, and of Paul (Phil. 4. 13).

III. A Man of Power. "He brought back all" (v. 16). Abram, as a separated man, dwelt in the presence of God. He went to battle as one who had *come out* from the holy, soul-inspiring presence. The victory is complete. Lot mingled with the ungodly, and he could not even save himself. It is the *separated one* alone who is able to save others. Abram's power lay in his life of faith. If we would have victory for God, then we must be separated unto God. Remember where and how Samson failed (Judges 16). The fruitful branch must abide in the vine.

IV. A Man of Independence. "I will not take anything that is thine" (v. 23). Abram took all he could get from the King of Salem, because he was the priest of the Most High God; but he would take nothing from the King of Sodom, lest he should say, "I have made Abram rich." GOD had enriched him, and he would take nothing likely to hinder Him from having all the honour. This is not the independence of pride and self-sufficiency, but that of a holy jealousy for the Name and character of God. It is the independence of entire dependence upon God alone. May our hearts be stirred up to the exercise of it. "The LORD is the portion of His people" (Deut. 32. 9).

V. A Man Approved of God. "Melchizedek met him and blessed him" (vv. 18 and 19). He also refreshed him with "bread and wine." Jesus Christ, the Priest of the Most High God, will so bless and refresh all who, like Abram, go forth in His Name to walk, to work, and to war. What a privilege to meet the *Blessing Priest* when returning faint and weary from the struggle of faith! Many a battle the separated man of God will need to fight on behalf of others, but Jesus, the succouring King of Peace, will meet him with His help and blessing, and at last with His "Well done," which brings eternal benediction.

ABRAHAM ENCOURAGED.
Genesis 15. 1-6.

A WORD in season; how good it is! God's words are always in season. He knows how to speak a word to them that are weary. His consolations are neither few nor small.

I. The Time. "After these things the Word of the Lord came to Abram." After the battle and rescue of Lot from the hands of the four kings. It is no unusual experience for the man of God to tremble, even after a great victory has been gained. The achievements of faith never bring *self-confidence*. Abram may have feared the return of the kings with renewed force; he may have been vexing his soul at refusing the gifts of the King of Sodom; but God's "Fear not; I am thy reward," would be a word full of consolation and comfort. Let us look at—

II. The Message. This message contains—

1. A REVELATION OF GOD'S LOVE. "Fear not." This is the language of One who, in love and grace, had considered all his need. Jesus said, "Give ye them to eat," for "*He Himself* knew what *He would do*" (Luke 6. 6). This message reminds us of the fulness of the blessing of the Gospel of Christ. Fear not; He who gave His Son for us, how shall He not with Him also freely give us all things?

2. A REVELATION OF GOD'S POWER. "I am thy shield." The Omnipotent, Personal God declares *Himself* as the protection of the man who walks by faith. GOD is our refuge. Your life is hid with Christ in God. I am thy shield. Christ shelters from sin by the shield of His Blood (Exodus 12. 13). Christ shelters the weak and faltering with the shield of His intercession (Luke 22. 32).

3. A REVELATION OF GOD'S FULNESS. "I am thy exceeding great reward." It is still the desire and delight of God that His people should be satisfied with HIMSELF. The great ultimate purpose of the incarnation is that the believing soul should be rewarded with the revelation of God. These *unsearchable riches* are in Christ for us now. In Him dwelleth all the fulness of the Godhead. The greatest reward God can bestow upon us is a fuller and better acquaintance with Himself. For this the Holy Ghost has been given, that He might take the things of Christ and *show them* to us. This precious promise was given to Abram after he had refused the unhallowed gifts

of the King of Sodom (Gen. 14. 23). Every sacrifice for Christ's sake will bring exceeding great reward.

III. The Result. "He believed in the Lord" (v. 6). This is very beautiful. He accepted God's gracious message, and rested calmly on His Word, and we read, "And God counted it to Him for righteousness." His was the righteousness, not of works, but of *faith* (Rom. 4. 3). Faith in God has alwasy a transforming power. God justifies the believer in Jesus. He counts, or reckons, them righteous. Who shall condemn whom God counts righteous? This *believing in the Lord* implies the entire surrender of ourselves unto God, that He may work in us both to will and to dò of His good pleasure.

ABRAHAM WALKING BEFORE GOD.
Genesis 17. 1-5.

ABRAM was ninety-and-nine years old when the Lord appeared unto him. Not too old to have fellowship with Him. Age may shut us out from the joys and companionships of youth, but through grace it may ripen our friendship with God.

I. The Revelation. "I am the Almighty. *I am God all-sufficient.*" This is a divine plaster large enough to cover any human sore. A son had been promised Abram; he was now old, and no son had yet been given to him; but in this promise he had enough to brighten faith and trim afresh the flickering lamp of hope. This revelation of God, as our all-sufficiency, is made known to us in Jesus Christ. There is enough in Him to meet all our need, both as sinners and as servants. Weary, downcast Christian toilers, hear Him say, "Look unto Me; I am God all-sufficient." To brighten thy little dwelling there is plenty of light in this sun; to float thy little vessel there is plenty of water in this ocean.

II. The Commission. "Walk before Me, and be thou perfect." Perhaps Abram had been walking too much *before* Sarah. Seeking to please her, guided by her counsel, he had already turned aside from the life of faith in God (chap. 16. 1-4). This was a call—

1. THAT AFFECTED HIS LIFE. "Walk *before Me*." In all things he was to act as one who lived in the *immediate* presence of God Almighty. This is not a life of dread and awkward restraint, but a holy, joyful, divinely-satisfied life. It is, in fact, *the life* of faith. This is the high privilege of every Heaven-born son of God.

2. IT AFFECTED HIS CHARACTER. "Be thou perfect." That is, be *whole-hearted*. Not having a double heart (Psa. 12. 2), seeking to *please* both God and man. All perfection comes from Him who alone is perfect. The highest human perfection lies in a whole-hearted life before God.

III. The Submission. "And Abram *fell on his face*" (v. 3). The best answer to God's high calling is a humble and broken spirit. Abram did not say boastingly, like some of his descendants, "All that thou sayest will we do" (Ruth 3. 5). He bowed his face to the dust, and "*God talked with him.*" A deep, conscious sense of ignorance and weakness brings us into the right attitude to be *taught of God*. God always talks to the heart of the self-abased. When John fell at His feet he felt the touch of His gracious hand, and heard His comforting "Fear not" (Rev. 1. 17). May He give us that humbleness of heart, that calmness of spirit that bears the faintest whisper from the lips of the Holy Ghost.

IV. The Transformation. "Neither shall thy name any more be called Abram; but thy name shall be called

Abraham." Abram, the *exalted*, is changed into Abraham, the *fruitful*. He has bowed with his whole heart unto the will of God, and his character is transformed. It is not always so? Complete surrender brings a complete change of nature. Jacob became a prince, and *prevailed* when he *yielded* entirely to the heavenly wrestler. It is when we are *crucified* with Christ that Christ liveth in us (Gal. 2. 20). It is by yielding to the Spirit of Christ that we are transformed into His holy and heavenly image.

ABRAHAM RECEIVING AND SERVING.
Genesis 18. 1-17.

EVERY Old Testament incident yields some New Testament truth. Let us read this portion in the light of the New Revelation.

I. A Gracious Visit. "The Lord appeared unto him; ... and he lift up his eyes, and, lo, *three* men stood by him" (vv. 1 and 2). This is striking language, that Jehovah should manifest Himself in the form of *three*. Does this not suggest the *Trinity* of the Godhead? The whole Trinity is interested and exercised in seeking to bless and save man. The *Father* loved, and sent His Son; the *Son* loved, and gave Himself up to the death to redeem; the *Spirit* loved, and came to make His abode in the believing heart. This threefold salvation is summed up in the benediction, "The *grace* of the Lord Jesus Christ, and the *love* of God, and the *communion* of the Holy Ghost" (2 Cor. 13. 14).

II. A Hearty Reception. The manner in which Abraham received the visitors, and his various acts toward them, may serve us as an illustration of how a weary, longing soul may receive Jesus, and be drawn out in eagerness after Him.

1. THERE WAS A LONGING DESIRE. "He lift up his eyes and looked" (v. 2). A good work has been wrought *in* us before we will even *lift up* our eyes. The Lord is sure to appear in grace to the *looking* ones. They looked, and were lightened.

2. THERE WAS A READY MIND. "He ran to meet them." He was in haste to receive the visitors. When the heart is really *hungering* for the living bread it will receive it gladly. The soul that is sighing for Christ will hasten to Him.

3. THERE WAS A HUMBLE SPIRIT. "He bowed himself toward the ground." The more closely we come to Jesus, the heavenly Visitor, the more unworthy do we see ourselves to be. The way to God is a self-humbling way. The nearer we come to His light the more unseemly doth the garments of our own righteousness appear.

4. THERE WAS A WILLING CONFESSION. Abraham said, "My Lord." When a soul has found its way into the presence of Jesus Christ we expect to hear the language of confession and testimony. "My Lord!" These two little words imply two great thoughts—(1) *appropriation*; (2) *entire subjection.* He is mine and I am His.

5. THERE WAS A LOVE FOR FELLOWSHIP. "If I have found favour in Thy sight, *pass not away,* I pray Thee, *from Thy servant*" (v. 3). What could be more natural? The soul that has found the Lord yearns to abide in His presence. In His presence is fulness of joy. The lonely heart finds its home in the bosom of His love.

6. THERE WAS A DESIRE FOR THEIR REFRESHING. "Rest *yourselves,* . . . and comfort *your* hearts" (vv. 4 and 5). In our selfishness we are apt to be satisfied with *getting* His favour and blessing, and stopping short of seeking rest for

His soul and comfort for *His* heart. Christ gave us rest and comfort by giving Himself for us; let us give Him rest and comfort by giving ourselves to Him.

7. THERE WAS A READINESS TO SERVE. "Abraham ran and fetcht and gave" (vv. 6 and 7). Love lends swiftness to the willing feet. "The Lord loveth a *cheerful* giver" (2 Cor. 9. 7). "Whatsoever ye do, do it *heartily*, as unto the Lord" (Col. 3. 23). "The love of Christ constraineth us" (2 Cor. 5. 14).

III. **A Blessed Reward.** "The Lord said, Shall I hide from Abraham that thing which I do?" (v. 17). The devotion of Abraham is rewarded with a revelation of the *secret* purpose of the Lord. The secret of the Lord is with them that fear Him. The way into the deeper things of God often lies through self-sacrifice and active service. If we would know the hidden wisdom of God, and feed on the finest of the wheat, we must lay ourselves and all that we have at the feet of our Lord. Open your heart to Him, and His heart will be open to you.

THE HISTORY OF LOT.
Genesis 19.

THE history of Lot is the history of a backslider. When he turned away from Abraham he turned aside from faith. When he sought the well-watered plains he was seeking *his own* glory. While seeking *his own* interest his testimony as a believer in the Lord was despised. Then came failure and flight, but being the Lord's he himself was saved as by fire, though all his works were burnt (1 Cor. 3. 14, 15). Look at the—

I. **Choice He Made.** "He chose the plain of Jordan, and pitched *toward* Sodom" (Gen. 13. 10-12). Those who walk by *sight* and not by faith will always be influenced by *appearances*. The choice of Moses was the choice of faith (Heb. 11. 24, 25). If we follow the dictates of our own hearts we will be sure to pitch toward Sodom.

II. Position He Occupied. "Lot sat in the gate of Sodom." Having become a *companion* of the Sodomites, he now becomes a *partner* with them. When a Christian can find pleasure in the fellowship of the ungodly he will soon become a sharer of their iniquity. Worldly advancement is no evidence of growth in grace. Mixing with the world often means helping the ungodly (2 Chron. 19. 12).

III. Message He Received. "The Lord hath sent us to destroy this place" (v. 13). Wicked places and wicked things must all be destroyed. If all your wicked things were destroyed would you *lose* anything? How would it affect your *plans* and *purposes*? If our heart interests are entangled with the wickedness of this world we will suffer loss. Set your *affections* on things above, then, when every wicked place is destroyed your inheritance will remain untouched.

IV. Testimony He Bore. "Lot went out and spake unto his sons-in-law;... but he seemed as one that mocked" (v. 14). Our testimony for God will always be a mockery if we are living the selfish life. Who will believe that sin is bitter if we roll it under our tongue as a sweet morsel? Neither earnestness nor eloquence will make up for *inconsistency*. It is the *life* that is the *light*.

V. Reluctance He Showed. "While he *lingered* the men laid hold upon his hand" (v. 16). We are always slow to obey the call of God when our lives are entangled with the affairs of the world. The young man went away sorrowful, for he had great possessions (Matt. 19. 22).

Many perish in the full light of knowledge for lack of decision. Escape for thy life—tarry not.

VI. Request He Offered. "Behold this city is *near*; let me escape hither" (v. 20). He thought the *appointed* mountain of refuge too far away. Why should he wish to be saved as near the city of doom as possible? Why should we wish to be saved, and nothing more? Is there not a lurking unwillingness in the minds of many of God's people to flee to the distant mountain of entire *separation*? Lot was saved, but he was still near enough the place of death to fill him with fear (v. 30).

VII. Favour He Enjoyed. "I cannot do anything till *thou* be come thither" (v. 22). How precious even a poor backslider is to God! Judgment cannot fall on Sodom till he is outside. But think further how the presence of this worldly-minded believer among the ungodly was *hindering* God from carrying out His own purposes. Until he came out from among them the work of God was at a standstill.

A SOLEMN REFLECTION.
Genesis 19. 27, 28.

"ABRAHAM gat up early in the morning to *the place where he stood before the Lord*; and he looked toward Sodom; . . . and, lo, the smoke of the country went up as the smoke of a furnace." This was a sacred spot to him. Here the Lord met him, and here he made intercession for the righteous in Sodom. Now from this holy place he beholds the judgment of God. Those flame-girt columns of smoke declare the fulfilment of His word, and reveal His awful character when dealing in *righteousness* with sin and guilt. "Our God is a consuming fire" (Heb. 12. 29). It is when we stand like Abraham in these high and heavenly places, walking by faith in *fellowship* with the Lord, and in the

spirit of *intercession*, that we see and understand what a
holy, sin-hating God we worship. As we in imagination
stand with Abraham gazing on the fiery doom of Sodom,
let us reflect on the—

I. Awfulness of Sin. It constrained the Lord to come
down from Heaven to deal with it (chap. 18. 20, 21). The
cry of Israel in Egypt brought the Lord down to *deliver*.
The cry of Sodom brought Him down to *destroy*. The cry
of the world's need brought Jesus our Lord from Heaven
that He might deal with it. When God comes in grace He
deals with *sin*, putting it away by the sacrifice of Himself.
When He comes in judgment He deals with the *sinner*,
putting him away. "The wages of sin is death" (Rom.
6. 23).

II. Certainty of Judgment. "We will destroy this
place;... the smoke went up" (vv. 13-28). A man might
as well hope to escape from his own shadow as from guilt
and punishment so long as his sins are unforgiven. The
judgment of God may slumber, and guilt may lift up its
haughty and defiant head; but (1) *it is certain*; (2) *it may
be sudden*; (3) *it will be complete*.

III. Sovereignty of Grace. As Abraham looked with
tear-filled eyes upon the smoke of perishing Sodom he
might have asked himself, "Why am I not there? How
have I been saved from it? Why was I called out of Ur?
What better was I than many left in their sins?" The
answer is, "*By grace* are ye saved" (Eph. 11. 8).

IV. Security of Believers. "I can do nothing till *thou*
be come hither." "I will not destroy it for *ten's sake*."
God will not destroy the righteous with the wicked. All
who belong to Him are under a *special* providence. God
said to Moses, "Separate yourselves *from among* this con-

gregation, that I may consume them" (Num. 16. 21).
Before the flood came the righteous were shut up in the ark.
Before the judgments are poured out on the earth the
Church will be translated to Heaven. "Neither shall any
man pluck them out of My hand" (John 10. 28).

V. Importance of Witness-Bearing. The Sodomites,
like the men of this world, were under condemnation, but
believed it not. God has not left us in ignorance of our
doom if we reject His Son. "He that believeth not is condemned *already*" (John 3. 18)

VI. Value of Present Opportunity. Soon our day of
testimony will be over. Soon those among whom we live
will be clothed in white robes before God, or rapt up in
the smoke of torment. Lot's *twenty years* in Sodom were
fruitless tc God. Now the day of his privilege is gone, and
his very companions perish in their sins. Behold, now is
the accepted time both for salvation and service (see Jude
20-23).

HAGAR THE HELPLESS.
Genesis 21. 14-19.

"WHAT aileth thee, Hagar?" Human ailments are very
many, and may overtake us, as they did Hagar, in a very
unexpected way. Who could be happier than she while
nursing the son of Abraham? But the birth of *Isaac* (type
of that which is born of the Spirit) brings trouble and
separation to *Ishmael* (that which is born of the flesh).
Poor Hagar, crushed in spirit, wanders forth into the
wilderness, where, like the weary dove outside the ark,
she is ready to perish, but the merciful hand of God is
stretched out, and she is received into the favour of Him
who seeks to save the lost. Notice—

I. Divine Question. God called, and said, "What
aileth thee, Hagar?" (v. 17). How timely and tender is

the *sympathy* of God! This is no formal question of curiosity, but the loving inquiry of One whose heart yearns to help the needy. When Jesus said, "What will thou that I shall do unto thee?" (Luke 18. 41) He was opening the door into His own divine fulness. Hagar's ailment, in a typical sense, is a very common one.

1. SHE WAS AN OUTCAST. "Cast out this bondwoman" (v. 10). "Abraham sent her away" (v. 14). She was shut out from the Master's house and presence. Why? Because her son mocked at Isaac—the gift of God. Those who were found sneering at the Word of Christ were all put outside, "And He put them all out, and took her by the hand, and called, saying, Maid, arise" (Luke 8. 54). Sin always separates and leads from the house of blessing to the desert of sorrow and misery.

2. SHE WAS DESTITUTE. "The water was spent in the bottle" (v. 15). The resources of an outcast are speedily exhausted. The prodigal's fortune was soon spent (Luke 15). When the sinner gets to an end of himself he has nothing left but prayer. His *wit's end* is often his best end. It is when all self-created streams are dried that the longing eye seeks the Living Fountain.

3. SHE WAS HELPLESS AND HOPELESS. "She went a good way off, and said, Let me not see the death of the child" (v. 16). She now sees nothing but the grim face of death before her. Her parting with the lad must have been like wringing the last drop of blood out of her agonising heart. It is possible to see and feel the greatness of our needs, so that we are afraid to listen to their voice. Stifling their cry does not improve our condition. She is a true and painful picture of one who is "without strength." "For when we were yet without strength, in due time Christ died for the ungodly" (Rom. 5. 6).

II. Divine Word of Comfort. "The angel of God said, Fear not, for God hath heard." What a beautiful fulfilment of "He knows how to speak a word *in season* to them that *are weary*" (Isa. 50. 4). Man's extremity is God's opportunity. It was "while we were yet sinners Christ died for us" (Rom. 5. 8). The divine "Fear not" is always accompanied with the divine fulness (Isa. 41. 10).

1. THE PROVISION. "She saw a well of water" (v. 19). She was sitting perishing in an agony of thirst while a well of salvation was close at hand. Spiritually this is the state and condition of many perishing for lack of knowledge while the Word of Truth is lying at their side, and even ringing in their ears.

2. THE PREPARATION. "God opened her eyes." It was not enough that the well was there; her eyes must be opened to see it. The great provision of the Gospel is twofold: 1, The outward work of Christ on the Cross; 2, the inward work of the Holy Spirit in the heart. The well of atonement cannot satisfy without the eye-opening power of the Spirit of God. "Open Thou mine eyes" (Psa. 119. 18).

3. THE ACCEPTANCE. "She went and filled the bottle with water." She could not *make* the well, but she could *take* the water freely offered to her. We are not asked to make salvation, but to take it (Rev. 22. 17). What a revelation this was to Hagar: 1, *Of her own blindness*. It was only when her eyes were opened that she discovered how blind she had been. 2, *Of the goodness of God*. He made the provision, and imparted to the needy one the very capacity to apprehend it. God opened her eyes, but she must fill the bottle. It is an awful responsibility to have the opened eye and yet to refuse the blessings revealed. In the Fountain opened for sin and uncleanness there is enough to fill every bottle to satisfy every heart.

4. THE RESULT. "She gave the lad drink." In accepting the divine provision she saved both herself and her son. "Believe on the Lord Jesus Christ, and *thou* shalt be saved, and *thy* house" (Acts 16. 31).

THE SACRIFICE OF ABRAHAM.
Genesis 22. 1-14.

HE who is to be the father of the faithful has to face the father of all the trials of faith. We see the workings of great faith in the actions of Abraham.

(1) *He reasoned not*; he consulted no one.

(2) *He staggered not* under the crushing weight of such a demand.

(3) *He was prompt*; he rose up early in the morning.

(4) *He was deliberate*; preparing the wood beforehand.

(5) *He was fully determined*; bade the young men keep back that they might not hinder him. This is a very fruitful portion. Look at the—

I. **Father's Sacrifice.** "Take now thy son." Think of the preciousness of this son. All the hopes and desires and affections of the father are centred in him. In offering up his son Abraham was giving up his all. He had absolutely nothing left but his God. Yet this is enough for faith. God gave up His Son, although all His affections and purposes were centred in Him. We can never understand the greatness of His sacrifice until we can understand the greatness of His love for His beloved Son. Like Abraham, in giving His Son He gave HIS ALL.

II. **Son's Submission.** It is significantly stated that "they went both of them together." In a deep and real sense this was true of Jesus Christ and His Father. In making an atonement for sin "they went *both of them together*." "I delight to do Thy will, O my God" (Psa. 40. 8). The purpose of the Father and of the Son was one. Like the Lord Jesus Christ, Isaac submitted—

1. To be Burdened. "Abraham took the wood and *laid it upon* Isaac, his son." What a burden in the eyes of the father! It was the cross of sacrifice, the symbol of death. What a picture of the only-begotten Son of God, with the burden of our iniquity laid upon Him, and laid on Him, too, by a loving Father! "The *Lord hath laid on Him* the iniquity of us all" (Isa. 53. 6). He also submitted—

2. To be Bound. "He bound Isaac his son, and laid him on the altar." As a young man, twenty-five years of age, he might have resisted; but he, like our Isaac, was led as a lamb, he opened not his mouth. Love and devotion were the cords that bound the Son of God to the altar of sacrifice.

III. **Sacrificial Requisites.** Isaac carried the wood, while he himself was to be the burnt-offering; but let us not fail to observe what was in the father's hands.

1. The Fire. "Abraham took the fire *in his hand*." There is something awfully solemn about this. "Our God is a consuming fire" (Heb. 12. 29). "Who shall dwell with devouring fire?" (Isa. 33. 14). Does not this suggest the holy, testing, consuming character of God when approaching the altar of expiation?

2. The Knife. "He took the fire and a knife." If the fire represents the holiness of God, then the knife may well symbolise the sword of justice. "Awake, O sword, against the man that is *my fellow*" (Zech. 13. 7). The

knife was quivering in the air when Jesus cried, "My God, my God, why hast Thou forsaken Me?" (Psa. 22. 1). In these days men are ready to forget that every sacrifice to God must have to do with the divine knife and fire.

3. THE ALTAR. "Abraham built an altar." Isaac did not make the altar; it was prepared by the father. My soul, tread softly here. This was solemn work for Abraham. In eternity God in His own heart and mind prepared the altar for Christ. He was the *Lamb slain* from the foundation of the world.

4. THE CORDS with which Isaac was bound to the altar, typical of the nails which bound Christ to the Cross. Not the nails, but love bound the Saviour. It was the love of the Father to the Son, the love of the Son to the Father, and the love of both to man—a threefold cord that is not easily broken.

IV. **Doctrine of Substitution.** "He took the ram and offered him *in the stead of his son*" (v. 13). The scene on Mount Moriah, as typical of the greater scene on Mount Calvary, could scarcely have been perfect without the thought of *substitution* being made prominent. The figure now changes. The ram becomes the *burnt-offering*, and the *submissive one* goes free. You observe this sacrifice was provided by God. We have still Jesus before us, not as the *Son* now, but as the Substitute of one condemned to die. Man found a Cross for Christ, but it was God who found THE RANSOM—"Jehovah-Jireh." "He *spared not* His own Son (like Abraham's), but delivered Him up for us all" (Rom. 8. 32). "Christ our Passover is *sacrificed for us*" (1 Cor. 5. 7). Ask Isaac, as he gazes on the ram burning in his stead, if he believes in *substitution*. "Behold the Lamb of God which taketh away the sin of the world" (John 1. 29).

THE BRIDAL SEARCH.

Genesis 24.

THIS is one of the most wonderful seed-plots in the whole field of Revelation. It is an epitome of the scheme of salvation, and an outline history of the Church of God. May our eyes be opened to behold these wondrous things. Here we may see—

I. **Abraham; or, The Father's Purpose.** "Thou shalt go and take a wife unto my son Isaac" (v. 4). The thought of a bride for Isaac originated with the father. It was the outcome of his love for his son, and a desire to bring into great blessing one who was as yet a great way off. What a picture of Christ and the Church (Eph. 5. 32). God the Father saw that it would be good for His Son to have a Bride with Him in the glory of His Father's presence. This purpose was declared, and the covenant made before the world was formed. The Church, as His Bride, was chosen in Him before the foundation of the world. O the unsearchable riches of His GRACE! O the unfathomable depths of His kindness toward us!

II. **Isaac; or, The Son and Heir.** "Unto him hath he given all *that he hath*" (v. 36). Isaac, like Jesus, came into possession of his *inheritance* after passing through the bitterness of death (Gen. 22. 9, 10). In the experience of both father and son Isaac *virtually* died and rose again. Now he becomes heir to all. Jesus Christ "humbled Himself, and became obedient unto death; . . . wherefore God also hath highly exalted Him" (Phil. 2. 8, 9). Now it hath "pleased the Father that in Him should *all fulness* dwell" (Col. 1. 19). "In Him dwelleth all the fulness of the Godhead" (Col. 2. 9). Unto Him hath the Father given all that He hath, that all the wants of His happy Bride may be fully satisfied. "Though He *was rich*, yet for your sakes

He became poor, that ye *through His poverty* might be
rich" (2 Cor. 8. 9). He emptied Himself that He might
get into touch with the poverty of His Bride. Ye are complete in Him.

III. Eliezer; or, The Spirit's Mission (Gen. 24. 2).
This old steward of the house of Abraham is a perfect type
of the Holy Spirit.

1. HE HAD AUTHORITY IN THE HOUSE. He looked
after the domestic affairs of Abraham. The Spirit is One
with the Father and the Son. He attended to the home
affairs of this world (Gen. 1. 2).

2. HE WAS SENT BY THE FATHER. "The Holy Ghost,
whom the Father will send" (John 14. 26).

3. HE WAS SENT IN THE NAME OF THE SON (John 14. 26).

4. HE DID NOT SPEAK OF HIMSELF (v. 33).

5. HE REVEALED THE THINGS OF ISAAC (v. 53; John
16. 14).

6. HE WITNESSES FOR HIS MASTER (v. 35).

7. HE GUIDES ALL THE WAY HOME (v. 61). "The
Comforter may abide with you for ever" (John 14. 16).

Every act of this servant seems instinct with deep
spiritual teaching. He would not eat bread until he had
made known his errand (v. 33). The Holy Spirit cannot
have fellowship *with us* until He has revealed *to us* the
character of the Father and of the Son. He said, "Hinder
me not" (v. 56). If the presence of Jesus Christ is to be
enjoyed we must be obedient to this Holy Messenger.

IV. Rebekah; or, The Bride of Christ. "Wilt thou
go with this man? She said, I will go" (v. 58). While
Rebekah is a type of the Church—called out by the Spirit

of God, and separated unto the Name of Jesus—yet we must not lose sight of our *individual* responsibility. The heavenly Eliezer is still calling out a people for His Name. In the Gospel we still hear the divine entreaty, "Wilt thou go with this Man?" This call—

1. Is GRACIOUS. It is not a question of character.

2. IT IS PERSONAL. "Wilt *thou?*" She alone could answer it.

3. IT IS URGENT. "*Hinder* me not." He may pass on to others.

4. IT IS A QUESTION OF THE WILL. "*Wilt* thou?" It is not a question of moral fitness. "Whosoever will." *Unwillingness* is the only unfitness.

5. IT IMPLIES SEPARATION. "Wilt thou *go?*" Count the cost (Ruth 1. 16). Are you prepared to leave all and follow Him?

V. Following; or, The Present Life. "Rebekah arose and *followed the man.*" She believed, and so she obeyed. She knew *whom* she was following—the messenger who had come forth from the father to guide her into the presence of the son. What attractions would the country through which they passed have for her while her guide talked to her of the goodness and glories of Isaac, and while her heart burned within for a sight of him whom, having not seen, yet she loved, and rejoiced in the hope of his fellowship! Such is our present privilege—guided by the Spirit, taught of Him by the way, and looking for the appearing of our coming Lord. Are we as intent pressing on for the prize of this high calling as Rebekah was?

VI. Canaan; or, The Future Home. "Isaac took Rebekah, and she became his wife" (v. 67). All the troubles of her weary journey are forgotten now. One sight of our glorified Lord will heal all the wounds and scars received by the way. She now rests in his love, and becomes a joint-heir of his riches. She endured, as seeing him who was invisible; now she is satisfied in his presence and likeness. It is a precious thought that at the end of our journey Jesus will be as *real* to us as Isaac was to Rebekah; that this union is a *personal* one, and that the joy will be for ever. If we follow the Spirit now we shall follow the Lamb then.

REHOBOTH; OR, VICTORY THROUGH YIELDING.

Genesis 26. 17-28.

To own a well in Palestine was to possess a fortune. To be in possession of the Well of Salvation is to own the good fortune of everlasting refreshing and delight. Observe the—

I. **Trial of Faith.** "Isaac's servants digged, and found a well; and the herdmen of Gerar did strive, saying, The water is ours." Well-digging—seeking to open up for ourselves sources of blessing—is a very common occupation. Not every well we dig will yield contentment. This one had to be named "Contention" (v. 20). They digged another; it also brought *strife* with increased force, and was called "Hatred." It was a severe trial to Isaac to spend so much labour on these wells and to let others claim the water. Isaac strove not, but meekly journeyed farther back into the valley. This is one of the hardest lessons we as Christians have to learn, to resist not the evil done against our own personal interests. It is so natural for us to "stand up for our rights." Fall back, and make room for God. "Not rendering railing for railing, but *contrariwise*" (1 Peter 3. 9).

II. Compensation of God. "They digged another well, and called it Rehoboth, for the *Lord hath made room* for us." By calmly *yielding* and trusting they found the—

1. PROVISION OF THE LORD. "The Lord hath *made room* for us." The Lord alone can make room *for us.* He knows when, and where, and what room we do need. When the Lord does make room for us He makes room for every gift and talent we have, room for every holy desire and every pure affection. It takes room of His making to meet all the needs of man as an immortal spirit. He has made room for us—

(1) *In the Atoning Death of Christ.*

(2) *In the Glorious Gospel.*

(3) *Room in His Loving Heart.*

(4) *Room in His Heavenly Home.* The Lord hath made room for us; let us enter in and take possession of His fulness in Jesus Christ.

2. PROMISE OF THE LORD. "The Lord appeared unto him, and said, I will bless thee." Isaac sought not his own, and the blessing of the *meek* came upon him. The herdmen of Gerar took the wells from him, but they could not rob him of the blesssing of God. Our afflictions and trials often drive us back to the place of blessing prepared for us by the Lord. The meek shall inherit—

3. PRESENCE OF THE LORD. "The Lord said, Fear not, I am with thee." Let us not strive nor cry when the men of the world seek to rob us of some of the wells of our earthly comforts. The bulls of Bashan often pitch the meek believer into fatter pastures. Abiding in His presence we shall be hid from the strife of tongues, and kept as the

apple of His eye. Take no thought for your life. "Seek ye first the kingdom of God, . . . and all these things shall be *added*" (Matt. 6. 33). The Lord will make room for us.

4. POWER OF THE LORD. "They said, We saw certainly that the Lord was with thee." When Christians are found seeking not their own, but the good of others, others will *see certainly* that the Lord is with them. Isaac showed his faith in God by refusing to strive for the wells he himself had dug. "My God shall supply all your need" (Phil. 4. 19). When shall this selfish, spirit-grieving hunt after worldly honours and preferments come to an end on the part of Christians? Has it come to an end with you? The Lord will make room for us; let us cast all our care upon Him. As a servant of Jesus Christ have you found your Rehoboth—room made for you by the Lord?

JACOB'S VISION.
Genesis 28. 10-22.

IT is now a proverb among men that "Man's extremity is God's opportunity." When in the midst of the fire and the lions God delivered His Hebrew children. It was while Stephen was being stoned that God opened the heavens before him. It was when John was an exile in Patmos that the Revelation came. It was after the sun had set on Jacob's path that he saw the ladder. The valley of Achor often becomes the door of hope. Observe—

I. The Benighted Wanderer; or, The Sinner's Condition. "He tarried there all night, because the sun was set." Jacob's plight was a sad one. As a terrified fugitive he was running for his life (vv. 27-41). Night overtook him in a "*certain place*." Ah, these *certain* places—places and experiences into which we often run unawares, but places appointed by God where we shall meet with Him. It may be a Chrsitian friend, a meeting-house, or a season of deep affliction. Jacob, like every other self-righteous sinner, was seeking to have a success by a life of deceit and unreality. Such a life is a life of misery through constant dread of discovery. Is the sun of thy hope setting? Is the night of dread and despair gathering around? Rest and look up!

II. **The Wonderful Ladder; or, The Way of Salvation.** "Behold a ladder set up on the earth, and the top of it reached to Heaven." This new and heavenly way was revealed to Jacob by God Himself. It is a lovely type of Him who is "the Way" (John 14. 6). This ladder, like the salvation of Jesus Christ, was "set up on the earth," indicating that it was a way of access for man. Its "top reached to Heaven." The ladder of Christ's Cross did not come short of the very Throne of God's Holiness. All men's ladders fail to reach Heaven (Rom. 10. 3). Jesus Christ, like Jacob's ladder, links earth to Heaven. "I am the Way" (John 14. 6). "There is none other Name" (Acts 4. 12).

III. **The Angelic Climbers; or, The Ministry of Angels.** "Behold the angels of God ascending and descending on it." The angels, "Are they not all ministering spirits, sent forth to minister for them who shall be heirs of salvation?" (Heb. 1. 14). As soon as the ladder is set up the angels are on it. How quick they are to take advantage of any opportunity of service! The angels have no way from earth to Heaven but this one way: they ascend and descend *upon* the Son of Man (John 1. 50).

IV. **The Gracious Promise; or, The Gospel Message.** "Behold, the Lord stood above it." God by the way of the ladder revealed Himself and His

will to Jacob. What a foreshadowing of God in Christ—
the New Way—reconciling us unto Himself. The Lord
stood above it, assuring us that Christ is the Way to God.
The Gospel of God, preached to Jacob, offered a threefold
blessing—

1. A POSSESSION. "The land whereon thou liest, to
thee will I give it." Those who trust Christ, the Living
Ladder, will receive an inheritance among the saints in
light.

2. PROTECTION. "I am with thee, and will keep thee."
At Jesus' feet this sweet promise is ours also, "The Lord,
thy keeper" (2 Kings 2. 2).

3. HIS ABIDING PRESENCE. "I will not leave thee."
Fear not. At the foot of the Cross there is the promise of
grace sufficient (Heb. 13. 5, 6). "I will not leave thee
until I have done that which I have spoken."

V. The Solemn Discovery; or, The Testimony of
the Awakened. "Jacob awaked, and said, Surely the
Lord is in this place." To those still asleep the Cross of
Christ is but as a confused dream; to those awake it is a
"dreadful place"—dreadful both to God and man; aye,
and to the devil also. The experience of Jacob at the foot
of the ladder has been the experience of many at the foot
of the Cross, and very much after the same moral order.
1, *The Lord is in this place, and I knew it not.* God in
Christ, on the Cross, and I knew it not. What a solemn
discovery! 2, *This is a dreadful place*—dreadful, because
it is the place where the awful question of sin has been
settled; where the wrath of God fell upon the head of His
Holy Son. 3, *This is the House of God.* Here God dwells,
in Christ, as a Refuge and a Hiding-place for sinful man.
4, *This is the Gate of Heaven*—the door of access into eternal

life and unfading glory. "If any man enter in he shall be saved" (John 10. 9).

VI. The Anointed Pillar; or, The Sacrifice of Praise. Gratitude and thankfulness constrained the privileged wanderer to lift up the pillars of praise to the Name of Him who had so graciously blessed Him. Only the presence of God can make a Bethel; only those to whom this presence has been revealed can really raise the anointed pillars of song. Where are the pillars that the goodness of God has constrained us to set up? Are they within sight of those who pass by? Every act of kindness done to others, for Jesus' sake, is a memorial pillar. The oil of grace makes every such deed holy and acceptable before God.

VII. The Willing Vow; or, The Covenant of Consecration. "Jacob vowed a vow, saying, If God will be with me, . . then shall the LORD be my God." Let us make this covenant without the "ifs," for the promises of grace are unconditional. Jacob on condition of prosperity was willing to give God a tenth part of his possession. This is good, but very Jacob-like. Any worldly man would gladly make such a bargain. Consecration goes deeper down than the tenth; it embraces all. "Ye are not your own; ye are bought with a price: glorify God in your body and in your spirit, which are God's" (1 Cor. 6. 19, 20). Therefore "present your body a living sacrifice unto God" (Rom. 12. 1). In so doing we shall "prove what is that good and acceptable and perfect will of God" (Rom. 12. 2).

THE MYSTERIOUS WRESTLER.
Genesis 32. 24-31.

It is now twenty years since Jacob made his covenant at Bethel with the God of all grace. Had God been faithful to His promise? Let Jacob testify, "With my staff I passed over this Jordan, and now I am become two bands" (v. 10). The blessing of God is not a passing emotion, but the abiding favour of His presence and power, therefore something that cannot fail (Gen. 28. 15). The blessing of God, it maketh rich. The various attitudes of Jacob as brought before us here are suggestive.

I. See Him Fearing. "He was greatly afraid and distressed" (v. 7). "And he sent them over the brook, and Jacob was left alone" (vv. 23, 24). He feared his brother, and tarried behind alone. The fear of man bringeth a snare, but by the infinite mercy of God Jacob fell into the arms of almighty grace and love. He was alone; now was God's opportunity to get into close contact with him. Lone souls are fit subjects for the fellowship of Heaven. Come ye yourselves apart that the Lord may have a better chance of dealing with the innermost thoughts of the heart.

II. See Him Resisting. "There wrestled a man with him." When Jacob was alone the Divine Overcomer draws near. All at once Jacob finds himself struggling against Him. This is so natural. In the pride of our heart our self-will refuses to bow submissively at the first manifestation of the divine will, when that will is to deliver us by yielding rather than by self-effort and carnal wisdom. The Jacob nature always strives to supplant the will of God by its own. Let us thank God that He contrives to wrestle with us till the day break. He knows that our only hope of success, as His servants, lies in our entire submission to Him.

III. See Him Crippled. "When He saw that He prevailed not, He touched the hollow of his thigh, and the hollow of Jacob's thigh was out of joint." The heavenly One wishes to prevail over our whole character and life that all may be filled with His power and blessing. The source of our strength must be touched, and broken, and withered, that His strength might be perfected in our weakness. Think of it! Our strength is just so much power of resistance. Peter's wisdom was a wrestling against his Lord (Mark 8. 32). Hath not the potter power over the clay? Submit yourselves to God.

IV. See Him Clinging. "I will not let Thee go except Thou bless me." Now that his strength is broken the resister becomes the clinger. This is the true attitude of blessing, clinging to the Overcomer. A broken and a contrite heart, O God, Thou wilt not despise. This submissive and helpless cry of entire dependence is always sure to bring forth such an answer as will for ever change our character and revolutionise our whole life. Clinging to the pleading Christ is the all-conquering attitude of a conquering soul. "By faith we cling to Thee."

V. See Him Changed. "Thy name shall no more be called Jacob, but Israel, for as a prince hast thou prevailed." The new name indicates the new nature; the new nature came not by struggling, but by yielding. The measure of our submission to Christ will be the measure of our victory for Him. Jacob has now gained his degree in the divine school, "P.G.M." (Power with God and with Men). Covet earnestly the best gifts. The way to prevail with men is to prevail with God; the way to prevail with God is to cling to Him with a stubborn trust.

VI. See Him Testifying. "I have seen God face to face." This is a great testimony. "I have seen God." No man can remain the same as before after he has seen God. The glory of such a vision is sure to blind the eyes to the sinful pleasures of the world by transforming the inner life. To see Jesus is to see God. "He that hath seen

Me hath seen the Father" (John 14. 9). "This is the true
God" (1 John 5. 20). Have you got into such close touch
with Jesus Christ, by the Holy Spirit, that you can truth-
fully say, "I have seen God?"

VII. **See Him Halting.** "As he passed he halted upon
his thigh." His walk evidenced the fact that he was a
God-conquered man. Does our walk and conversation prove
that we are princes with God by bearing the mark of a life
wholly surrendered to God? All God's conquered ones are
princes. It is surely significant that "As he passed the
sun rose upon him." The sun of God's light and power
will immediately rise upon us when we have yielded ourselves entirely up to the holy will of God. "His ways are
ways of pleasantness" (Prov. 3. 17). Thy will be done.
"Lift Thou up upon me the light of Thy countenance"
(Psa. 4. 6).

THE CALL TO BETHEL.
Genesis 35. 1-7.

TERROR laid hold on Jacob because of the bloody deeds
of his sons Simeon and Levi at Shechem. "I shall be
destroyed, and my house," he said. Is this the language
of "a prince with God?" Why this change? The God of
Bethel has been forgotten. If Jacob has forgotten his
covenant with God, God has not forgotten His promise to
Jacob. God said unto Jacob, "Arise, go up to Bethel."
Although we believe not, our gracious God still remains
faithful, and reminds us of the place of refuge for our
troubled souls. Look at the—

I. **Place Appointed.** "Go to Bethel." The very
mention of Bethel would be enough to arouse the drowsy
faith and slumbering thoughts of Jacob. Bethel was to
him both "a dreadful place" and "the gate of Heaven."
The gate of Heaven becomes the *House of God*, His place of

refuge and succour. It is beautiful to observe how the grace of God brings salvation to His thoughtless servant. Troubled Christian, go to Calvary. Go to the Throne of Grace, the House of God, the Gate of Heaven.

II. Command Given. "Arise, go to Bethel, and dwell there." Abiding at Bethel under the shadow of the Almighty he will be safe from the vengeance of the angry Shechemites. Bethel (House of God) is typical of the place or condition of fellowship with God. This we may always have by resting in Christ, who is the way to Heaven and the abode of God. God is in Christ, therefore abiding in Him we abide in the fellowship of the Father. It is God's will that we should dwell there. Let us dwell in this house for ever.

III. Preparation Made. "Jacob said unto his household, Put away the strange gods, and be clean and change your garments." Some of Jacob's household had brought the gods of strangers with them from the land of Mesopotamia. A separation must be made. If we would dwell in unbroken companionship with the God of Bethel there must be no other God among us, no usurping thought or thing. We must be clean, cleansed from all sin, and clothed in change of garments. Holiness becometh the House of God.

IV. Reason Urged. "I will make an altar unto God, who answered me in the day of my distress." God's call to Jacob reminds him of His former kindness to him in the time of trouble. The kindness of God showed us in the gift of His Son, and at the time of our spiritual distress should surely constrain us in the time of weakness and fears to arise and go to Him. "Lord, to whom can we go?" (John 6. 68). "He that spared not His own Son,... how shall He not with Him also freely give us all things?" (Rom. 8. 32). Not one hath failed of all His Promises.

V. **Effect Produced.** "They journeyed; and the terror of God came upon the cities." When the people of God set their faces to seek Him, and to be obedient to Him at any cost, it is impossible but the ungodly will feel the power of it. When God is sanctified in His people He will be exalted among the heathen. The reason why the ungodly are so brazen-faced in these days is because the people of God are so worldly-minded. Bethel is forgotten, and other gods have dominion in the camp.

VI. **Place of Blessing.** "Jacob came to Bethel, and built an altar; and God appeared unto Jacob again" (v. 9). When he came to the appointed place he inherited the promised blessing. God's Word will be fulfilled in us when by faith we take our stand upon it. It is impossible to dwell at Bethel and be a stranger to God, or to remain unchanged. God said unto Jacob, "Thy name shall not be called any more Jacob, but Israel." This was Jacob's second blessing. It was the breaking up of that self-seeking spirit which characterised him all along the past. Have we had such a vision of God that every idol has been buried, the altar of complete consecration erected, and our characters so entirely transformed that we have become dead to self-serving and alive unto God? If not, "Arise, go up to Bethel, and dwell there."

JOSEPH, THE PATIENT SUFFERER.
Genesis 37.

JOSEPH is a well-known and fruitful type of Jesus Christ. He was indeed despised and rejected; a man of sorrows and acquainted with grief. Like our blessed Lord, when cast out by man, He was exalted by God to be a Prince and a Saviour It is instructive and comforting to observe that in all His afflictions there were some compensating elements. If demons tempted Christ, angels strengthened Him. God has always some way of escape for His suffering ones (1 Cor. 10. 13). Every trial endured for Christ will bring in some way fresh supplies of grace and blessing.

I. **He was Despised by his Brethren, but Beloved by his Father** (vv. 3, 4). Like Christ, he came to his own, but his own received him not; but although his brethren despised him, he was acknowledged by the father as his beloved son, in whom he was well pleased. What a consolation to the timid Christians, persecuted it may be in their own home by their own kith and kin. "Beloved of the Father" (Gen. 38. 3). Let this sweeten every bitter trial. Remember it was the experience of our Lord and Master. "Neither did His brethren believe in Him."

II. **He was Hated for his Words, but Honoured with Visions** (vv. 8, 9). His words of wisdom and revelation were as goads in their hearts; they wounded their pride while they manifested the purpose of God. "They hated him the more; and he dreamed yet another dream." Stephen was hated and stoned by men; but God opened the heavens to his vision. We might be hated more for our words if we were like Joseph and Jesus, faithfully telling out the whole truth as revealed to us by God's Holy Spirit. If the Word is not preached the visions will cease, and that which we have learned will become stale and formal.

III. **He was Cast into a Pit, but there was no Water in it** (v. 24). The ungodly can have no power at all over us except it be given them of our Father in Heaven. The fire had no power over the three Hebrews, because their time of testimony had not yet come to an end. They cast Paul and Silas into prison, but there was nothing in it to damp the joy of their heart or hinder their fellowship with God. "They prayed and sang praises." They cast Christ into the pit of death, but it was to Him the place of eternal victory. Fear not.

IV. He was Sold as a Slave, but he was a Prosperous Man (v. 28; chap. 39. 2). Like our heavenly Joseph, he became of no reputation, being bartered for the price of a common slave. "But he was a prosperous man." "I have finished the work Thou gavest Me to do" (John 17. 4). The man is always prosperous who succeeds in doing the will of God. Sold for thirty pieces of silver, yet the pleasure of the Lord prospered in His hand. It does not matter what low value the world may set upon the servant of God, he will be a prosperous man in God's sight if he pleases Him.

V. He was Falsely Blamed, but the Lord was with Him (Gen. 39. 7-23). Many unrighteous and blasphemous charges were brought against the Holy Son of God. No Joseph beloved by the Father shall escape. The *pure in heart* not only see God, but suffer for His sake. If your heart be hot with zeal for God, men will charge you, if not with wrath and malice, at least with uncharitableness. But if they say all manner of evil against you *falsely*, rejoice and be exceeding glad (Matt. 5. 11, 12).

VI. He was Neglected by the Butler, but Remembered by his Master. If his companions in tribulation forgot him, the Lord whom he served remembered him, and made all things to work together for his good. We need not be discouraged, although those whom we may have helped, and from whom we might expect a word spoken in our favour, forget all about us in their eagerness to secure favour for themselves. The Lord knows where His faithful ones are. He needs no letter of commendation; He can easily create the circumstances which will make it necessary to call forth the hidden one. As Christian workers let us be faithful where we are, although it should be in some seemingly forgotten dungeon. It is possible for us so to live that we may become even indispensable to God. God's great ones are often prepared in pits and prisons. He knows what we are good for, and when and how to lift us up. "In all thy ways acknowledge Him, and He shall direct thy paths" (Prov. 3. 6).

JOSEPH, THE EXALTED HEART-SEARCHER.
Genesis 42-44.

JOSEPH came out of great tribulation to inherit the kingdom of privilege and honour. Like Jesus, he who was despised by his brethren was exalted by the King to His own right hand. As long as Joseph was in his state of humiliation he was rejected by his own. As long as Christ was in weakness He was despised by His own nation. While Joseph remained unknown to his brethren his dealings with them were perfectly mysterious. Is it not so still with our exalted Kinsman-Redeemer? Until we know Him His dealings with us by His Spirit seem strange and puzzling. Notice the—

I. **Attitude He Assumed.** "He spake unto them by an interpreter" (chap. 42. 23). They were not yet reconciled to him, so he could not talk to them as a friend face to face. The Holy Ghost is the great Interpreter of our heavenly Joseph's words. He speaks to us while in our sins by His convicting Spirit. While we are strangers to Him He can only deal with us as a ruler, not as our brother. We should be thankful that He is pleased to speak to us in any way.

II. **Manner of His Speech.** "He spake roughly unto them" (chap. 42. 7). "He spake *hard things*." The Lord

has to speak sharp things to us that we may be awakened
to a sense of our sinfulness. His brethren had never yet
confessed their sin. They must be made to feel the bitter
pangs of guilt ere they can know the depths of His forgiving
love. If Jesus by His Spirit speaks hard things to us, it is
that we might be prepared for His exceeding great kindness.

III. **Results that Followed.** "They said one to another, We are verily guilty concerning our brother" (chap.
42. 21). When He is come, the Interpreter, He shall
convince of sin. The work is now done; their sin has been
brought to remembrance, and made exceeding sinful in the
presence of him whom they sinned against. "*We* are *surely
guilty*." This is the opening of the door of the heart for
the entrance of the saving Word of Him who is alive from
the dead. Have you made this confession?

IV. **Privilege they Enjoyed.** "Joseph said, Bring
these men home, for they shall dine with me" (chap. 43.
16). They have acknowledged their sin. Now they receive his favour. What grace to be brought into the house
of Joseph the prince, and to dine with him! The Lord
Jesus Christ leads the penitent soul into His banqueting
house of love that all their needs may be fully met. But
as yet they know him not. It is possible to be feasting on
His mercies and yet be strangers to Himself.

V. **Compassion He Showed.** Three times do we see
Joseph weeping (chap. 42. 24; 43. 30; 45. 2). Oh, what
tenderness was in his heart, even when he spoke roughly.
How Christlike was all this! What a lesson for those who
deal with souls in His Name! If the tongue must speak
sharp, piercing words, let them come from a loving,
weeping heart. Think of Paul when he said, "I tell you,
even weeping" (Phil. 3. 18). "Jesus wept" (John 11. 35).
Our words are many, but our tears are few.

VI. The Victory He Gained. The one who sold him now says, "Let thy servant abide instead of the lad, a bondman to my lord" (chap. 44. 33). What a change has been wrought! He who persecuted his brother is now willing to be a bondslave in his brother's stead. What has brought about this moral transformation? The words and actions of him whom God hath highly exalted. Has the influence of Christ wrought such a good work in us? Are we prepared to give ourselves for the good of others?

VII. The Revelation He Gave. "Joseph said, Come near, I am Joseph, your brother" (chap. 45. 4). They have confessed that "God hath found out their iniquity" (chap. 44. 16). Thus enmity is slain, and now the full revelation is given them. Joseph was not satisfied until he manifested himself. Jesus Christ, like Joseph, offers us His gifts and tender invitations to come near that He might reveal Himself to us. This blessing, in all its mighty, melting fulness, can only be enjoyed by those who come near to Him. Such a revelation is needed to keep us low and trustful at His feet. He still says, "Come near, and I will manifest Myself." "Come unto Me, and I will give you rest" (Matt. 11. 28).

VIII. The Comfort He Administered. "Now therefore be not grieved; . . . for God did send me before you to preserve life" (chap. 45. 5). "Moreover, he kissed all his brethren; after that his brethren talked with him" (v. 15). How sublimely suggestive is all this! When the Lord makes Himself known to us then comes the sweet assurance of forgiveness through His own blessed Word. After that we are in a condition to talk with Him. Oh, how sweet and precious is this fellowship! How much we shall have to talk about when we see Him in the glory of His power, and are "*for ever* with the Lord."

JOSEPH, THE REVEALED KINSMAN.

Genesis 45.

THIS is a most thrilling chapter, read in the light of Christ's second appearing. Joseph's brethren sold him and cast him out. They would not have this man to reign over them; now he appears before them in the character as a ruler. They look upon him whom they have pierced with many a sorrow (Zech. 12. 10), and wail because of him. Confessing their sin, they receive him as their kinsman, and own him as their lord. Afterwards they go forth to proclaim the glad tidings of his resurrection and glory. "Joseph is alive, and is governor over all the land!" Although Christ was despised and rejected by His brethren He shall appear in great power and glory, and shall be King over all the earth. Then His brethren (Jews) will acknowledge Him as the One "sold and rejected," and become the heralds of His power and glory, preaching the Gospel of the kingdom. Here notice—

I. The Revelation. "Joseph made himself known unto his brethren" (v. 1). No one could reveal Joseph to them but himself. Christ manifests Himself unto us. He shall be revealed from Heaven. The revelation of Christ to us is very much what the revelation of Joseph was to his brethren.

1. IT IS THE REVELATION OF ONE WHOM WE HAVE REJECTED. How often have we heard His pleadings through the preaching of His Word (chap. 42. 21). "Behold, I stand at the door and knock" (Rev. 3. 20).

2. IT IS THE REVELATION OF A GUILTY PAST. "They were troubled at his presence" (v. 3). When Christ is revealed to the soul our sins are sure to stand out before us. They are realised that they might be blotted out; uncovered that they might be buried for ever.

3. It is the Revelation of Real Kinship. "I am Joseph, *your brother*" (v. 4). Members of His flesh and of His bones. He was made in the likeness of sinful flesh that we might be partakers of His divine nature. What fulness of consolation wells up out of these simple words, "I am your brother!" My Father and your Father.

4. It is the Revelation of Great Grace. "Joseph said, Now therefore be not grieved" (v. 5). He is willing to *forget* the past. "Their sins and iniquities will I remember no more" (Heb. 10. 17). The revelation of Christ is the revelation of the infinite grace of God.

II. The Commission. Now that they have been reconciled to their exalted and kingly brother they receive a grand commission from him. "Haste ye, and go up and say." Does every revelation of Christ not imply a commission? "Let him that heareth say, Come" (Rev. 22. 17). "Go ye into all the world" (Mark 16. 15).

1. Proclaim that He is Alive. "They went and told, saying, Joseph is alive." He who passed into the pit and the prison is now lifted up to the throne. "If Christ be not risen, then is our preaching vain" (1 Cor. 15. 14). "The Lord is risen indeed" (Luke 24. 34).

2. Proclaim that He is Exalted. "God hath made me lord of all." The keys of the treasure-houses of Egypt hang on the girdle of Joseph. Our exalted Kinsman is the possessor of all. The keys of hell and of death are in His hands, and all the fulness of the Godhead dwells in Him. "All things are yours; for ye are Christ's, and Christ is God's" (1 Cor. 3. 23).

3. Proclaim His Willingness to Receive. "Go and say, Come unto me" (v. 9). Now that he is exalted he desires others to behold his glory and share his blessing.

What an invitation is this, "Come unto Me, and I will give you rest" (Matt. 11. 28). It comes from One who is mighty to save.

4. PROCLAIM HIS POWER TO SUPPLY ALL NEED. "I will nourish thee." Come, and abide with Him. "My God shall supply all your need" (Phil. 4. 19). Is not this a glorious Gospel? "I am not ashamed of the Gospel of Christ" (Rom. 1. 16). He saves the sinner and He *nourishes* the saved.

III. The Reception. How did Jacob receive the great and glad tidings sent by his long-lost son? Just in the same way that many receive the tidings of salvation through a once crucified but now risen Redeemer.

1. HE DOUBTED. "Jacob believed them not." To those who know not the character and purpose of God it seems too good news to be true (Acts 17. 32).

2. HE BELIEVED. "When he saw the wagons Joseph had sent to carry him, he said, It is enough." Ah, yes! when the eyes are opened to see the suitable provision made for us by our exalted Lord, and realise our own need, we can no longer doubt His message of love and mercy.

3. HE DECIDED. He said, "Joseph is alive; I will go." Faith leads to action. It is not easy to move people for God until their heart finds rest in His Word.

4. HE POSSESSED. "Joseph gave them a possession in the best of the land" (Gen. 47. 11). To receive Christ's invitation is to become the heir of an eternal inheritance (1 Peter 1. 4, 5). Our kingly Master always gives the *best*. "In Thy presence is fulness of joy; at His right hand are pleasures for evermore" (Psa. 16. 11).

JOSEPH, THE RULING PRINCE.
Genesis 47.

THERE was a famine in the land, but there was enough and to spare in the hands of him whom God had exalted, and who carried the royal seal. All the needy ones must "go to Joseph." The time of dire necessity only helped to show forth the unsearchable riches of the Great Deliverer. There is enough in Jesus Christ to satisfy every famishing soul. "Lord, to whom can we go? Thou only hast the words of eternal life" (John 6. 68). It is not without deep meaning that the famine came to an end only when the people had no more to give. When they came to an end of themselves then God stepped in and delivered them. Many are still struggling through a time of spiritual famine in their souls, because they have not yet ceased bartering with God for blessing. In this chapter we have Joseph honoured and served by those who once denied and persecuted him. We may see here in type our relationship to Jesus Christ as servants. There is—

I. **Great Privilege.** "He gave them a possession in the best of the land" (v. 11). In being brought into the land of Egypt they were brought under Joseph's rule; into the kingdom of Joseph. We as Christians have been brought into the kingdom of God's dear Son, within the sphere of His gracious rule. This is our Goshen, the frontier of Heaven. This blessed Land of Promise is the best of all lands, for here the Prince Himself exercises His Personal care over us. "He nourished them with bread."

II. **Honest Confession.** "And they said, Thou hast saved our lives" (v. 25). He saved their lives by making provision for them long before the famine came. Jesus made provision for us many years ago. He still keeps mercy for thousands; He only can save our lives. Have we honoured Him by such a testimony? Thou hast saved my life; saved by grace alone. Unto Him be the glory for ever.

III. Willing Service. "Let us find grace in thy sight, and we will be servants" (v. 25). If the grace of Joseph constrained them to consecrate themselves to the service of Pharaoh, how much more should the grace of the Lord Jesus Christ constrain us to yield ourselves unto God. "The love of Christ constraineth us" (2 Cor. 5. 14). "Present your bodies a living sacrifice . . . unto God, which is your reasonable service" (Rom. 12. 1).

IV. Ample Provision. "Joseph said, I have bought you; lo, here is corn for you, sow the land" (v. 23). Joseph not only bought them, but filled their hands with good seed that they may now become fruitful labourers. The parable is plain. Redeemed by His blood and filled with the seed of the Word we go forth as sowers that fruit may abound to the glory and praise of His Name. Let us never forget that He supplies the seed. In our emptiness let us come to Him who gladly fills the hands of those whom He hath bought. This is the consecrated life—filled with His fulness.

V. Special Reward. "Look out men of activity, and make them rulers" (v. 6). The diligent shall stand before kings. Men of activity for the cause of Christ will receive their reward in the day of His appearing. Our Joseph will look them out. Not a cup of cold water given in His Name will be forgotten. How many Christians are losing this honour by trifling away their precious time! The day will declare it. Let us not be weary in well-doing; remember the due season.

VI. Royal Honour. "Joseph took his brethren and presented them before Pharaoh" (v. 2). Our Kinsman,

Redeemer, and Prince is able also to present us faultless before the presence of His Father with exceeding joy. If He should ask you on that day, "What was your occupation?" As a Christian what would you answer? Could you say, "Thy servants were shepherds," men who fed the flock of Christ. Let us praise Him for the all-atoning blood, and for the almighty, indwelling Spirit by which we may be able to stand before the throne without fault. Be active for Him if you would be blameless before Him at His coming.

TYPES OF CHRISTIANS.
Genesis 49.

THIS is Jacob's dying and prophetic benediction, "I will tell you what shall befall you in the last days." Taught by the Holy Spirit, he is able to declare the consequences that will surely follow certain well-defined characteristics that had already appeared among his own family. The features of Jacob's sons, with their results, are still being manifested among the children of God. We have with us still the—

I. Unstable Reubens. Reuben had many excellencies, "excellency of dignity and of power," the first-born, and the child of great hope, but being "unstable as water" he did not excel. Reuben is a type of those Christians who have many excellent gifts, but who have one besetting sin that acts like a fly in the ointment. Reuben's sin cost him his birthright (1 Chron. 5. 1). Sin always engenders instability, and leads to the loss of our birthright, of spiritual power, and progress. Stand fast.

II. Self-Willed Simeons and Levis. "In their anger they slew a man, and in their self-will they digged down a wall." Jacob had to say of them, "Ye have troubled me" (chap. 34. 30). How much of the trouble that comes upon ourselves, and others, has its root and cause in the same evil source, SELF-WILL. No wonder Jacob said, "O my soul, come thou not into their secret." The conduct of these sons led to division and scattering (v. 7). There are always the fruits of a self-seeking spirit. Let the cursed self-will go to the Cross. "I delight to do Thy will, O my God" (Psa. 40. 8).

III. **Praising and Courageous Judahs.** Judah means the "praise of Jehovah." Judah is a lion's whelp. "The sceptre shall not depart from Judah." The praising and courageous Christian will always possess the sceptre of power. Like Judah, we shall be able to put the foot of victory on the neck of the enemy when we have more of the nature of the lion of the tribe of Judah in our lives and the praise of Jehovah on our lips. The sceptre of spiritual power has departed from many a once Judah-Christian because of cowardliness and unfaithfulness to God. The true Judahs are always leaders (Num. 10. 14).

IV. **Comforting and Consoling Zebuluns.** "Zebulun shall be for a haven." The words means "dwelling," or a place of refuge for the distressed. "Zebulun's border went up toward the sea." This son of Jacob may be taken as a type of the modern sons of consolation—ready to offer a hand of help or a word of comfort to souls who, like ships, are seeking refuge from the crushing tempest. Zebuluns are always in great demand. The ministry of kindness is always acceptable. "Comfort ye, comfort ye My people, saith your God" (Isa. 40. 1). "Blessed are the peacemakers" (Matt. 5. 9).

V. **Timid and Self-Oppressed Issachars.** "He saw that rest was good, and that the land was pleasant," and, being afraid to offend the enemy, "he bowed and became a servant to tribute." And so the dying father characterises him as a "strong ass." Strong, but stupid; one who possesses the power, but, through the fear of man, gets ensnared and enslaved. Issachar is typical of those who, though they have all the strength of Christ at their disposal, yet remain timid and weak and helpless, bowing to the yoke of every passion, the bond-slaves of the world, strong asses.

VI. Cunning and Sharp-Dealing Dans. "Dan shall judge, and shall be a serpent that biteth the horse heels, so that the rider shall fall." This is close, personal dealing. Dan may represent those Christians who have the wisdom of the serpent, or rather the cunning way of the adder, in knowing how to bring down the pride of the enemy. The spiritual Danites can discern and judge. They know how to apply the truth, so that the enemies of God are brought low. Such can serve God best through personal dealing.

VII. Overcoming Gads. Gad shall be overcome, "but he shall overcome at last." Every Christian who would be an overcoming Gad must first himself be overcome. We must be vanquished if we would be victors in the cause of God. Those who overcome by the blood of the Lamb have been overcome by the blood of the Lamb. Lives conquered by the grace of God become conquerors through grace.

VIII. Blissful Ashers. Asher means "blessed." "His bread shall be fat, and he shall yield royal dainties." He is a type of those blessed ones, so few in number, who are themselves satisfied with good things, and who are able to bring out of their treasures rich dainties for others. They have received the unsearchable riches of Christ; they are filled with the fulness of God, and so can minister kindly portions to others. Those who do not eat fat things will groan in their leanness.

IX. **Joyful Naphtalis.** "He is a hind let loose; he giveth goodly words." The happy, skipping hind escaped from bondage, and now, growing goodly antlers, is a fit figure of those bright, joyful Christians who always delight in the liberty wherewith Christ has made them free. They continue to revel in their first love; their words are goodly, and their appearance attractive.

X. **Fruitful Josephs.** "Joseph is a fruitful bough, whose branches run over the wall." Here we have the type of an ideal Christian. As a branch he abode by the well, kept within touch of the source of supply. He was fruitful, an evidence that as a bough he was fully satisfied. He was shot at, persecuted for righteousness' sake. Those fruitful for God are sure to be hated by the ungodly. His branches ran over the wall. The fruitful life is a blessing to others, even to those outside the wall of salvation. His bough abides in strength. Power for service remains as long as we abide by the well.

XI. **Discontented Benjamins.** "Benjamin shall ravin as a wolf: he shall devour and divide." Alas! that he should have so many successors in the camp of Christ; they are known by their fault-finding spirit. They are the tittle-tattle tale-bearers, always dividing the spoil, delighting to pass round the faults and failings of their brethren. From such, good Lord, save us!

LIFE IN EGYPT.
Exodus 1 and 2.

EGYPT, after the death of Joseph, is the type of a world lying in wickedness. Pharaoh, who knew not Joseph, represents the god of this world. The experiences of the children of Israel in Egypt give us a plain, though painful, picture of the experiences of backsliding Christians in the world. It becomes to them the "house of bondage." What a difference from the land of Canaan! "A land which the Lord thy God careth for; the eyes of the Lord thy God are always upon it, from the beginning of the year even unto the end of the year" (Deut. 11. 12). Notice their—

I. Sorrowful Position. They were—

1. FRIENDLESS. "Joseph died, and all his brethren, and all that generation" (chap. 1. 6). Those Christians who abide in the Egypt of this present evil world must sooner or later part with the fellowship of Jesus and the company of His brethren. The arm of flesh failed them when Moses fled (chap. 3. 15).

2. FAITHLESS. The tidings of deliverance had been sent, but they believed not (chap. 5. 21). It is with great difficulty that backsliders are awakened to a sense of God's forgiving and restoring love. They are slow of heart to believe.

3. HOPELESS. "They hearkened not for anguish of spirit" (chap. 6. 9). How true all this is of those in the world without Christ (Eph. 2. 12). Without faith they are without the Friend; without Him they are without hope; so taken up with the miseries of their condition that they will not hearken to the voice of God's mercy in the Gospel.

II. Bitter Service. They—

1. SERVED AN ENEMY. "They built for Pharaoh" (chap. 1. 11). They served one who sought their destruction. All their work went to strengthen the hands of their great oppressor, helping the ungodly. That is all we can do as long as we are outside the kingdom of God's dear Son (Matt. 12. 30).

2. SERVED WITH SEVERITY. "The taskmasters hated them" (chap. 5. 13). Theirs was a joyless, thankless work. What a cruel master is the god of this world! What a task to please those who are under his authority! Child of the world, you have a hard taskmaster! All work and no pay.

3. SERVED IN MISERY. "The taskmasters afflicted them" (chap. 1. 11). Constrained to labour, not by love, but by fear of the oppressor's lash. Poor sinners, struggling to supply your tale of good works, to earn a little peace of mind, you are under a law that cannot reward you with mercy (Rom. 7. 13-24).

III. Despairing Cry. It was—

1. EARNEST. "Their cry came up unto God" (chap. 2. 23). Their very misery helped to work out for them a great deliverance. Grace has gained a victory when the devil's bondslaves have realised that there is no help for them but in God (Psa. 32. 3-5).

2. HEARD. "God heard their groanings" (chap. 2. 24). The eye and the ear of God are quick to see and to hear the movings of the hearts of the oppressed. He is faithful to His promise, "Call upon Me in the day of trouble, and I will deliver you" (Psa. 50. 15). The father saw the returning prodigal while yet a great way off (Rom. 10. 9-13).

3. ANSWERED. "God looked upon them and knew them" (chap. 2. 25, margin). His tender look of love implies His full knowledge of our need. God looked down from Heaven and knew man's real need, so in love He sent His Son. The cry of perishing Israel was fully met with, "I am come down to deliver them" (chap. 3. 8). "The Son of Man is come to seek and to save that which was lost" (Luke 19. 10).

MOSES' BIRTH AND FAILURE.
Exodus 2. 1-15.

BIBLE characters, like old manuscripts, need close and patient study if the deep and precious teaching of their lives would be understood. Every Old and New Testament saint is the embodiment of some special feature of character which is to be an example or pattern for us (1 Tim. 1. 16).

I. His Birth. He was born a "goodly child." He was "exceeding fair" (Acts 7. 20). Miriam and Aaron, his sister and brother, were doubtless very comely in the eyes of their parents; but Moses, the man drawn out for God, was the fairest of all. All God's fair ones are drawn-out ones—out from the hiding-place of darkness and fear, out from the river of death and doom. He was hid by faith and saved by God (Heb. 11. 23).

II. His Upbringing. "Pharaoh's daughter said, Take this child and nurse it for me." In the providence of God his mother was chosen for his nurse. The goodly children of God are always well looked after. "All things work together for their good" (Rom. 8. 28). By and by he is taken up to the palace; is learned in all the wisdom of the Egyptians, and likely engages in military pursuits. Moses is like the clay in the hands of the potter, a vessel on the wheel of God's unerring providence being prepared and made meet for the Master's use. May we be willing to take on any shape or fashion His love and wisdom may care to impress. Thy will be done on the earth of this poor vessel.

III. His Sympathy. "When Moses was grown he went out unto his brethren, and looked on their burdens." What a sorrowful sight would meet his eyes! They were digging, kneading, moulding, carrying, building, while they sighed, and groaned, and wept. A man will not be

much use for God as long as he refuses to go out and look
upon the sufferings of the sin-burdened. Nehemiah
viewed the walls before the work was began. If the power
of the Gospel is to be valued, the awfulness of sin and the
helplessness of the sinner must be seen.

IV. His Choice. "He refused to be called the son of
Pharaoh's daughter, choosing rather to suffer affliction
with the people of God" (Heb. 11. 24-26). Having seen
his own relationship, and the miseries of his brethren, he
takes this bold and decided step for God and His people.
It may have cost him many a sleepless night. There was
much to be given up, but faith gained the victory. Our
sympathy for the oppressed and the perishing is not very
deep if it has not led us to a more definite consecration of
ourselves to God and His work.

V. His Failure. "He looked this way and that way,
and slew the Egyptian. Who made thee a prince and a
judge over us?" (vv. 12 and 14). When a man has to look
this way and that way before he acts it is clear that he is
not yet fit to be used of God. The fear of man still
ensnares him. Moses knew that he was called of God to
deliver his brethren. "For he supposed his brethren would
have understood how that God by his hand would deliver
them, but they understood not" (Acts 7. 25). The time
was not yet come, the vessel was not yet prepared. He
had given himself to God, but this effort was only the energy
of the flesh, the impatience of self-will. We have not only
to yield to God, but also to wait on Him. God's clock has
two hands—His promise and providence. Both are moved
by the same will—they always act in harmony.

VI. His Flight. "Moses fled from the face of Pharaoh."
How deep and bitter must have been his disappointment
after all his agony of soul and decision of purpose! Only

God is left. All the wisdom of the Egyptians is not enough; he must be taught of God. The withering up of our own self-sufficiency is needful if we would be strong in His might. "Looking this way and that way" is sure to end in fleeing from the face of man. "If any man would serve Me, let him take up his cross and follow Me"

THE CALL OF MOSES.
Exodus 3. 1-10.

In the first chapter we see a picture of *helpless bondage*, in the second, *failure and despair*; in the third, the *Almighty Deliverer* appears. The king had died, and the darkness of sorrow and oppression was fast thickening over Israel; but God knew where to find a man suited for His gracious purpose of deliverance. Moses is now eighty years old, but he is not too old for God; he is more fit for His work now that he has been bleached in the wilderness for forty years. It takes a good deal to dry up the old, sinful sap of self that is within us. Moses had attempted to save his brethren, but failed. Now he receives the CALL OF GOD for the work. He went unsent; now God sends him. In this portion we have—

I. **A Startling Manifestation.** "The angel of the Lord appeared unto him in a flame of fire out of the midst of a bush." "This great light." The flame of fire was the symbol of God's presence.

1. It Signified Purity. "Our God is a consuming fire" (Heb. 12. 29). "Who shall dwell with devouring fire? Who shall abide with everlasting burnings?" (Isa. 33. 14). Only the pure in heart. The presence of God in the soul devours the unclean desire of the heart. "Be ye holy, for I am holy" (1 Peter 1. 16).

2. It Signified Power "The bush burned with fire." When the Holy Ghost came down to empower the disciples

He came in the likeness of tongues of fire. If we are made
partakers of the divine nature we are made partakers of
an Almighty power.

3. IT SIGNIFIED MYSTERY. "And the bush was not
consumed." The holy, consuming presence was there,
yet the bush was preserved.   What a symbol of God in
Christ!   Great is the mystery of godliness—God manifest
in the flesh. What a picture of the believer! We have this
treasure in earthen vessels. God dwelleth in you.

II. A Timely Resolution. "Moses said, I will now
turn aside and see this great sight."

1. THIS TURNING ASIDE WAS NEEDED. Think of what
he would have missed if he had heedlessly passed on. To
meet with God, and be taught of Him, man has often to
turn aside, even from his lawful occupation, but especially
from the pleasures of sin and the reasonings of a carnal
mind. When you see a new light burning in the bush of
God's providence, or in a text of His Word, turn aside and
seek to know the full meaning of it.

2. HE TURNED ASIDE WITH A PURPOSE. "I will now
turn aside and see why the bush is not burned." Perhaps
he stood for a time wondering if he would turn aside, but
now his mind is made up, "I will seek it out." "Ye shall
find Me when ye shall search for Me with all your heart."
"My people doth not consider."

3. IN TURNING ASIDE HE HEARD GOD'S VOICE. "When
the LORD saw that he turned aside, He called unto him."
A man soon finds God when he leaves all to seek Him.
The voice of God is soon heard in the soul when we have
yielded to His invitation. God saw that he turned, and
immediately He manifested His presence. God sees every
turn we take, whether it is to Him or from Him, and He
acts accordingly.

III. A Gracious Revelation. In turning aside
Moses was turning to God; in turning to God he received—

1. A REVELATION OF HIS CHARACTER. "I am the God
of thy fathers." This was a declaration of the eternity of
His Name. When a sinner turns aside to see that great
sight on Calvary's Cross what a revelation of God is made
known to him!

2. A REVELATION OF HIS SYMPATHETIC INTEREST
"I have surely seen the affliction, and have heard their
cry, for I know their sorrows." God knew the sorrows, and
heard the cry of a groaning world. In answer, out of His
own bosom He sent His Son. Herein is love Christ is the
revelation of the love of God.

2. A REVELATION OF HIS SAVING PURPOSE. "I am come
down to deliver." God came down into the bush to save
His people through His servant Moses God has come down
in Christ to save through the Gospel. This was a twofold
deliverance: 1, To bring them out; 2, To bring them in
Out of Egypt into Canaan; out of the kingdom of darkness
into the kingdom of God's dear Son. To accomplish this
great salvation our gracious God had to humble Himself;
He had to come down. "Obedient unto death" (Phil.
11. 8).

IV. A Definite Commission. "Come now, and I will
send thee." The revelation of God always precedes a
commission by God. The coming of the Holy Spirit at
Pentecost meant not only power to the disciples, but also a
fuller revelation of the glory of Jesus Then they went forth.

1. THE TIME. "Come now." Now that ye have failed in
your own strength; now that ye have been brought very low
during these forty years, waiting in the wilderness; now
that ye have had a new and fuller vision of Myself, now
that ye know the desire of My heart concerning the people

2. THE PURPOSE. "Bring forth My people." "They are in bondage and misery, but they are Mine. Bring them forth by declaring My will and Word to them." "Preach the Gospel to every creature" (Mark 16. 15). He willeth not the death of any. He is to-day, through His sent ones, calling out a people for His Name.

3. THE AUTHORITY. "I will send thee." In chapter 2. 12 we see him going in his own name; now he has the authority and the power of God. Moses got his Pentecost at the burning bush—his power for service. Have you received this authority? There must be a yielding to His call before He sends forth in His Name. "Come, and I will send thee." ———

THE EXCUSES OF MOSES.
Exodus 3. 11-14; 4. 1-16.

AT the burning bush the call of God came to Moses clear and distinct, but often all is not done, even when the will of God is known and the way of action plainly indicated. We are so apt to look to ourselves for the proper feelings and fitness for the accomplishing of the good-will of God. Our Lord's greatest difficulty with His servants is to get them to believe that He is able to work in them both to will and to do of His good pleasure. Moses offered several excuses for not obeying.

I. **His Own Personal Unworthiness.** "Moses said unto God, Who am I that I should go?" (chap. 3. 11). This language reveals a very great change in the character of Moses since he left Egypt (chap. 2. 12). It is good to know our own unworthiness, as we must know it when, like Moses, we are brought face to face with God and His great work, but it is bad to make that an excuse for receiving the grace and honour He is offering us. If we as Christian workers valued the full importance of the work given us to do we would be more sensible of our own unfitness for it and more ready to confess it. But notice how God in His great grace meets this objection. "Certainly I will be with you." Just as if God was saying to him, "You say, 'who am I,' but it is not 'who you are,' but *'Who I am.'* I am with you, let that suffice." "All power is given unto Me. Go ye" (Matt. 28. 18, 19). When Moses opened his mouth wide, saying, "What shall I say unto them?" God filled it with, *"I am that I am."* Herein lies the secret of successful testimony for God: (1) He hath sent me; (2) His Word is in me; (3) His presence is with me; (4) He is *Almighty.*

II. **The Incredulity of the People.** "Moses answered, But, behold, they will not believe me, nor hearken unto my voice" (chap. 4. 1). He seems to have forgotten what we so often forget, that God had taken into account all the natural reluctance and hardness of the human heart. They will not hearken unto you; but if you are filled with the Holy Ghost they will be compelled to hearken to the God who is in you. It is not you this dark, ungodly age needs; it is the light that is in you. "Ye are the salt of the earth; but if the salt lose its savour (power of the Spirit), it is good for nothing" (Matt. 5. 13).

How did the Lord meet this second excuse of Moses? As He met the first, with a further manifestation of His own fulness. He gave him a threefold assurance in the rod, the hand, and the water (chap. 4. 2-9). The—

1. ROD TURNED INTO A SERPENT. The sign of His overcoming power, by bringing terrible judgments upon those who oppose His will.

2. LEPROUS HAND HEALED. The sign of His restoring power. He was able to heal withered and leprous Israel, and to restore them to liberty and rest.

3. WATER TURNED INTO BLOOD. The sign of His transforming power, able to change the hearts and characters of

those to whom He was sent. What voice has all this to us? Does it not remind us of the power that still belongs to the Gospel of the blessed God—power to overcome by conviction, power to heal diseases, power to transform lives. The Gospel is the power of God to every one that believeth.

III. The Infirmities of His Body. "O my Lord, I am not eloquent. I am slow of speech, and of a slow tongue" (Exod. 4. 10). Rapid and eloquent speech may have much influence with natural men, but the still, small voice was not heard in the storm or the earthquake. The power of God is something different from mere fluency of speech (1 Cor. 4. 19). Note how the Lord answered this objection, "Who made man's mouth? Have not I, the Lord?" God knew all about his physical infirmity, and was willing and able to make His strength perfect in weakness. It is not our infirmities but our unbelief that hinder us in the service of God. God has chosen the weak things. He suggests further—

IV. The Unwillingness of His Mind. "He said, O my Lord, send, I pray Thee, by the hand; Thou wilt send" (v. 13). As much as to say, "Send any one else, only don't ask me to do the speaking." This reads like a timid refusal to do everything God was asking him to do. The divine reply to this last denial was sharp and final. His anger was kindled, and He said, "Here is Aaron, thy brother. I know that he can speak well; he shall be thy spokesman." The unwillingness of Moses does not turn God aside from His purpose. If one instrument proves unfit He selects another; but Moses has lost the honour that would have been his if he had not been so slow of heart to believe. Is there any sphere of service in which you or I have become a cast-away for the same reason? Would we rather have a spokesman than be a mouthpiece? Let us walk worthy of God.

NEW TESTAMENT STUDIES.

THE TEMPTATION.
Matthew 4. 1-11.

THE word "tempt" has two different meanings, which come from two different sources: (1) To *try*, as God tempted Abraham; (2) to *entice*, as Satan tempted Christ. God's trials are all for good, Satan's always for evil. Concerning the Temptation, notice—

I. The Time. It was after the heavens had opened, and the Holy Spirit had come (chap. 3. 16, 17). It was after Paul had been caught up to the third heavens that the messenger of Satan was sent to buffet and try him. Note the order: (1) *Owned* by the Father, "This is My Son." (2) *Anointed* by the Spirit. (3) *Tempted* by the devil. Some know little of the tempting because they know little of the anointing.

II. The Place. The wilderness. Adam was tempted in the garden, surrounded by every outward comfort. Christ in the lonely desert, among the wild beasts. All Christ's battles had to be fought alone—alone in the wilderness with the devil; alone in the garden with the cup of death; alone on the Cross, "My God, My God, why hast Thou forsaken Me?" (Matt. 27. 46). Soul battles are all solemn.

III The Tempted One. Jesus, the Son of God. This shows how truly human Jesus was. God cannot be tempted. He was tempted in "all points, like as we are" (Heb. 4. 15). But just as highly musical ears feel more keenly painful discords, so much more must He, the pure and undefiled, have felt the force of this trial. The more intense our devotion to God the more intense will we feel the approach of sin.

IV. The Nature. It could only be from *without*, because Satan could find nothing *in* Him. It was threefold:

1. To SELF-SATISFACTION. "Command these stones to be made bread." The answer of the *hungry* Christ shows that there is something more precious than bread—the Word of God. Eternal life is in it.

2. To SELF-DESTRUCTION. "Cast Thyself down." The devil's elevations are all with the view of self-destruction. Pride goeth before a fall. Satan seeks to destroy in every Christian their sense of divine *sonship*.

3. To SELF-GLORIFICATION. "Worship me." I will give you all. He suggests an easy way whereby He might possess the kingdom of this world without dying for it. An unredeemed world Christ would not take. Beware of the devil's *easy* paths.

V. The Tempter. The devil. He is a person, a person of great power. Was the whole world his *to give*? Why did Christ call him "the *prince* of this world?" (John 12. 31). Is he not the *god* of this world? Does the whole world not lie in the lap of the wicked one? The world will be Christ's when He comes again.

VI. The Fight of Faith. The means of Christ's warfare, the Word of God. "It is written." He trusted in God. As a tempted man He fell back on the divine promise. Where else can we go? What else need we do? Fight the good fight of *faith*.

VII. The Victory. "The devil leaveth Him, and angels came and ministered unto Him." His faith is rewarded with strength from Heaven. The Christian's position, like Christ's, is between the love of God and the hate of the devil. Greater is He that is for us.

CHARACTERISTICS OF CHRISTIANS.
Matthew 5. 1-12.

He who spoke in times past by the prophets now opened His mouth. These first words of the Great Teacher, come from God, reveal the way of happiness—not through *doings*, but *being*. Happiness is found not in what we *have*, but in what we *are*. This blessedness belongs to every Christlike character.

I. The Christian's Character.

1. He is Poor in Spirit (v. 3). Not spiritually poor, because that through the poverty of Christ he is made rich. The *humble* spirit is indwelt by the God of grace and glory (Isa. 57. 15).

2. He Mourns (v. 4). Not for fear of missing the kingdom, but over everything that hinders his greater growth into the image of Christ; over the sins of others; over the enemies of the Cross.

3. He is Meek (v. 5). He would not be like his Master if he was not meek and lowly (Matt. 11. 29). Not rendering railing for railing, but *contrariwise* (see v. 39). A *peculiar* people.

4. He Hungers and Thirsts (v 6). Not after the pleasures of sin and worldliness, but after righteousness—righteousness unto God These cravings are the natural desires of the *new* man

5. He is Merciful (v. 7). He delights to show mercy because he himself has had great mercy showed him Christ prayed for His enemies, so does he.

6. He is Pure in Heart (v. 8). His heart is right with God. Wholly yielded up to His holy will. Delighting in all that is pleasing to Him Cleansed by the blood, and open to the light.

7. HE MAKES PEACE (v. 9). He loves peace because he has the peace of God ruling in his heart. He seeks to make peace by beseeching men to be reconciled to God.

8. HE SUFFERS PERSECUTION (v. 10, 11). If any man will live godly he must suffer persecution. "They persecuted Me; they will persecute you." Notice that these characteristics present us with a true portrait of the life of Jesus Christ. Are we like Him?

II. **The Christian's Prospects.** Each Christ-like characteristic, you observe, has its own *special* reward. It is always so.

1. HE SHALL BE COMFORTED (v. 4). This is the hour and power of darkness. Being poor in spirit the kingdom is sure, and all the comforts of the kingdom will yet be given.

2. HE SHALL INHERIT (v. 5). The saints have not much of the earth just now, but when He comes they shall inherit it (Rev. 20. 6). There is a good time coming (Dan. 7. 22).

3. HE SHALL BE FILLED (v. 6). "They shall hunger no more." We shall be satisfied when we awake in His likeness. Filled with all the fulness of God. Present hunger is the evidence of future filling. There is satisfaction for every holy longing.

4. HE SHALL OBTAIN MERCY (v. 7). The mercy of God, which covered his sin, can cover every fault and failing. Blameless.

5. HE SHALL SEE GOD (v. 8). Because his heart is pure he is an holy one (Heb. 12, 14). Holy eyes see holy things; a holy heart shall see a holy God. Holiness is capacity for God.

6. HE SHALL BE CALLED A CHILD OF GOD (v. 9). The world says, "pestilent fellows." Christ says, "Sons of God." Every one like the children of a king (Judges 8. 18).

7. He Shall be Rewarded (v 12). "Great is your reward in Heaven." Reviled on earth; rewarded in Heaven with an eternal weight of glory (2 Cor. 4. 17). Let not the fear of man rob you of your reward.

CHRISTIAN INFLUENCE.
Matthew 5. 13-16.

Salt and light represent what every Christian should be— a *penetrating* and *illuminating* influence, something both to be seen and felt, a power to attract and transform. Notice the—

I. Twofold Sphere.

1. The Earth. "Ye are the salt of the earth." The earth is the place of the curse, and may represent the heart of man as the *seat* of his affections and the *source* of his desires "Thy will be done *in earth*" (Matt 6. 10)—in the heart of man as in Heaven Purify the spring (2 Kings 2. 21).

2. The World. "Ye are the light of the world." The world here may mean the sphere of man's mind and thought. Apart from the light of revelation, this is a world of spiritual darkness. "No light in them."

II. Twofold Action.

1. It Permeates Like Salt. Invisible, but effectual in its working. Must first get into *touch* with the corruptions of ungodliness before it can heal. It represents unconscious influence.

2. It Illuminates Like Light. This is something to be seen The light is not something *put on*. It is the outcome of a flame kindled The Christian's *life* is the *light*. The life is the light of men. If there is abundance of life there will be a brightness of light. A living Christ within will make a steady light without.

III. Twofold Nature.

1. The salt must have *savour*. Salt is good, but *savourless* salt is good for nothing. The mere name and form without this is powerless. The *savour* is an emblem of the Holy Spirit. We may bear the name Christian and have the form of godliness, but without the Holy Ghost we are savourless salt, "good for nothing." "Have salt in yourselves" (Mark 9. 50). Salted with the fire of the Holy Spirit. It is the *savour* that is precious and powerful. "Be filled with the Spirit" (Eph. 5. 18).

2. The candle must have *light*. Here again the mere name and form are useless without the living flame. A candle must be lighted; it cannot light itself. *God hath shined* into our hearts, giving us the light. "Thou hast lighted my lamp, O Lord."

IV. Twofold Purpose.

1. To Salt the Earth. If Christians lose their savour, wherewith shall it be salted? If the world does not see Christ in the Christian, where will it see Him? If the ungodly don't feel the power of Christ's presence in the actions of His people, how will they feel it?

2. To Glorify the Father (v. 16). The light is to shine, not that men may praise the light, but that they may be *led* to trust and glorify the Father. Let your light *so* shine.

V. Twofold Hindrance.

1. In Losing the Savour. "If the salt lose its savour, it is *thenceforth* good for nothing," trodden under foot of men. Sad picture of a powerless Christian! A withered branch. Samson was savourless salt when the Spirit departed from him (Judges 16. 20). Quench not the Spirit.

2. IN HIDING THE LIGHT. If God hath shined *in* our hearts, it is to *give the light* (2 Cor. 4. 6). Let it shine forth in a bold, steady testimony for Christ. The fear of man is often the bushel that hides the light, or the bed of selfish ease. Remember that a covered light may be *suffocated*.

THE TWO WAYS.
Matthew 7. 13, 14.

THERE are only two religions in the world—that which has emanated from the heart of man, and that which has come out of the heart of God. The one is only an imagination, the other is a revelation. In these verses we notice two gates, two ways, two companies, and two ends. Specially observe two ways—

I. **The Way into Life.** What does this *life* mean? "The gate" suggests the idea of a city, a place of *safety*, *fellowship*, and *plenty*. The life which is in Christ is a life of—(1) Safety from sin and wrath; (2) of fellowship with God; (3) of satisfaction in the fulness of God. There must be a *passing* from death *into* life.

1. IT IS AN OPEN WAY. It may be strait, but, thank God, it is not shut. "Behold, I have set before thee an open door" (Rev. 3. 8). This way was closed up by sin, and fenced up by the law. Christ opened it through bearing our sins and becoming obedient unto death. It is a new and *living* way consecrated (set apart) for us. There are no back doors into the kingdom of God (John 14. 6).

2. IT IS A NARROW WAY. "Strait is the gate, and narrow is the way." Perhaps the gate on the side-walk may be referred to, where even camels were sometimes dragged through after stripping them of everything. Men needs a stripping to enter here. Self-righteousness is

not admitted. This gate is as narrow as the new birth. The straitness is not with God, but in man's utter unfitness. If the way be narrow it leads to a large place.

3. IT IS THE WAY OF THE FEW. "Few there be that find it," because few there be that seek it. "Seek, and ye shall find." There are few on it, because many shun it, preferring the darkness to the light, because their deeds are evil. Some put off, others hope to stumble into it by chance. This is no chance work. "Strive to enter." "Ye shall find Me when ye shall seek Me with *all your heart*" (Matt. 6. 33).

II. **The Way of Destruction.** The word "destruction" here means "loss," and is awfully significant. It is the loss of that which alone can save and satisfy. Like a watch losing its mainspring, like a plant losing the earth from its roots, a man losing all his privileges and hopes. This way is:

1. A BROAD WAY. It suits the carnal mind. There is plenty of room in it for all the sinner's likes and pleasures. The world, the flesh, and the devil have full scope here. It is broad enough for the staggering drunkard, for the dishonest and the unclean, for the scoffer and the proud and haughty religious formalist.

2. A CROWDED WAY. "Many go in thereat." It is easy going downhill. Generally man's first choice is the "broad way." The heart of man is deceitful and wicked, and naturally prefers the pleasures of sin to the fellowship of God. Some are being pushed along in the crowd without any serious thought. All are without God and without hope.

3. A FATAL WAY. There is but one only possible end to this way—"Destruction." As sure as a stone sinks in the sea will the man perish who loves and follows sin.

"The wages of sin is death" (Rom. 6. 23). "Turn ye, turn ye, for why will ye die?" (Ezek. 31. 11). "Behold, I set before you the way of life and the way of death" (Jer. 21. 8). Choose life.

THE TWO BUILDERS.
Matthew 7. 24-27.

THE sermon on the mount begins with the blessedness of the poor in spirit, and ends with the ruin of the proud, self-confident professor. The end of this sermon is the end of all Christian teaching. Life and death, righteousness to those who believe and obey, ruin to those who do not obey.

I. **A Suggestive Comparison.** He that *heareth* and *doeth* is *likened* to a *wise* man. The connection between hearing and doing is very vital. Those who have the blood-sprinkled *ear* must also have the blood-sprinkled *foot* (Lev. 8. 24). These *sayings* of Christ are for the *doings* of His people. The hearer only is a fool. He is like a man taking shelter in the *plans* of a building instead of in the house. The hearer only is like a cake unturned; like a man rowing with one oar. If the hearing does not affect the fingers and the feet it profits nothing.

II. **A Common Need.** A house. A house is one of the common necessities of man. "A wise man built his house." There is responsibility resting upon every man with regard to his own house. A house is:

1. A PLACE OF SHELTER. Man needs a hiding-place from the storm and the tempest of Jehovah's wrath against sin. The wrath of God abideth upon every unbeliever (John 3. 36).

2. A PLACE OF REST. A resting-place is needed from the busy, bustling, bothering cares and sorrows of this present

life. A man might as soon find heat in an iceberg as rest
in disobedience to the sayings of the Son of God.

3. A PLACE OF FELLOWSHIP. Man's needs will never
be fully met until he is brought into fellowship with the
Father and the Son.

III. **An Indispensable Prerequisite.** A Rock. Before a house of safety can be got the *Rock* must be found.
"That Rock was Christ" (1 Cor. 10. 4). The Rock is within
the reach of all if men would only *dig deep* enough (Luke
6. 48). This Rock is strong enough to bear all. None
doubt their foundation who build on Christ. Until He
is found all building is vain and ruinous.

IV. **A Threefold Trial.** Rain, floods, winds beat
upon the house. The rain tries the roof, the floods the
foundations, the winds the whole structure. Every stone
built on this Rock, that is, every deed done for Christ's
sake, every act of trust in Him will be tried by the threefold enemy of the soul—the world, the flesh, and the devil.
The foundation holds.

V. **A Presumptuous Effort.** . Building on the sand.
This man is wise enough to know that he needs a place of
shelter, but fool enough to believe that he can have it
without getting into *touch* with the great, eternal Rock.
He has no faith in what is *out of sight*. His whole work is
a matter of *appearance*. What a sad picture of all those
who trust their works without having a grip of the invisible
Christ (Heb. 11. 27). The life may be right and beautiful
in the sight of others, yet have no connection with Christ
the Rock.

VI. **An Irreparable Mistake.** It fell, and great was
the ruin of it (see Luke 6. 49). It fell in the time of his
greatest need. He hoped it would save him, but hoping,
without Christ, is vain and ruinous. The more beautiful

the life and works are, without Christ the foundation, the more dangerous and fatal. The greater the house the greater the ruin. Take heed *where* ye build (1 Cor. 3. 11).

THREE SUGGESTIVE ATTITUDES OF JESUS.
Matthew 11. 20-28.

I. Toward the Wilful Impenitent. "Woe unto thee" (v. 21),

1. THINK OF THEIR PRIVILEGES. What mighty works were done among them! How many miracles had they witnessed! And Christ Himself had lived among them. What are your privileges? Have you not seen His mighty works in others? Christ only knows the awful consequences of rejection.

2. THINK OF THEIR DOOM. "Woe unto you." Our responsibility will be according to our privileges.

II. Toward the Purpose of God. "I thank Thee" (v. 25). He thanks the Father for two things:

1. FOR HIDING THESE THINGS FROM THE WISE. Much divine wisdom is this. What would unrenewed men do with these holy things? Pearls before swine.

2. FOR REVEALING THEM UNTO BABES. To those willing to receive, to trust, and be thankful (Matt. 18. 3).

III. Toward the Heavy-laden Sinner. "Come unto Me." The sovereignty of God is no excuse for the sinner's delay.

1. THE INVITED. (1) *Labourers*—those trying to earn rest by their works, a poor-paying business. (2) *Burdened ones*—those staggering, helplessly and hopelessly, under the weight of sin and guilt.

2. THE PROMISE. "I will *give* you rest." He gives the labourer rest by doing the work for him. "It is finished" (John 19. 30). He gives the burdened ones rest by carrying their load. He bore our sins in His own body.

THE GRACE THAT GLADDENS.
2 Corinthians 12. 9.

NOTICE Paul's testimony. He has had a revelation from the Lord and a messenger from Satan. *Revelations* and *buffetings*, visions and thorns, make up much of the Christian's experience.

I. **The Promiser.** He said, "My grace." He who cannot lie, He into whose lips grace has been poured, He will give grace and glory—HE, the God Man, Mediator, in whom all fulness dwells.

II. **The Promise.** "Grace sufficient." Sufficient.

1. To SAVE. It is made perfect in *weakness*. It delights to forgive, to deliver, and keep.

2. To SUPPLY. To meet all need (Phil. 4. 19). It is a stream sufficient to turn every mill, to *satisfy* every longing of the trustful heart.

3. To SUPPORT. It bears up in midst of all trials and temptations, all the thorns and thistles in life; enables also to bear the unspeakable revelation without pride.

4. To OVERCOME. It slays the power of *sin* within, resists the devil without, and turns the dark shadows of death into forerunners of glory.

III. **The Result.**

1. GLADNESS. Most gladly will I glory. Glad because everything needed is promised by such a loving and faithful one (Rom. 8. 32).

2. POWER. Power of Christ resting upon him, because he rejoiced in his weakness, the weakness that enabled him to lean all the more on His mighty promise.

GREAT FAITH.
Matthew 8. 5-10.

ALL men have not faith; some have no faith (Mark 4. 40); some have little faith (Matt. 6. 30). This Centurion was one who had great faith. Those who have faith are rich. Faith will buy anything from God. This man's faith was—

I. **Great when you think of who he was.** He was a *Roman Centurion*—not a Jew, familiar with the Scriptures. How would his faith grow so great if he had not believed all that he heard of the truth concerning Jesus? Great faith is often fostered in the midst of the greatest difficulties. Poor circumstances are not specially favourable for poor faith. If your faith would grow exceedingly it must be exercised abundantly.

II. **Great when you think of the occasion of it.** His *slave* was sick. He believed that Christ's compassion was deep enough and broad enough to reach the poor and the ignorant. Not like the Pharisee (Matt. 9. 11). Great faith always brings the little and the disputed things to Jesus. Little faith never carries little troubles to God. It takes great faith to bring the trifling details of life to Him in prayer. Beware of the *little* foxes.

III. **Great when you think of the need mentioned.** "His servant was sick of the *palsy, grievously tormented.*" Afflicted both in body and soul, a helpless incurable, as far as human skill and power were concerned. But his faith in Jesus surmounted all. Nothing is too hard for Him. Great faith lays hold on the greatness of Christ. The power of Christ is sufficient for all the emergencies of a believer.

IV. Great when you think of the request made.
"*Speak* the word only." No visit asked; no means
trusted. All his desire will be met with *His word only*.
It is always so. Great faith asks for no signs, but is
satisfied with the *promise* alone, knowing that He is
faithful.

V. Great when you think of the argument used,
"I am *not worthy*; I am a man *under authority*." Great
faith is always humble, for it sees so much grace and goodness in Jesus that proud, boastful self is ashamed. "Speak
the word only, and the demon and disease will go as
quickly as my servant obey me." Great faith is the most
childlike of all. "Lord, increase our faith."

**VI. Great when you think of the results that
followed.** "As thou hast believed, *so be it done* unto
thee" (v. 13). His simple but large-hearted faith was
answered at once, and answered to the full. There was
nothing left to be desired. So wonderfully gracious is our
loving Lord He never sends the hungry empty away.

**VII. Great when you think of the commendation
given.** "I have not found *so great faith*." Jesus knows
exactly the measure of our faith. What a precious thing
it is in His sight! He does love to be trusted. He is so
pleased with it that He saves all who believe (Acts 13. 39).
"Without faith it is impossible to please Him" (Heb.
11. 6). Give Him this pleasure.

EVIL: ITS NATURE AND REMEDY.
Matthew 8. 28-33.

THIS incident has been sneeringly called "The pig affair."
But in these two demon-possessed men we have some of
the most terrible and heart-humbling revelations that we
have in all the Bible. Look at evil as personified in these
wholly-possessed ones.

I. Evil may be Closely Connected with Man. These men were "possessed" (v. 28). Evil takes possession of the sinner, controls his actions and thoughts, and completely masters his whole life. Sin is an awful tyrant, a perfect despot; it claims and affects every power and faculty of the being.

II. Evil is Allied with Death. "They dwelt among the tombs" (v. 28). They preferred the company of the dead to that of the living. They loved darkness rather than the light. Such is the effect of an evil heart. The things that holy men dread are loved. The company of those who are dead in sin is chosen rather than the company of those who are alive unto God. They love death; separation from God.

III. Evil is the Enemy of Liberty. "No man could pass that way" (v. 28). Sin always hinders true liberty. There are many still who are afraid to pass the tomb (grave) because of evil. As long as there is unforgiven sin in the heart there will be fear. Perfect love casteth out fear.

IV. Evil Shuns the Presence of Christ. "What have we to do with Thee?" (v. 29). All living in sin, and satisfied with it, hate the holiness of God. They will have nothing to do with Christ, yet they are afraid of being tormented by Him. They can see no hope in the Holy One of God.

V. Its Influence is only Toward Destruction. When the demons entered the swine they did with them what they were trying to do with the men—drove them quickly into destruction. Evil always chooses the shortest and steepest way to ruin. It is easy running downhill.

VI. Its Power is too Great for Man. Those possessed ones had no power of resistance whatever; they could do nothing to save themselves. No more can ye. Sin, like a poison, becomes an integral part of the being; it cannot be shaken off like a viper.

VII. Its only Cure is to be Cast Out. It cannot be tamed or reformed. Christ said to the demons, "Go." The mighty, never-failing, cleansing Word of the Son of God alone can change the heart and *separate* the sin from the soul, as the demons were separated from the men. He speaks, and it is done.

VIII. Its Conqueror is often Unwelcomed. "They besought Him to depart out of their coasts" (v. 34). Those who don't want victory over their sins don't want the Lord Jesus. If you want sin put away, receive the Lord Jesus. If you want to die in your sins, let Him depart, and He will go. Welcome the sin-separating Saviour.

_____

THE CALL OF THE PUBLICAN.
Matthew 9. 9-13.

GREAT multitudes followed Jesus (chap. 8. 1), but He knew the worthlessness of mere popularity. This river of public favour would soon dry up. "He came not to be ministered unto, but to minister, and to *give his life* a ransom for many" (Matt. 20. 28). Let us see here the—

I. Call of Grace. "Jesus said unto him, Follow Me" (v. 9). If Christ had been seeking popularity among men He never would have called a hated tax-gatherer as a personal friend. He cannot but be true to Himself. Grace came by Jesus Christ. As water seeks the lowest place, so grace seeks the neediest soul. He saves, not because we are rich, or righteous, but because we are *sinners*. All men are at liberty to follow Him, but He *calls sinners* to repentance.

II. Obedience of Faith. "He arose and followed Him" (v. 9). Matthew may have known and heard much about Jesus before this. Now the call comes for instant *decision* for Christ. It is possible to believe much about Him, and yet in heart not to be one with Him. "He left all and followed Jesus." *Following* is the evidence of faith. Discipleship may often mean "a leaving all." It was so with Abraham. He believed God and went out.

III. Proof of Love. "He made Him a great feast" (Luke 5. 29). "Jesus sat at meat in his house." Feasting and following Christ have a wonderful heart-opening effect. It is a blessed experience—Jesus resting with us in the home of the heart. "If *any man* open the door I will come in." Jonathan loved David, and stripped himself (1 Sam. 18. 4). Let us lay all at His feet—this gives refreshing to His soul.

IV. Place of Hope. "Many came and sat down *with Him*" (v. 10). The place of hope for sinners is at the feet of Jesus. There is room and welcome for all here. There is mercy with Him. Sit down with Him in His rejection, and you will sit with Him in His resurrection glory.

V. Manifestation of Pride. "The Pharisees said, Why eateth *your* Master with publicans and sinners?" (v. 11). Why did they not ask the Master Himself? The self-righteous never like to plead their own cause before God. Pride blinds the eyes from seeing the great depths of divine grace. Jesus came to seek and to save the lost. Are you a seeker or a faultfinder?

VI. Condition of Need. "The whole need not a physician, but they that are *sick*" (Mark 2. 17). The Pharisees, like thousands still, were not sin-sick, but self-satisfied. Such have no room for Jesus. Like the Laodiceans, they have need of nothing; or, if they do want

Christ, it is as a teacher, not as a SAVIOUR. Christ's work
is a great *remedy* which can only have effect where there is
disease.

VII. Purpose of Christ. "I will have mercy, and not
sacrifice" (v. 13). He will have mercy on sick sinners.
He will not have the sacrifice of the self-righteous. Take
the place of the guilty, then you come in for His mercy.
Ye who would be saved by your works "Go and learn what
this meaneth."

COME, TAKE, LEARN.
Matthew 11. 28-30.

THIS invitation of Christ implies His deep, conscious
fitness to bless all men in all ages. He knows every need
of man, and He knows, as none else can, the great and
holy claims of God. Put these two sayings together, "All
things are delivered unto Me of My Father" (v. 27).
"Come unto Me" (v. 28).

I. We are Invited to Rest. What an opportunity for
a sin-burdened heart! Jesus gives rest from guilt, from
the fear of death, and the dread of judgment. He *gives* it;
He does not sell it. He does not give it as a prescription,
but as an actual, conscious possession. This rest is for
heavy-laden ones, whether they be saints or sinners.
Weary workers, disappointed and downcast because of
fruitlessness, hear Him say unto thee, "Come unto Me."
Everything that is a *burden* to us should bring us to Christ
for rest and relief. Are you feeling your task *heavy* upon
your heart and strength? Take advantage of this loving
offer.

II. We are Invited to Serve. "Take *My* yoke upon
you." There are different yokes. Yokes we put upon
ourselves, and Satan's yoke. What is Christ's yoke?
It is the yoke He Himself willingly took on, the yoke of
His Father's will. "I delight to do Thy will, O My God"

(Psa 11. 8). To take on this yoke means a life of entire submission to the work and will of God. Paul had this yoke on when he prayed men, *in Christ's stead*, to be reconciled to God. The yoke of Christ means yoked with Christ, co-workers together with Him. We take it upon us when we come to the *help of the Lord* against the mighty. Every soul who has received rest from Him may find a life of restful activity in His yoke. His yoke is easy to the *willing* mind; His burden is light to the *loving* heart. The yoke of service is not thrust upon us; we are invited to *take* it. It will be to our eternal loss if we do not.

III. **We are Invited to Learn.** "Learn of Me." To learn of Christ we must get close to Him. To get close to Him we must needs be yoked with Him. The yoke of service comes before spiritual wisdom. We learn best while in the yoke. Paul had to cry out, "Lord, what wilt Thou have me to do?" (Acts 9. 6) before he received his divine commission. In the school of suffering and testimony for Christ the deeper things of God are learned. The reason why many Christians make no progress in grace and heavenly-mindedness is because they are ashamed of Christ's yoke; and not keeping company with Him, they cannot be taught by Him. We enter the school of Christ when we enter the yoke of Christ. There are many branches of learning here. With Him we learn to be patient in suffering, to walk humbly, to trust implicitly, to love intensely, and to rejoice exceedingly (Eph. 4. 20-23).

THE CHARACTER OF CHRIST.
Matthew 12. 18-21.

IN these verses we have a beautiful and correct photograph of our Divine Lord. Taught by the Spirit of God, their clear eyes saw Him distinctly, although afar off. Sirs, if ye would see Jesus, look at Him standing before you here as—

I. The Chosen One. "My Servant whom I have chosen." This choice was made before the foundation of the world (Eph. 1. 4). It was a choice constrained by infinite grace—chosen as the Lamb to be slain. Although men disallowed Him, He is still the chosen of God, and precious. Let us fall in with God's choice.

II. The Obedient One. "Behold My Servant." This is the Servant who could neither fail nor be discouraged (Isa. 42. 4). He delighted to do His Father's will. He said at the beginning of His service, "I must be about My Father's business" (Luke 11. 49); and at the close, "I have finished the work which Thou gavest Me to do" (John 17. 4). "He was obedient unto death" (Phil. 2. 8), because His love was stronger than death.

III. The Beloved One. "My Beloved, in whom My soul is well pleased." There is strong consolation for us here; in that Christ was, as the Servant of God and in the *likeness of men*, well-pleasing to the soul of Jehovah. It opens wide the door whereby we may be accepted in the Beloved.

IV. The Anointed One. "I will put My Spirit upon Him." At Jordan this Scripture was fulfilled when the Spirit as a dove came upon Him. There and then He was sealed by God the Father (John 6. 27), owned and fitted for the great work He had to do. This every Christian needs.

V. The Revealing One. "He shall show judgment." The truth is made known through Him, because He is the Truth. To come into contact with Christ is to come into the judgment (truth) of God, both concerning ourselves and Himself. Christ as the wisdom of God speaketh the words of God (John 3. 34).

VI. The Lowly One. "He shall not strive nor cry." How could He, when He had committed Himself unto Him who was able to keep. He never sought the favour of men for His own sake. "I am meek and lowly in heart" (Matt. 11. 29). When a Christian *strives* and cries it is an evidence of weakness and unbelief. "The servant of the the Lord must not strive" (2 Tim. 2. 24).

VII. The Sympathising One. "A bruised reed shall He not break, and smoking flax shall He not quench." He will not break the bruised reed of a weak, feeble, musicless Christian life. In tenderness and patience He will bind up. He will not quench the smoking flax of a flickering, powerless, Christian *testimony*, but will pour in a fresh supply of the Spirit of Grace. The lack of oil (Spirit) makes a smoky testimony.

VIII. The Conquering One. "He shall send forth judgment with victory." His truth shall triumph. "He shall see of the travail of His soul, and shall be satisfied" (Isa. 53. 11).

IX. The Trustworthy One. "In His Name shall the Gentiles trust." His Name is as a nail in a sure place; it bears all that is hung upon it. Not like the rotten pegs men make and fix for themselves (Acts 4. 12).

THE SOWER.
Matthew 13. 1-8; 18-23.

THE Sower is the Son of Man; the seed is the Word; the soil is the human heart. The SOWER! What a beautiful name for the Preacher! He went forth to *sow*; not to criticise, or make a display. All who are *burdened* with precious seed long to scatter it. The prophets of old knew what the burden of the Lord meant. May His message so burden us that we shall go forth weeping! The four different kinds of ground represent four distinct ways in which the Word of Life is treated by those who hear it.

I. The Wayside, or Indifferent Hearer. The "wayside" is—

1. A HARD PLACE. The indifferent hearer may be a regular hearer, but his heart is like a public footpath, open to every passer-by, and beaten hard with the feet of selfish thoughts. The heart that is open for the pleasures of sin will be hard for the Word of God.

2. A DANGEROUS PLACE. Exposed to the "fowls of the air" and the feet of *every* passer-by. No matter how precious the seed, it can only fall *on* it; it cannot fall *into* it. The seed is always in danger of being lost until it is *hid* (Psa. 119. 11). Fowls have quick eyes. The wicked one detects the precious Word lying on the thoughtless heart and "catcheth it away." The loss is never felt, because its worth has never been enjoyed.

3. A HOPELESS PLACE. Here the living seed can find no *shelter*. Although it may remain for a time, it has had no *entrance*, and so can show no life. Indifferent hearers can profit nothing.

II. The Stony Ground, or Emotional Hearer. Here the word is—

1. JOYFULLY RECEIVED (v. 20). There being no *depth* of earth it is easily moved. The shallow-hearted hearer is often very emotional. Their thin layer of feeling is easily wrought upon. Tears are quickly shed, and as quickly dried up. They hear the Word gladly; but, alas! their heart seems to be in their eyes.

2. QUICKLY STARVED. There is "no root." It soon sprang up, but its life was all on the *outside*. No downward growth, because there was no deepness of earth.

Beneath the thin covering of emotional feeling there lies the hard, unyielding rock of a stubborn will. No room for the *root* of the matter.

3. COMPLETELY SCORCHED. "It was scorched and withered away" (v. 6). There being no *inward* nourishment it is soon overcome by *outward* circumstances. Unless the heart is filled with love to God the Word will not root and grow, and stand "rooted in love." Persecution soon withers the pretentious. But what withers the rootless strengthens the rooted.

III. The Thorny Ground, or Double-Minded Hearer. Here we have—

1. SOIL ABUNDANT. Where there is plenty of depth for thorns there is depth enough for seed. In the heart of the double-minded the plough of the convicting Spirit may have been, for there is readiness to receive the Word of the kingdom, but only to give it a place with the thorn of worldly things.

2. SOIL PREOCCUPIED. "Thorny ground." That which is first is natural. The thorns and the briers usually have the first place in the heart of man. But that which is first must be taken away if that which is second and spiritual is to possess and prosper. "Ye cannot serve God and mammon" (Matt. 6. 24).

3. SOIL UNFRUITFUL. The seed will not choke the thorns, but the thorns the seed. The sins that are allowed to harbour in the heart will surely manifest themselves, although they may be out of sight for a time, like the thorns covered by the passing plough. "Cares," which choke the hopeful Word, are deadly enemies, although often excused. Cast out these murderers if you would be fruitful in every good work.

IV. The Good Ground, or Honest Hearer. This is—

1. A PREPARED HEART. "Good ground." Ground that has been the object of special care. A heart that has been ploughed and torn by the Spirit of God. Here the weeds and thorns have been *cut up* at the roots and gathered out. The heart that is truly anxious for spiritual things has no room for the "cares" and "riches" that hinder the one thing needful.

2. AN UNDERSTANDING HEART (v. 23). If the seed of the Word is to be fruitful it must have *full liberty* in the soil of the heart. It must have soil congenial to its nature. Without meditation the Word will get pot-bound (Psa. 1. 2). The understanding of the Word is the germinating of the seed.

3. A FRUITFUL HEART. "Some an hundredfold, some sixty, some thirty." There are degrees of fruitfulness even in good ground. The individual seeds of special truth will be better conditioned in some hearts than others. The same truth in one man's life may bring forth an hundredfold, while in another only thirty. The measure of understanding has much to do with the measure of fruitfulness. The character of the fruit betrays the nature of the soil. The great object of the Sower is *fruit*. All is loss and failure that is not fruitful. Let us *abide* in Christ, and our lives shall not be barren (John 15. 7, 8).

THE TARES.
Matthew 13. 24-30; 37-43.

IN the parable of the tares we have a revelation of the kingdom of Heaven in the field of the world. Christ's own interpretation of it is beautifully clear and simple. The kingdom represents the dispensation of the grace of

God. It came with Christ Jesus, and continues till the end of the age.

I. The Sower, or Planter of the Kingdom, is the Son of Man (v. 37). All the affairs of this kingdom are in the hands of Jesus Christ. As precious seed it was brought forth as a burden in His bosom. It is not *of* this world, but from Heaven. It is righteousness, and peace, and joy in the Holy Ghost. It is the ministration that exceeds in glory (2 Cor. 3. 9).

II. The Field, or Place of the Kingdom, is the World (v. 38). The world is called "His field" (v. 24). The field is great, but He has seed enough for every corner of it. His large, compassionate heart and eye take in the whole (John 3. 16). Much of the field is still in waste. May the world of our inner being be possessed by it !

III. The Seed, or Subjects, are the Children of the Kingdom (v. 38). The seed with which He sows the field has cost Him much—redeemed with His own precious blood. Every seed is a living one, and as closely connected with the Sower as children are to a parent. Each seed is sent forth into the soil of the world to grow and manifest His own hidden life and beauty. To this end it must die. "Except a corn of wheat fall into the ground and die, it abideth alone" (John 12. 24). We must die unto sin before we can live unto God.

IV. The Tares, or Hinderers, are the Children of the Wicked (v. 38). Where did the tares come from? "An enemy hath done this" (v. 28). There is everlasting enmity between the tares and good seed (Gen. 3. 15). The title "children" reveals their very close connection with the devil (Eph. 2. 2). While growing together in the field there may be a seeming likeness, but their *origin* and character are entirely different. Regeneration is the only remedy for the tares (John 3. 5).

V. The Enemy, or Usurper, is the Devil (v. 39). It was while men *slept* he sowed the tares. He loved the darkness rather than the light, because his deeds were evil. It is when Christians cease to watch that the devil comes, and his awful work is silently and quickly done. When the tares spring up many say, "There's your Christians." No! An enemy hath done *this*. Every seed sown by the Son of Man is good.

VI. The Harvest, or Separation, is the End of the World or Age (v. 39). "Let both grow *together* until the harvest" (v. 30). So the grace of the Master spares the tares for a time; but sparing grace is not saving grace. While abiding among the wheat their *privileges* are the same, but the *nature* of the tares unfits them for the heavenly garner. The end will come as sure as the seed-time, when all that offend shall be gathered out.

VII. The Reapers, or Servants, are the Angels (v. 39). They said, "Wilt Thou that *we* gather them up?" He said, "Nay! the reapers are the angels." These impartial servants will in no wise be hindered in their mission. Their first work is to put away all scandals and them which do iniquity.

1. THEY ARE GATHERED. The offensive and the worthless are brought together. No comfort, no hope, because they are many.

2. THEY ARE BOUND INTO BUNDLES. As straw binds straw, so both doth evil and evil-doer. No more liberty or fellowship with the wheat.

3. THEY ARE CAST INTO THE FIRE. A fearful plunge: eternal separation; awful doom! The tares are not made for the fire, but the fire for the tares. The Lord knoweth them that are His.

THE MUSTARD SEED.

Matthew 13. 31, 32.

WHERE there is life there is growth. The kingdom of Heaven, as represented in the Person of the Lord Jesus, is a living thing. Notice it's—

I. **Outward Appearance.** "The *least* of all seeds." The kingdom of Heaven is like to a *grain* of mustard seed. The Lord Jesus Christ Himself was the living grain. His kingdom was the least of all kingdoms. It began with a handful of illiterate men. He was despised and rejected of men. No beauty in Him for the carnal eye.

II. **Inward Vitality.** It is a *seed*, not a stone. There is within it a vital principle capable of wonderful manifestations. A seed needs to be planted under favourable conditions before its hidden power and fruitfulness can be seen. The living seed of the truth as it is in Jesus Christ must fall into the soil of a broken and believing heart before its life-giving power will be realised. In the life of Jesus we see the *blade*; in His resurrection the *ear*; and on the day of Pentecost the *full corn* in the ear. The atmosphere of worldliness is not favourable for the development of this tender plant. The power of this seed lies in the presence of the quickening Spirit.

III. **Manifest Progress.** "It became a tree." Its *vitality* is *apparent* to all now. The corn of wheat has fallen unto the ground and died. Much fruit has appeared. Every soul quickened from the dead is a branch. The fowls of the air lodge in the branches. But the fowls are *no part* of the tree; they are only *lodgers*. The tree is perfect without them. The tree of the kingdom has many lodgers—those who identify themselves with it only for their *own* convenience. Are you a BRANCH or a *lodger*?

THE LEAVEN.

Matthew 13. 33.

Two different methods of interpretation have been applied to this parable. Much depends on how we view these seven parables, whether separately or dispensationally.

I. The General Interpretation. Looked at separately, it is said—

1. That the MEAL IS THE WORLD—something bad, and all alike bad, needing a new and transforming principle put into it.

2. THE LEVEN IS THE GOSPEL, and must be hid within before it can effect any change.

3. THE WOMAN IS THE PREACHER, the one who hides the Gospel in the hearts of men.

4. THE RESULT—"the whole is leavened." The world becomes permeated with the Spirit of Christ. As an *exhibition* of Gospel truth all this is beautiful, and may be much blessed. But as an *exposition* of the parable it may be very faulty.

II. The Difficulties in the Way of Accepting this View.

1. It changes the SCRIPTURAL USE of meal and leaven. It makes the meal bad and the leaven good. Everywhere else meal is good and leaven is bad.

2. The meal is VERY FAVOURABLE to leaven, whereas *the world* is for ever *opposed* to the Spirit of the Gospel of Christ.

3. The HIDING of it suggests secrecy and craft, a thought never associated with the *preaching* of the Word, but closely connected with the work of Satan, who sowed the tares "while men slept."

4. The MANNER in which leaven works is more suggestive of sin than grace. It *mixes with* the meal, and gradually operates by the law of *contagion*. We do not see sinners converted in this way. Grace does not run in the blood. We do not see whole streets, and towns, and cities being *leavened* with the Spirit of Jesus.

5. The PURPOSE OF LEAVENING also suggests the idea of making the meal, or bread, more *palatable to man*. The great purpose of the Gospel is to make men more favourable to God.

III. The Other Interpretation views *the kingdom* in this parable as in a state of further development in the course of time, and may represent things as they are pretty much in our own day. Those who look at it in this way see—

1. The LEAVEN, as a *good thing* that has become *polluted*; as the truth of God, perverted by the carnal wisdom of men.

2. The MEAL, as a good thing that has been *corrupted* by the leaven of false teaching. As the meal is very susceptible to the leaven it may represent professing Christendom being corrupted by doctrines that are not of God. This corrupting process does work like leaven.

3. The WOMAN who *hid* the leaven in the meal, as typical of those who are *acknowledged* as religious teachers. It was the woman's work to hide leaven in meal. Their business is to *hide*, to promulgate things contrary to Christ while acting as the servants of Christ.

4. The RESULT. "The whole was leavened." They see here the universal corruption of Christendom as such—a Church that has become unfaithful, and so unfit for the Lord's use; a Church saying that it has need of nothing, while Jesus Christ stands without (Rev. 3. 17-20).

THE TREASURE.
Matthew 13. 44.

SOME seem to see in this parable: (1) The FIELD, as the Scriptures, that must be searched; (2) The TREASURE, as salvation that must be found; (3) The SELLING ALL, as the condition on which salvation is possessed. We much prefer to put it thus—

I. The Field is the World. It is expressly called so in verse 38. It is a large field, loved by God (John 3. 16), and claimed by Jesus Christ (John 1. 10). He is the propitiation for the sins of the whole world. He bought the field. Satan offered it to him on the cheap, but He would not have it on such conditions (Matt. 4. 8, 9).

II. The Treasure is the Church. The people of God are called His own "peculiar treasure" (Exod. 19. 4-6). The Lord's treasure is His people. This treasure was hid in the field of the world, but promised to Christ before the world was. "All that the Father hath *given* me shall come to Me." Those which Thou hast given Me "*out of the world*" (John 17. 6).

III. The Price was Himself. "He selleth *all that He hath*, and buyeth the field." Salvation cannot be *bought* by anything the sinner can sell. "The gift of God is eternal life" (Rom. 6. 23). Jesus did sell "all that He had" to purchase the treasure of His believing people. "He who *was rich*, yet for your sakes He *became poor*, that ye through His poverty might be rich" (2 Cor. 8. 9). "Christ loved the Church, and *gave Himself* FOR IT" (Eph. 5. 25). He purchased it with His own blood (Acts 20. 28). The *hiding* of the treasure may suggest the mystical character of His body—the Church known to Him, but not yet manifested to the world.

THE PEARL.
Matthew 13. 45, 46.

THE scope of this parable is very much the same as the last; but there is this marked and beautiful difference, that while the "treasure" is His possession, the "pearl" is for *personal adorning*. The Church here is not only a "purchased possession," but a pearl of great price and *beauty* to adorn His person and reflect the *glory of His character*. If CHRIST is the pearl, then the sinner, as the merchantman, has to buy Christ by selling all that he has. It is quite clear that this is not the teaching of the Scripture. The price is paid by Jesus Christ as the Redeemer, not by man, the already bankrupt sinner (1 Peter 1. 18, 19).

I. **The Merchantman is Christ.** He is a merchantman, a man well up in the business of carrying on heavenly trade. He has a great business on hand. "Wist ye not that I must be about My Father's business?" (Luke 11. 49)—seeking goodly pearls.

II. **The Pearl is the Church.** The Church is the Lamb's wife, and has been purchased with a great price. As Boaz found Ruth, and redeemed her to himself, the Bride of Christ is a priceless pearl to Him. She will be to Him as diadem of glory through all the coming ages. "Come, and I will show thee the Bride, the Lamb's wife" (Rev. 21. 9-27). "A purchased possession" (Eph. 1. 14).

III. **The Price was His Own Life.** "He sold all that He had" (2 Cor. 8. 9). He died for us. "Ye are bought with a price, therefore glorify God in your body and in your spirit, which *are God's*" (1 Cor. 6. 20). "Ye are bought with a price; *be not ye the servants of men*" (1 Cor. 7. 23). Christ may truly say of His Church:

> "I've found the pearl of greatest price,
> My heart doth sing for joy."

THE NET.
Matthew 13. 47-50.

THE key to this parable has been laid beneath the door (v. 49). It is the last of a series of seven parables, bringing us up to the close of the period of the kingdom; to the end of the age, when the whole system will be tested and judged.

I. The Net. The net is something prepared and fitted for a special purpose—to catch fish. It is emblematic of the Gospel of the grace of God. The net itself makes no distinction of the fish, for it *receives all* who come. The invitation of the Gospel is universal; it is to every creature. Whosoever will may come. Like the sunshine and the rain, it comes to both bad and good.

II. The Sea. The net was cast into the sea. The sea represents the sphere in which men live and move, and corresponds with the "earth" and the "field" in the other parables. It indicates a state of changeableness, restlessness, and danger. Into this sea the net of the Gospel, prepared by the grace of God, has been cast. The purpose is to gather out a people unto His Name.

III. The Gathering. "And gathered of every kind" (v. 47). Was this the intention of the great Fisherman? Was the net made for both "good and bad?" Does it not seem that the net is put to a wrong use when used, as here, for a *drag-net*? When the Lord told His disciples to cast their net on the right side of the ship they did not get one bad fish. The Gospel is put to a wrong use when it gives an equal place to both good and bad. In these days *quantity*, not *quality*, is the aim of the net-spreaders. But the sifting-time is coming.

IV. The Time of Drawing. "When it was full they drew it" (v. 48). The net of God's saving grace will not always be in the sea of this world. There is a time—it may be near at hand—when it will be full. This time will be the *end of this age*, when the fulness of the Gentiles be come in (Rom. 11. 25). When the Gospel net is drawn, then present privilege and opportunity of salvation will be gone.

V. The Place of Sifting. "They drew to *the shore*" (v. 48). The bad and the good could sport *together* while in the sea, but it will be different on the shore. The wheat and the tares were allowed together until the end came. As they came near the shore the more did the bad and the good *crowd* together. There is a great cry for *union* in the present time. Let us take care it is not the crushing together caused by the net being drawn out.

VI. The Separation. "They gathered the good, and cast the bad away" (v. 48). So shall it be at the end of the age. They shall sever the wicked from among the just (v. 49). Their *character* determines their destiny—*good or bad*. The Lord knoweth them that are His. The bad may boast, while in the sea, that they are just as good as their neighbours, but they shall not escape.

VII. The Final Destiny.

1. THE GOOD are put into *vessels*. These vessels were prepared for them before the net was drawn. "In My Father's house are many mansions. I go to prepare a place for you" (John 14. 2).

2. THE BAD were cast into the fire (v. 50). "Cast the bad away." Oh, think of it! Away from what? Away to what? "Ye must be born again" (John 3. 7).

THE UNEXPECTED APPEARANCE.
Matthew 14. 22-27.

THE hungry multitude had just been fed and sent away. His own soul now hungers for secret communion with His

Father. "Man shall not live by bread alone" (Matt. 4. 4).
He constrains His disciples to go before Him to the other
side, and when the evening is come we see Him *alone* on
the mountain.   Here is a picture of Christ's present
position and of His Coming again.   Jesus is now on the
mount of intercession before the Father.   His disciples
are still being tossed with tempest on the sea of this
troublous world.   But one day He will appear again and
deliver His Church out of all its troubles.   As Peter went
to meet Him on the waters, so shall we meet Him in the
air (1 Thess. 4. 17).   When Jesus came back to the boat He
brought Peter with Him.   When He shall appear then we
also shall appear *with Him* in glory.   Then those who see
Him will also confess, "Of a truth Thou art the *Son of
God*" (v. 33).   This is a very fruitful theme.   Let us gather
some practical lessons—

I. The Obedient will be Tried.   "Jesus *constrained*
them to go before Him unto the other side" (v. 22).   Perhaps it was with reluctance that they went, but they
obeyed, and while doing His will they were severely tested.
The trial of your faith is precious, more precious than tried
gold.   Observe the nature of their trials—

1. THAT IN WHICH THEY TRUSTED WAS LIKELY TO FAIL
THEM. "The ship was tossed with waves" (v. 24).   Every
object of the believer's confidence will have a tossing.
Jesus Himself had it.   The little ships of our own making
are too slim to bear the stress of strong temptation.   In
following Jesus let us beware of trusting anything apart
from Himself.   The arm of flesh, our own understanding or
past experience, if trusted, can only bring the soul into
dread and danger.

2. THAT WHICH MIGHT HAVE HELPED WAS AN ACTUAL
HINDRANCE. "The wind was contrary" (v. 24).   We, too,

while seeking to do the will of our Lord may expect to meet with many a storm of opposition. The wind which wafted them across the lake now hinders their progress. The favour of men, which may have helped us at one time, may press against us at another. It is as fickle as the wind. But there is a deep need for every contrary wind in the experience of God's people. It only hindered these disciples from getting beyond the sphere of His own wonder-working power. It made them *tarry till He came*. Blessed detention!

3. THAT THEIR MOST STRENUOUS EFFORTS WERE OF LITTLE AVAIL. "He saw them *toiling in rowing*" (Mark 6. 48). Ignorant of the Master's purpose to bless them among the billows, they toiled and struggled as earnest, honest men to save themselves. But they spent their strength in vain, as every one will do who seeks deliverance by their own works (Rom. 3. 20).

II. **The Obedient will be Helped.** "Jesus *saw them* toiling in rowing," and made haste to their help. Comforting thought! He sees every stroke of the oar. He hears every groan of the heart, every half-choked sigh, and is an eye-witness to every bitter tear. Our fruitless efforts may prove a blessing by bringing Jesus Christ into closer touch with us. He came—

1. AT AN UNEXPECTED TIME. "In the fourth watch." As in nature, so may it be in our spiritual experience—the darkest hour is the hour before daybreak. He came in the hour of their greatest need—when their strength was exhausted, when all hope was gone. In perplexity cast the anchor of faith, and wait for the day.

2. IN AN UNEXPECTED WAY. "Walking on the sea." The great, surging billows, the source of the disciples' fear and dread, were now *under His feet*. He comes as the

OVERCOMER to their help. They found their salvation where you and I will always find it, not in *toiling*, but in *trusting*. "My ways are not yours."

3. WITH AN UNEXPECTED BLESSING. "Be of good cheer. It is I; be not afraid." He does not at once remove the *cause* of their trouble (wind and waves), but He gives them rest *in the midst* of the storm. He may not take away the thorn, but He makes His grace sufficient (2 Cor. 12). He did not save from the fiery furnace, but He walked with them *in it*. This is the greatest blessing.

A SUPERNATURAL WALK.
Matthew 14. 28-34.

JESUS appeared to His storm-tossed disciples walking on the sea. To this purpose of His followers the wind was contrary, but the contrary wind was an opportune time for the Lord. They saw His wonders in the great deep of their distress.

I. **A Bold Request.** "Peter said, Lord, if it be Thou, bid me come unto Thee *on the water*" (v. 28). This was a great petition, but not too great. "If it be THOU." He is able to do exceeding abundantly above all we ask. Should our love to Christ not constrain us to walk even as He walked? What although other disciples shrink from such a prayer; let us seek the privilege of walking with Him, even where human wisdom and fleshly feelings cannot find a footing.

II. **A Gracious Invitation.** "He said, Come" (v. 29). The door is now open for the faith of Peter. He is invited to walk where none but the feet of faith dare go. The Christian's walk is a supernatural one. He walks by faith. This, in the eyes of the wise men of the world, is like walking on the sea. They cannot understand it. Every believer is invited by Christ to walk with Him on the deep as He walked.

III. A Successful Venture. "Peter went *out of the ship*, and walked on the water" (v. 29). The seemingly impossible can be accomplished through simple faith in the Word of Christ. There must be a going *out* if there is to be a going *on*. The life of faith implies the complete abandonment of every other source of confidence—out of the ship of self on to the Word of Christ. Jesus is not fully trusted until both hands are off every earthly prop.

IV. A Momentary Failure. "When he saw the wind boisterous he was afraid" (v. 30). Perhaps he expected the storm would cease when he stepped out on the invitation of the Lord Jesus. Our troubles don't all cease the moment we trust Christ. Our faith will be tried. Peter was afraid, and began to sink, because he was getting more concerned about himself than the Word of his Master. Even walking in Christ's *ways* will become a terror and a labour when our eyes are off Christ Himself.

V. An Earnest Prayer. "Lord, save me" (v. 30). "Let him that thinketh he standeth take heed lest he fall." Let him who is falling not hesitate to cry out for salvation. Out on the depths of the life of faith, where no unbeliever ever stood, Jesus will make us realise that, apart from His continual help, we can do nothing but tremble and sink. Peter was wise in crying as soon as he began to sink. Many wait until they are up to the neck.

VI. A Speedy Deliverance. "Immediately Jesus caught him" (v. 31). Instant confession brought instant salvation. He leaps to the help of His needy ones (S. of S. 2. 8). Peter was not sent back to the ship. There is no help for the troubled and tempted believer in the old life. Jesus *caught* Peter, so he found refuge in the "arms of Jesus." These strong and willing arms are still outstretched (Psa. 138. 7).

VII. A Gentle Rebuke. "O thou of little faith, wherefore didst thou doubt?" (v. 31). The tenderness of Jesus is very manifest. He will not break the bruised reed. We might think Peter's faith was anything but *little* when he boldly stepped out on the swelling waves. Oh, how precious a thing faith is! If we have trusted Christ let us trust Him wholly. None perish that Him trust. Abraham staggered not, but was strong in faith.

VIII. A Blessed Result. "When *they were come* to the ship the wind ceased" (v. 32). Peter now walks *with Jesus*—saved from fear, where before he had feared and sank. His walking *to* Jesus was a testing time, but his walking *with* Him is calm and peaceful. The wind is still as boisterous as ever, but he fears no evil, for the Lord is with him. The near presence of Christ is the secret of a restful and triumphant Christian life. When Jesus came into the ship the wind ceased. Let Him into the heart; He maketh the storm a calm.

THE WOMAN OF CANAAN.
Matthew 15. 22-28.

JESUS had said, "Him that *cometh* unto Me, I will in no wise cast out" (Matt. 11. 28); but difficulties have often to be faced and surmounted in the coming.

I. Her Character. With regard to her nationality, she was—

1. A WOMAN OF CANAAN. A representative of a class that were without hope, having no promise, and without God in the world (Eph. 2. 12). Such were some of us.

2. A WOMAN IN DEEP ANXIETY. "Her daughter was vexed with a devil" (v. 22). Her own soul was thereby grievously vexed. Her great need and conscious helpless-

ness drove her to Jesus. Blessed thirst that draws us to such a fountain. Our poverty, like the prodigal's, is often the means of driving us home to the house of plenty.

II. Her Request. Such soul-agony must cry out. It was—

1. A CRY FOR MERCY. "Have mercy on me" (v. 22). The prayer will always be short when *mercy* is felt to be the first need. Secure His mercy and you have lifted the sluice for the outflowing of infinite blessing. If mercy is your first plea it will not be your last.

2. A CRY TO THE LORD. "Have mercy on me, O Lord" (v. 22). "To whom can we go but unto Thee? Thou hast the words of eternal life." Mother *Nature* is deaf to the cry of the needy.

III. Her Difficulties. The first trial she met with was—

1. THE SILENCE OF JESUS. "He answered her not a word" (v. 23). Does it not seem alarmingly strange that Jesus should hold His peace at such a time? There is a needs be. We must not deal with Jesus as one would do in *trying* an experiment. The silence of the Saviour may lead to deeper searchings of heart. Although He gives no *word* we may still hope in His *character*. Other difficulties were—

2. THE CONDUCT OF THE DISCIPLES. "They said, Send her away" (v. 23). Between the silence of Jesus and the surliness of His followers her faith would be severely tested. The *conduct* of many of Christ's disciples is more likely to drive away than attract to the Master; their words and actions are sad representations of His gracious character. Are we commending Him by showing *love* for the perishing?

3. HER OWN UNWORTHINESS. "Jesus said, I am not sent but unto the lost sheep of the house of Israel" (v. 24).

She did not belong to the house of Israel; therefore as a heathen Gentile she had no *claim* on Him as the *Son of David*. She was knocking at a closed door. If *as sinners* we would buy from *Him*, we must buy *without money*. "Nothing in my hand I bring."

4. THE RIGHTEOUSNESS OF GOD. "It is not meet to take the children's bread, and to cast it to dogs" (v. 26). Deep ploughing this; yes, but the shafts are in the hands of Infinite Love. The promises given only to saints will not be cast to sinners. God cannot be unrighteous, even in saving a soul. She was not a Jewish *child*; therefore by *birth* she had no hope. In Christ we meet with a *just* God and a Saviour.

IV **Her Argument**. "Truth, Lord; yet the dogs eat of the crumbs which fall" (v. 27). As much as to say, "That's the truth, but as LORD Thou canst give *me* also what I need." This was a powerful plea, because it was—

1. THE ARGUMENT OF FAITH. "O woman, great is thy faith" (v. 28). She laid fast hold upon His character, not as Son of David, but as the Son of God—as Lord over all, blessed for ever. It was also—

2. THE ARGUMENT OF A BROKEN SPIRIT. She humbly took her place among the undeserving dogs, that the grace of the Lord might reach even to her. *Grace* delights to flow *down* and fill the needy. A broken and a contrite spirit He will not despise.

V. **Her Success**. Hers was the triumph of faith.

1. SHE GAINED THE NEEDED BLESSING. "Be it unto thee even as thou wilt" (v. 28). Her "Lord help me" is answered by His offer of Omnipotent fulness. Faith may be tested, but it will not be disappointed. Though He tarry, wait. She knew His Name, and trusted in Him, and He did not forsake her (Psa 9. 10).

2. SHE EMBRACED A PASSING PRIVILEGE. While Jesus was passing by she "came out and cried" (v. 22). This was her only opportunity, and she made the most of it. Take heed lest you are letting yours slip. "Behold, now is the accepted time; behold, now is the day of salvation" (2 Cor. 6. 2). _____

THE GREAT PHYSICIAN.
Matthew 15. 29-31.

CHRIST's public ministry began with the baptism of the Holy Spirit. Does not every real ministry begin with this? His first recorded utterance is, "The *Spirit* of the Lord is upon me. *He* hath sent me to heal, to recover the sight of the blind, and to set at liberty the bruised" (Luke 4. 18). This is His diploma.

I. **The Position of the Healer.** "He *went up* into a mountain and *sat down*" (v. 29). The actions as well as the words of Christ were prophetic. While He sat upon the mountain great multitudes came unto Him, and He healed them all. What a picture of Christ's position and power! He has *gone up* into the mount of Heaven, and is *sat down* at the right hand of God to give gifts unto men. Whosoever will may come. None are cast out. He heals them all. He now sits as He did on that mount by the Sea of Galilee, *waiting to be gracious*. No question asked, no fee required, no prescription given, but instant help and healing imparted. Before God Jesus sits as the only hope and health for a perishing world. "Look unto Me and be ye saved, for I am God" (Isa. 45. 22).

II. **The Character of the Healed.**

1. THE LAME. Those whose legs are unequal, and whose walk is very unsteady, who have many an up and down. There are many lame Christians vainly trying to walk like those whose legs are equal. It is no use trying to conceal

the limp. If there are failure and weakness bring them to Jesus. He maketh the lame to walk.

2. THE BLIND. Those who walk in darkness. Their outward life may be without a limp, but their minds are darkened. They have no assurance; they know not where they are going. They depend on human hands to guide them; they have not the eye-salve of the Holy Spirit. He can make the blind to see for themselves.

3. THE DUMB. This is a type of those who can both *see* and *walk*, but whose *lips* are sealed. They know the truth, and their actions may be faultless, but their *tongues* are dumb for God—moral beauties, but spiritual dummies. This great Physician can also make the dumb to speak.

4. THE MAIMED. This is a very plentiful class, and very pitiful. They once had hands and feet and tongues for God, but sin has maimed and marred their members, so that they are now useless in the service of Christ. They once had power, but the Holy Ghost is grieved, and their testimony is maimed (see Judges 16. 20). "I will *heal* your backsliding" (Jer. 3. 22).

5. THE NONDESCRIPT. "And many others." Among this lot there would likely be found "all sorts"—the sick, the sad, the fevered, and the broken-hearted. Christ can heal every ailment. Everything that hinders our joy in God and our testimony for Him may be confessed as a disease. Is it care, anxiety, temper, fear, despondency? *He healeth all thy diseases.*

III. **The Place of Healing.** "They cast them down at Jesus' feet" (v. 30). The place of blessing is at the feet of Him who is able to tread upon the surging waves of humanity's sorrows (Matt. 14. 25). Those bleeding feet on Calvary's cross proclaim victory through His blood over every sin to all who believe. The way into this place of perfect healing is to *get down, down* to Jesus' feet.

IV. The Results that Followed—

1. THE HEALED BORE TESTIMONY. They saw the dumb *speaking*, the lame *walking*, the blind *seeing*, the maimed to be *whole*. Every one used the gift received to the glory of the Great Healer. What a change! The power of Christ could not be hid in the lives of the healed ones.

2. THE MULTITUDE GLORIFIED GOD (v. 31). Why has the multitude ceased to wonder and glorify God now? Have we not the same all-sufficient Saviour to-day waiting to make us perfectly whole, that our lives might be worthy of His Almighty grace and healing power. "Let your light so shine before men, that *they may see* your good works, *and glorify your Father* which is in Heaven" (Matt. 5. 16).

THE TRANSFIGURATION AND ITS LESSONS.
Matthew 17. 1-9.

JESUS had just begun to show unto His disciples how He must suffer many things, and be killed (Matt. 16. 21); but before the awful darkness gathers over the Cross He here gives them a passing glimpse of His great glory. We need such manifestations to support us in the hour of sorrow and trial. When we come to this mount we are apt to be so blinded with the "glory of the light" that we cannot see the helpful lessons we might learn. We might learn that—

I. To be Alone with the Lord is a Glorious Privilege. "Jesus *taketh* Peter, James, and John, and was transfigured *before them*" (vv. 1, 2). "They went apart *with Him* to pray" (Luke 9. 28); and, while alone with Him, they beheld His glory, and were eye-witnesses of His majesty. This was a premature outburst of the *hidden* glory of the Man whose face was more marred than any man's. If we would know Jesus Christ in all His glorious fulness, let us be much alone with Him on the quiet mount of prayer. We hope to be alone with Him in eternity; why not seek much of His presence now?

II. The Lord is Infinitely more Glorious than Men see Him to be. "While He prayed His face did shine as the sun, and His raiment was white as the light" (v. 2). There was a double glory—that which shone out of Heaven from the Father, and that which shone out of Himself as the image of the Father. The carnal eye saw no beauty in Him, but He was glorious within all the same. The hidden glory of Christ and the hidden glory of the Christian will both in one day yet be manifested. The same "Lord the Spirit" who hath transfigured our souls will also transfigure our bodies (2 Cor. 3. 18; 1 John 3. 1, 2).

III. The Death of Christ is the Most Important Subject under Heaven. "Moses and Elias talked with Him" (v. 3); and Luke says, "They talked about the decease to be accomplished at Jerusalem." The death of Christ had a wonderful significance—to Heaven, earth, and hell. Think of the contrast between the *subject* of their talk and the *appearance* of the One appointed to die on a cross. What would Moses and Elias think of our present-day religious talkers who deny the atoning death of Jesus?

IV. The Glory of the Lord can be but Little Appreciated in our Present State. "The *voice* that must accompany the glory terrified them. They fell on their face, and were sore afraid." Moses had to be hid in a cleft of the rock to see the back parts of the divine glory; Paul, caught up into Paradise, heard and saw what was *unspeakable*. The High Priest never attempted to explain the "Shekinah glory." Enough for us that God graciously gives us as we are able to bear.

V. The Lord only is Sufficient to Comfort the Troubled heart. "He *touched* them, and *said*, Be not afraid...They lifted up their eyes, and saw Jesus only" (v. 8). When the living Word of God touches the sorrowful or terrified soul it is enough. Although all else should fail, and every comfortable feeling flee, "If I've Jesus, Jesus only, then my sky will have a gem." The *touch* and the *word* of Jesus are sufficient to bind up every wound.

VI. The Resurrection of the Lord is the Foundation of the Gospel. "Tell the vision to no man until the Son of Man be risen from the dead" (v. 9). The Gospel of the glory must come *after* the Gospel of the Cross. "If Christ be not risen, then is our preaching vain" (1 Cor. 15. 14). But Christ *is risen*; therefore tell out the vision of His glory. He is exalted to be a Prince and a Saviour.

VII. To Hear the Word of the Lord is a Divine Command. "This is My beloved Son, *hear ye Him*" (v. 5). We should hear Him because the Father is "well pleased" with everything He says. Hear—

1. THE VOICE OF HIS WORD. He is a great Teacher come from God, with God's message to sinful men.

2. THE VOICE OF HIS WORKS. "The works that I do bear witness of Me" (John 5. 36). Works of miracle and mercy. "Believe Me for the very works' sake" (John 14. 11).

3. THE VOICE OF HIS BLOOD. The blood that *speaketh* better things than that of Abel. Jesus' blood speaks of *satisfaction* to God and *peace* to man.

4. THE VOICE OF HIS SPIRIT. That Spirit who maketh intercession for us with *groanings* which cannot be uttered, and who seeks to transform us into the image of Christ. Hear ye Him, and be made like Him.

THE UNFORGIVING SERVANT.

Matthew 18. 23-35.

PETER had just been asking, "How often shall I forgive?" and even hinted that he was willing to go the length of seven times. But Christ's seventy times seven would teach us to exercise the love that was after His own heart— the "charity that never faileth." In this parable two great truths are brought out: (1) The need of being forgiven; (2) the need of forgiving others.

I. His Deplorable Condition. His true state was only discovered when he began to reckon with his Lord. A day of reckoning will come when every hidden thing will be revealed. See him—

1. AS A GREAT DEBTOR. "He owed ten thousand talents" (v. 24), about three million pounds. Our debt to one another may be measured by one hundred pence, but our debt to God is infinite. How much owest thou my Lord? Thou shalt love the Lord thy God with all thy heart, soul, mind, and strength. How much of His goods have we squandered?

2. AS A HELPLESS BANKRUPT. "He had not wherewith to pay" (v. 25). In the eyes of his fellowmen he is rich and honourable; in the presence of his Lord he is a wretched insolvent. He has sinned, and has come short, far short. To meet all the demands of a holy Lord God by our own selfish efforts is a miserable and hopeless task. "By the deeds of the law there shall no flesh be justified in His sight" (Rom. 3. 20). Without strength.

3. AS ONE UNDER CONDEMNATION. "His lord commanded him to be sold" (v. 25). All his past service only merited his condemnation. This is a sharp rebuke to the self-righteous. This is the revelation that comes to us

when by the Holy Spirit the soul is brought face to face
with the righteous claims of God. "By the law is the
knowledge of sin" (Rom. 3. 20).

4. As an Earnest Petitioner. "He fell down, saying,
lord, have patience with me, and I will pay thee all"
(v. 26). He is in downright earnest, but it is a self-
righteous and presumptuous prayer. He is not able to
pay, yet he only pleads for patience. He makes confession
of his failure, and promises to do better in the future. It
is the old trick of the carnal and unbelieving heart, which
refuses to ask forgiveness. He still hopes to be justified
by his works. But when will an imprisoned man be able
to pay his debt? Not of works.

II. His Merciful Lord.

1. Had Compassion on Him. "His lord was moved
with compassion" (v. 27). It was good for him that he
met his lord in a day of grace. Poor debtor, in his reckoning he left no place for the love of his lord. "Behold, now
is the accepted time" (2 Cor. 6. 2). Let us bless God that
we have seen and felt His infinite compassion through the
grace of His Son.

2. Pardoned Him. "He forgave him the debt" (v. 27).
This was much more than he expected. This was the only
remedy, and it was a gracious one. Not a word of rebuke,
not a word about continued patience. Ah! He knows what
we need, as poor, penniless paupers in His sight. "He
forgiveth all thine iniquities" (Psa. 103. 3). "Your sins
and iniquities will be remembered no more" (Heb. 10.
17). "Who is a God like our God, who pardoneth iniquity,
transgression, and sin?" (Micah 7. 18). He is now
saved by grace.

3. Delivered Him. "He loosed him" (v. 27). He not
only got his debt cancelled, but he was, as a matter of

course, loosed from the sentence of condemnation passed upon him. Being forgiven, he is now free from the law. Blessed change! Not under the law, but under grace. Salvation is twofold: (1) He forgiveth all their iniquities; (2) He redeemeth thy life.

III. His Selfish Behaviour. "He took his fellow-servant by the throat, saying, Pay me that thou owest." He had mercy shown him, but he shows no mercy. The spirit of his lord had not possession of him, and not being filled with his spirit he soon has to forfeit the fellowship and favour of his master. As those who have received mercy, let us take heed lest we frustrate the grace of God, and as a servant become a castaway. We may learn here the—

1. MANNER OF BROTHERLY FORGIVENESS. "Shouldst not thou have had compassion; . . . from your hearts forgive." If the love of God is shed abroad in our hearts we will have compassion on the erring, and be willing to forgive them from the heart. Freely ye have received, freely give.

2. EXAMPLE OF BROTHERLY FORGIVENESS. "Even as I had pity on thee." May the pity of the Lord Jesus Christ toward us fill up the measure of our pity for others. "As the Father loved Me, so have I loved you, so ought ye also to love one another. By this shall all know that ye are My disciples, if ye love one another" (John 13.34,35).

3. MISERY OF THE UNFORGIVING. "The lord was wroth, and delivered him to the tormentors." The unforgiving servant cannot abide in the fellowship of his Lord. One hard, unkindly thought toward a fellow-Christian worker is enough to bring the soul into the hands of the tormentors, and to rob us of the smile of the Master's face. Sin always betrays us into the hands of the tormentors. The torments

of an evil conscience and a proud, covetous heart are neither few nor small. "Be ye kind one to another, tender-hearted, forgiving one another, even as God for Christ's sake hath forgiven you" (Eph. 4. 32).

THE LABOURERS;
OR, LESSONS FOR CHRISTIAN WORKERS.
Matthew 20. 1-16.

THOSE who leave all *for* Jesus will find their all *in* Jesus (chap. 19. 27). Peter said, "What shall we have *therefore?* Seeing we have left so much, how much shall we get?" This savours too much of the language of the mere hireling. To labour only for reward is a mean motive for serving Christ. To correct this grovelling spirit, and to enlighten the darkness that fosters it, this parable seems to have been given. Notice—

I. Some Things about the Labourers. The—

1. PLACE OF LABOUR. "His vineyard" (v. 1). This is the place where much patient labour is urgently needed, or much fruit will be lost. Those who labour among the trailing vines must be careful about their *walk.* The tender grapes must be gently handled. To gather fruit for Christ the gentleness of Jesus is needed. Note, further, that every labourer in the vineyard must have the Master's call.

2. HIRING OF THE LABOURERS. This was done at five different times. Look at it dispensationally, "early in the morning" (v. 1) may represent from Adam to Noah, the third hour from Noah to Moses, the sixth hour from Moses to David, the ninth hour from David to Christ, the eleventh the present, till He comes again. Or it may suggest the various stages of life from youth to old age. How few are found at the eleventh hour, but even then the full reward of eternal life is given to all who believe and obey.

3. REWARDING OF THE LABOURERS. "Call and give them their hire." Every one *called* to labour shall be called to their reward, "beginning at the last." The most hopeless at the eleventh hour becomes the most hopeful in the evening. Here grace reigns. Labour on. Idlers in the market-place are less responsible than idlers in the vineyard.

4. DISSATISFACTION OF THE LABOURERS. "The first supposed that they should have received more." These find their counterpart in the "elder brother" mentioned in Luke 15; those hired at the eleventh hour in the prodigal son. We cannot anticipate disappointment in Heaven; but are there not many on earth who grudge the chief of sinners an equal share of the grace of God with themselves?

II. **Some Things about the Master.** Here observe His—

1. JUSTICE. "Friend, I do thee no wrong" (v. 13). The selfish servant cannot understand the grace of Christ. Those who labour only for wages cannot enjoy the favour of God. If we knew Him better, we would murmur less at His doings. "I have not the gifts of So-and-so." "Friend, I do thee no wrong."

2. FAITHFULNESS. "Didst thou not agree with me for a penny? Take that is thine" (v. 14). He gave all that He promised. The penny seems to have been their own terms; the others went on His terms, "Whatsoever is right I will give you," and had no desire to grumble. Trust His grace, and you will have good cause to praise and rejoice.

3. SOVEREIGNTY. "Is it not lawful for me to do what I will with my own?" (v.15). What unhallowed feelings arise in our hearts when we see a brother or a sister, with scarcely any experience—just an hour in the vineyard—

being more honoured of the Master than we are, who have borne the burden and heat of the scorching drought. So it seemeth good in Thy sight.

4. Judgment. "Is thine eye evil, because I am good?" (v. 15). The evil eye can see but little good in the grace of Christ. "An evil eye makes a darkened body" (Matt. 6. 23). It contrasts badly with the unmerited goodness of the Master. Our thoughts at the best come far short of the exceeding riches of His grace. Lord, give us the single eye to Thy glory.

THE TWO BLIND MEN.
Matthew 20. 30-34.

"Behold two blind men." There are many important lessons for us in this short narrative. Here we see—

I. **A Sorrowful Picture.** "Two blind men." They were—

1. Poor. They sat by the wayside, evidently begging. They were men who had no promise to live on, no prospect to cheer them. Such were all of us, at that time having no promise, and without hope. All who are without Christ are poor indeed.

2. Blind. They had no eyes even to look on the passing Saviour. Picture of those who are destitute of spiritual vision, walking in darkness, and having no light.

3. Helpless. Although there were two of them, the one could in no wise help the other. All are alike guilty and impotent before the Lord. Help must come from above.

II. **A Passing Opportunity.** "Jesus passed by." In the coming near of the Son of God lies man's only chance of getting deliverance from the power of darkness. These men embraced their opportunity by putting themselves "in the way." Jesus has come near by the light of His Word. Flee not from Him by preferring the darkness (Hosea 7. 13).

III. An Earnest Prayer. "They cried out, saying, Have mercy on us, O Lord." See their—

1. BOLDNESS. "They cried out." It was nothing to them who heard their voice. They were poor men, crying out of the depths of their dire and conscious need.

2. FAITH. "They cried, saying, Lord." They acknowledge Him as Messiah and Master. Dost thou believe on the Son of God? Hast thou confessed Him?

3. PETITION. "Have mercy on us." They confess their helplessness and need by begging for mercy. The prayer of the self-righteous is, "I am not as other men" (Luke 18. 11), or, "Have patience with me, and I will pay thee" (Matt. 18. 26). "God be merciful to me." (Luke 18. 23).

4. WISDOM. "When they heard, they cried." They did not wait for a more convenient season. "Faith cometh by hearing" (Rom. 10. 17). "Hear and your soul shall live" (Isa. 55. 3).

IV. A Rebuking Crowd. "The multitude rebuked them." Anxious and inquiring sinners are often rebuked by a multitude of false fears and feelings, but perhaps a greater obstacle lies in the multitude of inconsistent disciples—those who outwardly follow Christ, but who have no sympathy with Him in His great work of saving sinners. Do with the hindrances that arise through the failings of some professing Christians what these blind men did with the rebuking multitude, "Cry the more."

V. A Willing Saviour. "He willeth not the death of any." He—

1. STOOD. The cry of need has a magical power to arrest the passing Saviour, and draw out the living waters of divine compassion. He stood. What a privilege! "Behold, I stand at the door and knock" (Rev. 3. 20).

2. CALLED. Liberty of access is now given. Nearness invited, He seeks the fellowship of those whom He blesses. He that stands at the door and knocks still calls, "If any man hear My voice, and open the door" (Rev. 3. 20). He has made room for you; make room for Him. ·

VI. A Gracious Offer. "What will ye that I should do unto you?" (v. 32). He invited them. Now He throws the door of infinite fulness open before them, that all their needs may be fully met. Oh, what a wonderful Saviour is Jesus! The rebuking multitude cannot hinder Him from pouring out the treasures of His love and grace upon all who come. "Come unto Me, and I will give ye—." What will ye?

VII. A Perfect Cure. God's remedy for needy man is a wonderful compound of infinite love and precious blood. The order here is very beautiful—

1. HE HAD COMPASSION. The need of the blind men touched the very depths of His heart, and His whole soul moved out in mighty, misery-melting mercy.

2. HE TOUCHED THEIR EYES. The presence of Jesus is always a conscious presence. To be blessed we must come within His touch. Here the dead live, and sin is blotted out. His gentle yet almighty hand is laid on the cause and source of their misery. He opened Lydia's heart.

3. THEY RECEIVED SIGHT. What a change! Old things have passed away, all things became new. Salvation is a very great and conscious blessing we know.

4. THEY FOLLOWED HIM. He touched them. Now they keep in touch with Him. Blessed life! "Follow Me!" "Wilt thou go with this Man?" (Gen. 24. 58).

THE TWO SONS.
Matthew 21. 28-32.

THIS parable begins with Christ's "What *think* ye?" and is eminently fitted to make us *think*. Some perish for want of thought, and many more for wrong thinking. The priests and elders had been asking Him, "By what authority doest Thou these things?" Christ answers their question by holding up this parable as a mirror before their eyes that they might be convinced of their sins. The way to understand the authority of Christ is to discover our real state before Him. Those who pride themselves in their own supposed goodness will always remain in ignorance of Christ's authority and saving power.

I. **What the Father Commanded.** "Son, go work to-day in My vineyard" (v. 28). The Father's vineyard needs workers; who should be more interested than the Son? Observe the—

1. GROUND OF THE FATHER'S CLAIM. "Son," (v. 28). Plenty of hirelings may be got for wages, but love ought to constrain a son. "The love of Christ constraineth us" (2 Cor. 5. 14). If we are the sons of God, surely our Father has the first claim upon our time and strength and substance. Our Father may *hire* strangers to serve Him (Isa. 7. 20), but sons are *commanded*.

2. DESIRE OF THE FATHER'S HEART. "Work" (v. 28). What a grief it must be to our God to see so much work to be done and so many of His sons idle! Work is pleasing to the Father, good for the vineyard, and profitable for the Son. The idle soul shall suffer hunger (Prov. 19. 15). Our Father has a multitude of talkative sons, but the labourers are few.

3. URGENCY OF THE FATHER'S REQUEST. "To-day." The time for serving the Lord is always NOW. Some of the

younger sons say, "Wait till I get a little more experience." Some of the older sons say, "It is not worth my while beginning now;" or they are thinking about retiring from the vineyard. Go, work to-day, this present day of salvation, for "the night cometh when no man can work" (John 9. 4). "Wherefore the Holy Ghost saith, To-day" (Heb. 3. 7).

II. **What the Sons Said.** In the case of the first we have—

1. A DECIDED REFUSAL. "I will not" (v. 29). This language reveals the spirit of selfish indifference to the Father's desire. In plain words it is this: "I have something else of my own to look after, and have not time to work in your vineyard." What cares the selfish Christian for the perishing millions, or the grieving of the Father's heart, if their own little plans and purposes can only be attended to. This language also betrays a heart in open rebellion. "I will not." A life opposed to the Father's will and out of sympathy with the Father's purpose. The other son answered with—

2. A READY CONSENT. "I go" (v. 30). He speaks with marked respect, "I go, sir." Judging from his talk he has a great reverence for his father and a great zeal for his work. His words are smoother than butter. The descendants of this oily-lipped professor have not yet ceased from among us. Yet his instant decision and prompt reply to the father's urgent command should be copied by every son. "If ye love Me, keep My commandments" (John 14. 15).

III. **What the Sons Did.** There is often a vast difference between a man's profession and his actions. "Whither of them twain did the father's will?" It is not which of them talked the best or made the loudest profession? By their deeds are they justified or condemned. His Word is fulfilled in our doing of it, not in our talking about it.

1. The One Repented and Obeyed. Repentance always precedes the doing of the will of God. The bold, self-willed rebel is the first to yield and obey. Don't despair of the restoration of the loud-mouthed, disobedient backslider, or of the conversion of the defiant sceptic. "Afterward, he repented and went." Those who go willingly into the vineyard of God's service will find grace sufficient and a holy joy in pleasing Him.

2. The Other Promised and Failed. "He said, I go, sir, and went not." All who go not at God's bidding into the field of service for Him are disobedient and rebellious children, no matter how nicely they may talk about "the Lord's work." Talking about ministers, churches, and religion is not working for God any more than warming your hands at the fire is gathering grapes. Not every one that saith, "Lord, Lord," shall enter into the kingdom, but he that doeth the will of My Father. "Whatsoever He saith unto you, do it" (John 2. 5).

THE WICKED HUSBANDMEN.
Matthew 21. 33-41.

In this parable Christ rebukes the unfruitful profession of the rulers of His people. They had rejected the Corner-stone, as builders, and their work had come to naught. So the vail of their temple was rent in twain from the top to the bottom, and the kingdom of God was taken from them and given to another nation (the Gentiles, v. 43). Religious knowledge, enthusiasm, and scrupulous observances are all empty and lifeless when Jesus Christ is rejected or denied His proper place—a lamp without a light, a body without a spirit. We observe here—

I. Labour Expended. The householder himself was at all the expense of the "planting," "hedging," "digging," and "building" (v 33). Think of what God had done for

Israel as a nation. He dug them out of Egypt, planted them in a good land, and hedged them about with promises and privileges, yet it proved an empty vine. God, as the Householder, wrought all this work—there were none to help Him. Think of the labour expended by our Lord Jesus Christ, that we might bring forth fruit to the praise of His Name. Oh, what praying, suffering, groaning, sweating, dying, He gave Himself.

II. Privilege Enjoyed. "He let it out to husbandmen, and went into a far country" (v. 33). These husbandmen did not purchase the vineyard; through the grace of God it was let out to them. Israel was honoured, as being the tenant of divine wisdom and knowledge, but because of unfaithfulness they have been expelled. This privilege now belongs to all who are in Christ Jesus. While the Master is in the far country these priceless blessings are let out to us by the grace of God. We have not bought them; we do not deserve them; they are the gifts of God—the tokens of His infinite love.

III. Fruit Expected. "He sent his servants, that they might receive the fruits" (v. 34). Although the Master is in the far country (Heaven) He is still mindful of His vineyard. In asking the fruits He is only asking His own. The vineyard was His. "Ye are not your own, for ye are bought with a price; therefore glorify God in your body and your spirit, which are God's" (1 Cor. 6. 19, 20). The much labour of Christ for us should produce much fruit through us.

IV. Selfishness Exhibited. "The husbandmen took his servants, and beat, and killled, and stoned them" (v.35). There is here no sign of gratitude for great privileges bestowed; no concern about the Master's interests. The grace of God has been in vain to them. It is sad to

find this same selfish spirit among those who profess to be
the servants of the Lord Jesus Christ. They are ready to
take every earthly blessing and advantage God may give
them, but they will yield Him nothing. They will even
wear the Name of Christ for their own personal interests.

V. Forbearance Manifested. "He sent other servants, and last of all He sent His Son" (v.36). What longsuffering, what patience with insult and cruelty, what
willingness to forgive, what reluctance to punish! What
a hideous contrast between the selfish greed of man and the
lovingkindness of God! "They will reverence My Son."
The appearance of His Son brought out the awful enmity
of the human heart against God. Such is GRACE—giving
His best gift to the least deserving.

VI. Rebellion Declared. "When they saw the Son
they said, This is the Heir; come, let us kill Him, and let
us seize on His inheritance" (v. 38). "We will not have this
Man to reign to reign over us." "We have no king but
Caesar" (John 19. 15). So Jesus, as the Son of Sovereign
Grace, is cast out, and the Father, as the Householder, is
defied. We will reign as gods without Him is still the
language of many a highly-favoured but God-hating sinner.
Yet, O the depth of the mystery, that through the death of
the Son we may indeed seize on His inheritance. Heirs
of God.

VII. Destruction Assured. "He will miserably
destroy those wicked men" (v. 41). Privilege may exalt to
the gate of Heaven, but if neglected and abused will crush
into the depths of hell. These 1880 years' wanderings of
the Jews on the face of the earth, without a king and without a country, is a divine and solemn witness and warning
that God will judge sin. When the Lord Himself appears
to reckon with the husbandmen it will be a time of dread-

ful awakening to those who have been in the vineyard only for their own selfish ends. Carefully note that the Householder asked for the fruits *before* He came. His coming was the time of judgment for His servants. "We must all appear before the judgment-seat of Christ, that every one may receive the things done in His body, according to that he hath done, whether it be good or bad" (2 Cor. 5. 10).

THE MARRIAGE FEAST.
Matthew 22. 1-14.

THE scope of this parable is very wide; it seems to embrace the whole of this present dispensation. The "certain King" is God the Father; the "Son," Jesus Christ; the "marriage," the new relationship into which the Son was about to enter; the "servants," the apostles of Christ; "those that were bidden," the Jews, who, as a nation, had received notice long before; the "other servants," perhaps those who went forth after Pentecost; the "dinner," the provision made by God in the death of His Son for hungry, perishing souls; they "made light of it," the rejection of Christ by the Jews, His called ones; the "city burned," destruction of Jerusalem by the Romans thirty years later; "Go into the highways," the universal invitation of the Gospel; the "wedding furnished," the calling out and completion of the Church; "the King came in to see the guests," the second Coming of Christ; "Bind him, and cast him into outer darkness," the separation of the chaff from the wheat; He shall thoroughly purge His floor. The Gospel of the grace of God is here beautifully set forth. Observe the—

I. Provision. "Behold, I have prepared My dinner; all things are ready; come" (v. 4). The provision was wholly His own. "My oxen, my fatlings are killed." He spared not His own Son, but freely gave Him up to the death for us all. "Behold the Lamb of God." The provision was very great; it included "all things." All things are yours if ye are Christ's. Those who came to this feast found what sinners find on coming to Christ—

1. REST on a Princely couch.

2. SHELTER under a Princely roof.

3. SATISFACTION at a Princely table.

4. FELLOWSHIP with Princely friends.

II. **Invitation.** "Come unto the marriage" (v. 4). This invitation is for all. Whosoever will may come; both bad and good were called. The Gospel invitation takes no notice of our character; the vilest as well as the most virtuous must accept the invitation on equal terms. None deserve it. It is the goodness of God freely offered to all. The pompous prince and the poverty-stricken beggar are both alike indebted to the mercy and grace of God for salvation. Because of this many "make light of it." To make light of the invitation is to make light of the God who gives it. That is no light matter.

III. **Inspection.** "The King came in to see the guests" (v. 11). All who accept the invitation expect to see the King; with joy they wait for His Coming. Those who are living in rebellion against His will, despising His grace, may well dread His appearing. He comes to see and to welcome all those who have believed His Word through His servants. Jesus Christ manifests Himself to those who yield to His call, and accept His offered mercy. Believe, and thou shalt see the glory of God.

IV. **Detection.** "He saw a man which had not on a wedding garment" (v. 11). Only one, but the quick eye of the King soon found him out. The man was conspicuous, not for what he had, but for what he had not. "A wedding garment." The garment was part of the King's provision, but he refused it. It is not enough that we merely believe the invitation of the Gospel; we must lay hold of the righteousness of God, which is offered us in Christ Jesus, and upon all them that believe. Remember that mingling among the people of God does not fit us for meeting the King. You may escape the detection of the servants, but the Searcher of hearts will find you out.

V. Interrogation. "Friend, how camest thou in hither, not having a wedding garment?" (v. 12). He does not take him by the throat. This is the language of tenderest compassion, but he is faithful and just. It was not the King's fault, but perhaps he was priding himself in his own good-looking garments, prepared for the occasion, and all duly paid for. He belongs to the family of those "who go about to establish their own righteousness" (Rom. 10. 3). "Prepare to meet thy God" (Amos 4. 12).

VI. Conviction. "He was speechless" (v. 12). He was self-condemned before a court from which there was no appeal. He may have been making fine speeches before the King came in, but now his mouth is stopped. There is no one to plead his cause; in his behalf all his friends are speechless. Oh, friend, boast of nothing now that you will not rejoice in when the King comes. This man does not even ask for mercy, so utterly hopeless is his case now. It is a solemn moment when all the refuges of lies are swept away by the power of His presence. "What wilt thou say when He shall punish thee?" (Jer. 13. 21).

VII. Expulsion. "Then said the King, Bind him, and take him away, and cast him into outer darkness" (v.13). The man who despises the King's garment will never taste His feast. Think of what he was taken away from. Away from all his opportunities and companions, into the outer darkness, the darkness of hopeless despair, that is, outside the kingdom of God's dear Son. What a change! What a disappointment! Out from the presence of a feast into the place of weeping. There will be great and sudden changes when He shall appear. Put on the Lord Jesus Christ. ———

THE LAST DAYS.
Matthew 24. 37-39.

"But as the days of Noah were, so shall also the Coming of the Son of Man be." Then, according to the teaching of Jesus Christ, Noah was a real person, the flood was a great fact, and the second Coming of Christ as the Son of Man will be an unfailing certainty. What the state and conditions of the world will be when He comes is here clearly revealed, "As the days of Noah were, so shall the Coming of the Son of Man be." Nothing could be more simple than this.

I. **As there was great and growing wickedness in the days of Noah, so shall also the Coming of the Son of Man be.** The world did not go on growing better and better up till the days of Noah. No, but it grew worse and worse, till God saw that the wickedness of man was great in the earth, and that every imagination of the thoughts of his heart was only evil continually (Gen. 6. 5). So shall it be when the Son of Man comes. "As in the days of Sodom" (Luke 17. 29, 30). In the last days, "Perilous times" (2 Tim. 3. 1); "Not endure sound doctrine" (2 Tim. 4. 3); "Damnable heresies" (2 Peter 2. 1); "Strong delusion" (2 Thess. 2. 11); "Scoffers, walking after their own lusts" (2 Peter 3. 3); "Many departing from the faith."

II. **As there was faithful warning in the days of Noah, so shall also the Coming of the Son of Man be.** Noah was a preacher of righteousness (2 Peter 2. 5). For a hundred and twenty years, while the Ark was a preparing, "he condemned the world" (Heb. 11. 7). Every board put in the Ark was a note of warning that judgment was coming. So shall also the Coming of the Son of Man be. There never was a time in the history of the Church when the "Coming of Christ" was so generally believed and so clearly preached as now. The cry, "Behold, the Bridegroom cometh!" (Matt. 25. 6) is being heard by the waiting virgins.

III. As they were overtaken with sudden and universal surprise in the days of Noah, so shall also the Coming of the Son of Man be. "They knew not until the flood came and took them all away" (v. 39). They were marrying and giving in marriage until Noah entered the Ark and the Lord had shut the door. They believed not the testimony of Noah. The habits and sins of society remained unchanged and unrepented. So shall also the coming of the Son of Man be. When He comes shall He find faith in the earth? He shall come suddenly. "For as the lightning cometh out of the east, and shineth even unto the west, so shall also the Coming of the Son of Man be" (Matt. 24. 27). Who shall stand when He appeareth?

IV. As all who entered the Ark in the days of Noah were saved, so shall also the Coming of the Son of Man be. The Lord said, "Come thou and all thy house into the Ark" (Gen.7.1). Noah and his family obeyed the call; then "the Lord shut him in"—"kept by the power of God through faith unto salvation" (1 Peter 1. 5). So shall it be when the Son of Man cometh. "Caught up...to meet the Lord in the air, and so shall we ever be with the Lord" (1 Thess. 4. 17). All who are now in the kingdom of God's dear Son shall be taken away before the judgment of God falls upon the disobedient and the unbelieving. "They that are Christ's at His coming" (1 Cor. 15. 23). Just as Lot was taken out of Sodom before the deluge of fire came. He that hath this hope purifieth himself.

V. As all outside the Ark were visited with judgment in the days of Noah, so shall also the Coming of
the Son of Man be. "The flood came and swept them all
away" (v. 39). The Ark, as a means of salvation, was
beyond their reach whenever the door was shut. Their day
of opportunity was now gone. So shall also the Coming of
the Son of Man be. Selah—pause and think. "Tribulation
and anguish" (Rom. 2. 9); "Weeping and wailing and
gnashing of teeth" will be the portion of every Christ
rejecter when He comes. Those who have not on the
wedding garment when the King comes will be cast forth
into outer darkness. "Be not deceived; God is not
mocked." "As it was in the days of Noah, so shall it be
when the Son of Man cometh."

FOOLISH VIRGINS.
Matthew 25. 1-12.

FROM the closing verses of the preceding chapter we learn
that the purpose of this parable is to teach the servants of
God the necessity of being always ready for their Master's
appearing, and that readiness consists not in idly staring
into Heaven, but in actively doing those things that are
pleasing unto Him. They are always ready who are always
doing His will: "Blessed is that servant whom when his
Lord cometh shall find so doing" (Matt. 24. 46). The good
wife may watch for her husband because she longs to see
him, but if he, when he comes, finds the house untidy and
the supper unprepared, would he be satisfied with her
watching? These foolish virgins represent those who have
the appearance of being ready, but who will be found
unprepared. Notice their—

I. **Blameless Character.** They were "virgins," their
characters were without reproach, blameless in the sight
of men; they are typical of a large class of professing

Christians whose outward life and conduct are unstained with iniquity. They are found in every sphere of Christian work; their motives are never for a moment questioned. They love the company of the virtuous and the wise, and even the truly wise love to have their help and fellowship; they are very courteous, congenial, and liberal-minded.

II. **Noble Intention.** "They went forth to meet the Bridegroom" (v. 1). The others are going, so they go too. They would like to see the Bridegroom, and to share the marriage feast. They make some little sacrifice for the hope that is in them; they never question their fitness. The counterpart of these is still to be found among us; religious people whose moral lives are beautiful, who have been good all their days, who never question their condition before God, nor imagine that they must be "born again." Their intentions are good, but they are blind to their own real need.

III. **Thoughtless Neglect.** "They took no oil with them" (v. 3). All their hope was in their lamps of profession. This could only last for a very brief season. They would not go without their lamps—lamps could be seen, but the invisible oil was unheeded. Type of those satisfied with an outward resemblance to the real while strangers to the Holy Spirit of promise. Oil in the vessel is suggestive of the Spirit of God in the heart, which is the true witness that we are the children of God. This will stand when all outward evidences faint and fail.

IV. **Helpless Indifference.** "They all slumbered and slept" (v. 5). The Bridegroom tarried, and they grew tired, and sank into a state of insensibility. The waiting time is a testing time for all. The time the Bridegroom tarried was a time of grace and opportunity for the foolish virgins; now was their time to go and buy the oil they

needed, but they slept. Even a little lawful indulgence
with self-satisfaction may prove ruinous. Our Lord has
tarried now for more than 1900 years; what a long
opportunity for lamp-trimming! When the wise sleep, it
is no wonder that the foolish become unconscious of
their danger. "What meanest thou, O sleeper?"

V. Anxious Request. "Give us of your oil, for our
lamps are gone out" (v. 8). The midnight cry is an
awakening cry. There will be many alarming discoveries
made when Jesus comes. The midnight cry of warning is
followed with the cry of alarm, "Give us of your oil." No
oil, and the Bridegroom at hand. No fitness to go in, and the
door of Mercy about to close. This oil cannot be borrowed;
it must be bought of Him who alone can sell it (Luke 11.13).
No mortal can give to another that which will fit him for
the appearing of the Lord. "Buy of Me" (**Rev. 3. 18**),
saith He. "One thing thou lackest" (Mark 10. 21).

VI. Earnest Endeavour. "They went to buy" (v. 10).
They are indeed in dead earnest as they run to the nearest
village, wiping the sweat from their faces, but their earnestness does not save them, for "while they went to buy the
Bridegroom came." They were busy seeking when they
should have been rejoicing. Men may use the right means
at the wrong time. Those that were ready went in; those
who were getting ready were shut out. Hoping to be ready
is no fitness for His coming. "Behold, now is the
accepted time" (2 Cor. 6. 2). "Be ye also READY"
(Matt. 24. 44).

VII. Fearful Disappointment. "Afterward came the
other virgins, but the door was shut" (v. 11). The only
answer that came to their urgent appeal, "Lord, Lord, open
to us," was, "I know ye not." Notice, a personal acquaintance with Jesus Christ by the power of the Holy Ghost is
the prime necessity for future fellowship with Him. The

foolish virgins hoped to get in, but they were shut out. Out among the scoffing and the unclean, who never expected to be in, their virgin names did not save them. Only those who had met the Bridegroom entered with Him. "Acquaint now thyself with Him, and be at peace" (Job 22. 21). "If any man have not the Spirit of Christ, he is none of His" (Roman 8. 9).

THE TALENTS.
Matthew 25. 14-30.

In the parable of the "virgins" we are taught the great necessity of individual readiness when Christ comes. This parable teaches the need of trading with His gifts till He comes. In both we are shown the twofold attitude of waiting and working. The man who hid his talent in the earth was also waiting, and may have been longing for his Lord's coming, but, like the foolish virgins, found himself unprepared. In gathering up the truth taught here, observe the—

I. **Calling of the Servants.** "He called his own servants, and delivered unto them his goods" (v. 14). Those called to this more honoured service were His own servants —those who had previously given themselves to Him. They were the disciples of Jesus Christ, whom He called and delivered unto them His goods ere He took His journey into the far country of the Father's presence. His servants are not sent a warfare on their own charges. In John 17 we see what these goods were, the "words," the "joy," and the "glory." With these they were to occupy His place on the earth till He came. "As My Father hath sent Me, even so send I you" (John 20. 21). The power to trade with His goods was given at Pentecost.

II. **Measure of the Gifts.** "To every man according to his several ability." All have not the same ability,

because all have not the same faith. Great faith is great
ability. If the man who got only one talent had got the
ten he doubtless would have misused them all. It is the
Lord Himself who divides to every man. He knows how
much our faith is able to receive and use for His own glory.
"Unto him that hath shall be given." Even one talent is a
great gift. Every gift of God is precious. "According
to your faith, so shall it be unto you."

III. Using of the Talents. All who receive the gift of
God are compelled to do something with it—either to trade
with it or bury it. He that received the five and he that
received the two used them, and in the using they were
doubled. Think of the two great talents God hath given
us—His Son and His Spirit. What spiritual wealth and
power are here! The more we use them in our life and
testimony the more will their preciousness and blessing be
multiplied in our personal experience. But one "hid his
Lord's money." Was it pride or shame that made him
bury it in the earth? Are there not many still who
bury the gift of the Spirit in the earth of a worldly
life—those who deliberately hide their spiritual gift from
the eyes of men, who trade with their own natural talents,
and so cover up their Lord's money.

IV. Coming of the Lord. "After a long time the Lord
of these servants cometh, and reckoneth with them."
The Lord will come again. Nineteen hundred years may
seem a long time, but it is a time of grace and opportunity.
The Lord's money is enough for His servants to trade with
till He does come. When He comes it is first to reckon with
His servants, not to judge the ungodly (2 Cor. 5. 10).
Those who are always trading with the Master's gifts are
always ready for His appearing. If we would succeed in
the Master's business we must see that we trade with the
Master's money. His grace is sufficient.

V. Rewarding of the Diligent. "Well done, good and faithful servant." Eternal life is the gift of God to all who believe, but rewards are only for the servants who have been "good and faithful." The promise is not to the successful, but the good and faithful servant will in God's sight always be successful. This reward was threefold—

1. COMMENDATION. "Well done." An abundant entrance.

2. EXALTATION. "I will make thee ruler." A place of distinction and honour.

3. COMMUNION. "Enter thou into the joy of thy Lord." A condition of fulness of blessing. Happy fellowship.

VI. Doom of the Unprofitable. "Cast the unprofitable servant into outer darkness." He was a servant, but as such his life and work were failures, because he used not the gift bestowed upon him by his gracious Lord. This is the secret of every servant's unprofitableness to God— neglecting the gift of the Spirit. There are seven steps in the downward career of this man. Look at the privilege he enjoyed. Numbered with His servants, and the possessor of a special gift from his Lord. The steps are—

1. WILFUL NEGLECT. He hid his Lord's money.

2. HARD THOUGHTS ABOUT HIS LORD. "I know thee an hard man."

3. SLAVISH FEAR. "I was afraid."

4. SLOTHFULNESS.

5. WICKEDNESS.

6. HIS TALENT TAKEN FROM HIM.

7. CAST OUT. As a fruitless branch he was cut off. Like the foolish virgins, he did not enter into the joy of his Lord.

We then, as workers together with Him, beseech you also that ye receive not the grace of God in vain.

BIBLE READINGS.

FRUITFULNESS.

I. Before Fruit there must be Life. "*Severed* from Me," says Christ, "ye can do nothing" (John 15. 5). He is the Living One, and is come that we might have life. We never look for fruit from a dead tree. A soul dead in sin (Eph. 2. 1) can never bring forth the fruits of righteousness. There must first be a *planting* into Christ (Rom. 4. 5). "He that hath the Son hath life" (1 John 5. 12).

II. There must be Entire Surrender to the New Conditions. If the roots of the tree do not strike out into the new soil in which it has been transplanted it will not prosper.   In Philippians 3. 9, 10 Paul speaks of being found *in Him*, the source of life, then he says: "That I may *know* Him"—a growing acquaintance with Him. The branch must be entirely passive to the power of the vine. Yield yourselves unto God, as those that are alive from the dead (Rom. 6. 13). The fruit of the self-life is corrupt. Crucify the flesh with its lusts; grow in the knowledge of God. This whole-hearted surrender to the grace and power of the Spirit of God opens the way into the heart and life so that God can enter in and work mightily (Eph. 3. 16, 17).

III. Fulness must come before Fruitfulness. The branch will not bear fruit until it has been *filled* to overflowing with the sustaining sap. The cup will not run over until it has been filled. If rivers of water are to flow out of us the unfailing spring must rise up and fill all within (John 7. 38, 39). A dissatisfied heart will bear but a poor, dissatisfying testimony for Christ. If the roots of our being are spread out by the river, by the way of the Holy Spirit, then we shall not cease from yielding fruit (Jer. 17. 8).

IV. The Character of the Fruit.

1. It will be NEW fruit (Ezek. 47. 12). It does not belong to the unregenerate man. It is not the fruit of the flesh; not the outcome of an energetic self-life. The corrupt tree has been made good by being created anew by the Spirit of God. It is fruit unto holiness (John 1. 13).

2. It will be fruit ACCORDING TO THE NATURE OF THE TREE. You cannot gather figs from thorns, or grapes from thistles. The fruit of the SPIRIT is love, joy, peace, etc. (Gal. 5. 22), not the fruit of the *Christian*. The fruit of the Spirit, you observe, is just the *likeness* of Christ. Ye are partakers of the divine nature. As fruit is the result of the living, moving sap within, so the image and characteristics of Christ are wrought in the believer by the living, moving Spirit within. From *Me* is thy fruit found. It is the work of God, and the *evidence* of a soul being fully possessed by Him. Where there is the fulness of the indwelling Spirit there must be the manifestation of the Christ-likeness. Death is the way to life and fruitfulness. "Except a corn of wheat fall into the ground and die it abideth alone; but if it die it bringeth forth much fruit" (John 12. 24).

A BIBLE CHRISTIAN.

A SECT called "Bible Christians" had their origin in England in the year 1815. They took this name because they professed to stick fast to the Bible. Every Christian is a "Bible Christian," holding fast to Christ and His Word of truth. Every other Christian is a sham. A "Bible Christian" is a Christian after the order of the Bible. He is—

1. ONE WHO TRUSTS IN CHRIST (Eph. 1. 12). One who has been convicted by the Spirit, made to feel his need of Christ, and who has, by a deliberate act of His own will, transferred all his confidence to Him. He has a settled faith in Him as the almighty and infallible Son of God.

2. ONE WHO HAS LIFE THROUGH CHRIST (John 6. 37). He was alienated from the *life of God*, but now he is by faith engrafted into it. Through receiving Him who is the "Living Bread" life has been imparted, a new creature formed—born of God—partaker of the divine nature. This is life eternal.

3. ONE WHO HAS LOVE TO CHRIST (1 John 4. 19). Love is the first evidence of a regenerated heart. When the love of God is shed abroad in the heart it will rise up in all its strength and fulness to Him from whence it came. It is a love that now believes and rejoices with joy unspeakable (1 Peter 1. 8).

4. ONE WHO HAS FELLOWSHIP WITH CHRIST (1 John 1. 3). This fellowship is sweet because there is intense love on both sides. "Lord, to whom can we go?" (John 6. 68). There is none on earth the new-born soul desires besides Him. "If *Thy* presence go not with us, carry us not hence" (Exodus 33. 15). "Abide in Me" (John 15. 4).

5. ONE WHO WORKS FOR CHRIST (2 Cor. 6. 1). "Whose I am, and whom I serve" (Acts 27. 23). Belonging to Him and living for Him it is his privilege not only to work *for* Christ but to work *with* Him. This is the more excellent way: God working *in* us both to *will* and to do of His good pleasure. Delivered to serve.

6. ONE WHOSE RESOURCES ARE IN CHRIST (Col. 2. 9, 10). All the fulness of the Godhead is *in Him*, and ye are *in Him*. Abiding in Christ he receives, as a branch in the

vine, all the fulness of Him who is his life, his strength, his power, his all. The unsearchable riches of Christ! What are they? All is yours, for ye are Christ's.

7. ONE WHO WILL BE REWARDED BY CHRIST (2 Cor. 5. 10). Every Christian will be saved, but every Christian will not be rewarded. Rewards are only given for works done in His Name and for His glory (1 Cor. 3. 13-15). Salvation is a *gift*. Rewards must be earned. Christ Himself will fix the value of every deed done (Matt. 25. 19-25).

8. ONE WHO WILL SPEND ETERNITY WITH CHRIST (John 17. 24). This great privilege is promised in John 14. 3, prayed for in John 17. 24, and realised in Revelation 5. 9. A little girl said she lived where mamma lives. Our fitness to be with Him will be our *likeness to Him* (1 John 3. 2). For ever with the Lord.

VISITED AND REDEEMED.
Luke 1. 46.
A PROPHETIC SONG.

I. **The Visitor.** The Lord God. (1) *The need of a Visitor.*—Man's lost and helpless condition. (2) *The Promise.*—"I will surely visit you." (Exod. 3. 16). (3) *The Wonder.*—"What is man that *Thou* visitest him?" (Psa. 8. 4). (4) *The manner.*—"God was *in Christ* reconciling the world" (2 Cor. 5. 19).

II. **The Visited.** His People. (1) They knew *Him not* (John 1. 11). (2) They knew not *their time* of visitation (Luke 19. 44). (3) They rejected Him (John 19. 14).

III. **The Purpose.** To Redeem. (1) Who? Thy Maker is thy Redeemer (Isa. 54. 5). (2) How? By giving Himself a ransom (Matt. 20. 28). (3) What from? (Titus 2. 14). (4) What to? To God, to holiness, and to service (Luke 1. 74, 75).

EZEKIEL'S CALL AND COMMISSION.

THERE are four distinct positions in which we find
Ezekiel that seem to characterise the state and privilege
of the Christian in a very striking way.

I. We see Him as an Exile. "I was among the captives" (chap. 1. 1). He had his place among those who
were helplessly shut out. This is a humbling position,
but we must take our place among sinners and rebels if we
would see the salvation of God. No good can come by
denying that we are captives. It is no use boasting of
liberty when we know that our lives are enslaved by lust
and sin, by the pleasures and fashions of the world. While
among the captives he said, "The heavens were opened,
and I saw visions of God" (chap. 1. 1). The heavens will
always open and visions of God be given to those who
acknowledge their true state before God and look up.
The sum of the likeness was "the likeness of a man" (v. 5).
All satisfying vision is in the revelation of Him who is
the Man Christ Jesus. In Him we get a vision of God. He
is the image of the invisible God. "He that hath seen Me
hath seen the Father" (John 14. 9). What a vision
this is! It is the opening up before our eyes of the love,
mercy, power, and glory that dwell in the great and
gracious heart of God. "Blessed are the pure in heart, for
they shall see God" (Matt. 5. 8).

II. We see Him as an Ambassador. Having seen
God, he is now to be prepared as a messenger for God.
We testify what *we have* seen.

1. HE IS CALLED. "Stand upon thy feet, and I will
speak unto thee" (chap. 2. 1). He is now face to face with
God, and must have to do with *His Word*. God speaks *to*
us before we are sent to speak *for* Him.

2. He is Helped. "The *Spirit entered* into me when *He spake* unto me" (v. 2). The Spirit always enters when God speaks. His Word is with power. The result of both is *a setting up*. We are never properly set up till we have heard the Word of God in the power of the Holy Ghost. After this we are in the right attitude to hear (v. 2).

3. He is Commissioned. "And He said, Son of man, I will send thee" (vv. 3, 4). The commission comes after being taught of God by the entering of the Holy Spirit. The Holy Ghost—the great Teacher come from God—'rested upon the early disciples before they became witnesses FOR HIM. The secret of authority and power for service lie in these words, "I send thee."

4. He is Filled with His Message. "Son of man, eat this roll, and fill thy bowels with this roll that I give thee" (chap. 3. 1-3). Even the Word of God will not have much power at our lips if we have not eaten it for ourselves. The truth as it is in Jesus must be in us as the strength and satisfaction of our own hearts if it is to influence others.

5. He is Encouraged. "Son of man, be not afraid of them, neither of their words" (chap. 2. 6). It is so needful that the servant of God should find all his succour in Himself, because the words and faces of those to whom He is sent are often very stout. He is to "speak My words, whether they will hear, or whether they will forbear" (v. 7).

6. He is Led and Empowered. "The Spirit lifted me up, and I went in bitterness, but the hand of the Lord was strong upon me" (chap. 3. 12-14). Filled with the Word of God, and led by the Spirit of God in bitterness and sorrow. How Christlike is this experience before us here. Ezekiel was obedient to the guiding Spirit, and the hand ot almighty power was upon Him. The *willing* servant will have his reward (1 Cor. 9. 16).

III **We see Him as a Watchman.** In chapter 3. 17 we hear God saying to him, "Son of man, I have made thee a *watchman*." To be a watchman for God we must have the eye-opening, soul-transforming vision of God (Acts 9. 1-15). We must be lifted *high up* by the Holy Spirit, far above all principalities and powers. Those in the valley cannot see afar off. We need to be raised and seated with Christ in the heavenlies before we can seee men and things as they really are in the sight of God. The work of the watchman is—

1. A WORK OF WARNING. "To warn the wicked of his wicked way" (v. 18), and also to warn the backsliding righteous man (v. 20). Sinners are to be warned to flee from the wrath to come, and Christians to beware of becoming a *stumbling-block* by an un-Christlike life. It also is—

2. A WORK OF GREAT RESPONSIBILITY. "His blood will I require at thy hand" (v. 20). Are our hands and garments clean?

IV. **We see Him as a Sign.** "I have set thee for a sign" (chap. 12. 1-7). In these verses the words "in their sight" occur seven times. Ezekiel was to live *before* the people as a sign for God. Ye are epistles of Christ, known and read of all men. Every Christian is to be a sign to the world of the grace and power of God. The *life* is the light. A *sign* is a silent testimony. It may be the look of love, or the sigh of sympathy. A tear has often melted the hardened heart. God commanded the prophet, saying, "Sigh, therefore, thou son of man; sigh before their eyes" (chap. 21. 6). It is easier to be a watchman than a sign; easier telling men what they ought to do than sighing over their sins and wickedness. Paul was a true sign when he wrote, "I tell you, even weeping" (Phil 3. 18). The

men who sigh and cry are marked men (chap. 9. 4).
"Blessed are they that mourn, for they shall be comforted"
(Matt. 5. 4). May God by His Holy Spirit lift us up into
the compassion and tenderness of Him who wept over
Jerusalem!

THE IMAGE OF GOD.

IT is interesting to notice how the image of God is connected
with *four* prominent men in the Scriptures. Observe—

I. The Image of God Created in the First Man.
"The first man Adam was made a living soul" (1 Cor. 15.
45). "God created man in His own image" (Gen. 1. 26).
He did not rest satisfied until His own likeness was manifested. This was the great end of creation, to reproduce the
image of Him who created. The first man was to save all
who believe (1 Tim. 4. 10); He came like God—

1. IN BEING A SPIRIT. His life was a separate thing from
the mere animal creation. God created the beasts, but He
did not *breathe* into them the breath of His own life, as He
did to man. Adam only was capable of *knowing* God.

2. IN BEING IMMORTAL. The deeper and more real life
of Adam was independent of outward and material things.
In receiving the breath of God he was a partaker of the
divine.

3. IN BEING HOLY. He was, as yet, an utter stranger
to anything unlike or displeasing to God.

4. IN BEING SATISFIED. Between the Holy Creator and
the new created likeness there was perfect harmony and
mutual delight. God saw Himself in man, and man saw
himself in God. In each other's image there was complete
satisfaction.

5. IN HAVING DOMINION. Adam was the crown of creation, exalted high over all, ruling in the power and authority of the Almighty Maker of all.

II. The Image of God Destroyed in the Old Man. In Ephesians 4. 22 we are told, "Put off the old man, which is corrupt." Compare the first new man Adam with this old man. What a change! Where is the holiness, the happiness, and the harmony? Sin has poisoned and polluted all. Nothing left but an immortal spirit at war with God. This old man is so utterly ruined that there is no hope for him. We are to put *him* off with his deeds (Col. 3. 9). Where are we to put him? The only place fit for him is the cross. "Your old man is crucified with Him" (Rom. 6. 6). The absence of the image of God means corruption and death.

III. The Image of God Manifested in the Second Man. "The *Second* Man is the Lord from Heaven" (1 Cor. 15. 47). As if all who came between were unworthy of the Name. In Jesus Christ the image of God reappears in perfect beauty. He is the brightness of the Father's glory, and the *express image* of His Person (Heb. 1. 3). He is the image of the invisible God (Col. 1. 15). Man lost the holy likeness; God alone could restore it. When we see Jesus we see the Father, and see what man should have been and what man should be, walking in holiness and in humble, joyful, unbroken fellowship with God. Christ came to seek and to save that which was lost. By His death, resurrection, and holy Spirit He *renews*, restores, and rejoices.

IV. The Image of God restored in the New Man. "And have put on the New Man, which is renewed in knowledge *after the image of Him* that created him" (Col. 3. 10) We put on the Lord Jesus Christ (Rom. 13. 14), and are *created in* Christ Jesus (Eph. 2. 10). "If any man be *in* Christ he is a new creature" (2 Cor. 5. 17).

Take note that this restoration work can only be done by the God whose image is to be created, and that it is a *creation* rather than a reformation. Those who go about to establish their own righteousness will never establish themselves in the likeness of God. This is not a matter of so many deeds or actions, but a renewing of *the spirit of the mind* by the regenerating power of the Holy Spirit, "Ye must be *born* again" (John 3. 7). Let your prayer be, "*Create* in me a clean heart, O God, and *renew* a right *spirit within* me" (Psa. 51. 10).

THE CHURCH.

THERE are two great wonders in the world—the Jew and the Church. The first is a witness to the Christ rejected; the second to the Christ risen.

I. Its Marvellous Character.

1. IT IS A DISTINCT BODY. There is the Jew, the Gentile, and the Church of God (1 Cor. 10. 32). The Church is neither Jew nor Gentile, although both may be in it. The Jew looks for a coming Messiah; the Church for a Bridegroom. The Gentile cares for none of these things.

2. IT IS HIS OWN MAKING. "Upon this Rock *I will build My* Church" (Matt. 16. 18). He Himself, as the Christ, the Son of the Living God, is the foundation laid in Zion—a stone tried, precious, and sure (Isa. 28. 16). He also does the *building* by His Holy Spirit, planting believing souls into Himself, as *living* stones into the living foundation. It is God that worketh in you.

3. IT IS CALLED OUT FOR HIS OWN NAME. "God did visit the Gentiles, to take out of them a people for His

Name" (Acts 15. 14). The Church of God, like His people of old, have been *formed for Himself* to show forth His praise (Isa. 43. 21). This work of *out calling* has been committed to the Holy Ghost, is going on just now, and will continue until the fulness of the Gentiles be come in. Make your calling sure.

4. IT IS FILLED WITH HIS FULNESS (Eph. 1. 22, 23). Each individual member of His body is brought into contact with the power and wisdom of the Great Head. Grow up *into Him* in all things (Eph. 4. 15). All fulness dwells in Him. Abide in Him. The world cannot see the invisible head, but it does look upon His visible body. How needful that it should be true to Him!

II. Its Present Privileges.

1. IT OCCUPIES TILL HE COMES (Luke 19. 12-15). It has been left in the place of service, entrusted with gifts, to be used during the Lord's absence, and to be accounted for when He comes. Its true position is " *In Christ's stead* " (2 Cor. 5. 20), occupying Christ's place till He come. Is the mind and purpose of our absent Lord being fulfilled in us now? Are we occupying for Him, or for ourselves?

2. IT SUFFERS FOR HIM. Suffering is part of the heritage of the Christian. "Even hereunto were ye called" (1 Peter 2. 20, 21). If any man will live godly he must suffer. The members of the body are so closely connected with the *rejected* head that they *must* suffer. Blessed fellowship. "If ye be reproached for the Name of Christ, happy are ye, for the Spirit of Glory and of God *resteth upon* you. Therefore glorify God on this behalf" (1 Peter 4. 14-16).

3. IT IS A CO-WORKER WITH HIM (2 Cor. 6. 1). "Labourers *together with God*" (1 Cor. 3. 9). Surely the members of the body ought to labour together with the

head. What if they should not? If the service of the hand or
foot is not controlled by and in harmony with the will of
the head, what is it worth? As Eve was to be an helpmeet
to Adam, so the Church is to be to Christ. His will is to be
done in us and through us. The head has no other means
of working but by the use of the members of the body.

III. Its Future Prospects.

1. IT LOOKS FOR HIM. He has said, "I will come again."
"This same Jesus shall so come *in like manner* as ye have
seen Him go" (Acts 1. 11). They wait for His Son from
Heaven (1 Thess. 1. 10). The Bride longs for the Bridegroom. Love yearns for fellowship.

2. IT EXPECTS TO BE CAUGHT UP BY HIM. The Lord
Himself shall descend, and we shall be caught up together
to meet the Lord (1 Thess. 4. 16). In olden times powerful
men would *steal away* their brides. It will be a rapturous
experience to be caught up in the arms of our Beloved and
borne to the home of eternal rest.

3. IT EXPECTS TO BE MADE LIKE HIM. "We look for
the Saviour, who shall change our vile body that it may be
fashioned like unto His glorious body" (Phil. 3. 20, 21).
We are to be like Him now in the *inward spirit*, fashioned
by the Holy Spirit. Like Him then in outward form, when
the sons of God are manifested (1 John 3. 1-3).

4. IT EXPECTS TO BE MARRIED TO HIM. "The marriage
of the Lamb is come, and His wife hath made herself
ready" (Rev. 19. 7). Just now the Church, like Rebekah,
is on her way through the desert to meet and marry the
Father's beloved Son, into whose hands all things have
been committed (Gen. 24).

5. IT EXPECTS TO REIGN WITH HIM. "They shall reign
with Him" (Rev. 20. 6). "Know ye not that the saints

shall judge the world" (1 Cor. 6. 2).   "Thou hast made
us unto our God kings and priests, and we shall reign on the
earth" (Rev. 5. 10). What a high calling this is! He that
hath this hope in him *purifieth Himself*, as He is pure, a
hope that maketh not ashamed.

SEVEN ATTITUDES TOWARDS GOD.
1 Thessalonians.

IN this epistle we observe seven things the Thessalonians
did. Seven different attitudes, or relationships, which
should characterise every Heaven-born son of God. We
read of them—

I. **Receiving the Word of God** (chap. 2. 13). This is
the first great necessity. "Receiving the Word of God, not
as the word of men, but as it is in truth the Word of God."
It is by the Word of Truth that He by His own will begets
us (James 1. 18). The Word is often received in much
affliction (chap. 1. 6). This is the result of the ploughing
of the Holy Spirit—preparing the soil of the heart for the
incorruptible seed (1 Peter 1. 23).

II. **Turning to God.** "They turned to God from idols"
(chap. 1. 9). These idols of their own making represent the
desires of their own carnal minds. They turned *from* them
to God. The living God now takes the place of sinful
self. If the heart would be satisfied with God it must be
turned entirely to Him. When the stream of God's truth
is tasted it constrains to turn to the fountain. We shall
never know the depth of the love of our God until we
plunge into it.

III. **Dwelling in God.** "The Church which is *in God*
the Father, and in the Lord Jesus Christ" (chap. 1. 1).
Having received the Word of Truth, and turned to God,
they find their abode and resting-place in God. Those who

turn to God with all their heart will never seek to turn
away from Him. In Him we find our life and strength, as
the branch in the vine. In Him we are planted by rivers of
water, so that the roots of our desires are abundantly
satisfied (Jer. 17. 8).

IV. **Serving God.** They "turned to God from idols to
serve the living and true God" (chap. 1. 9). Their service
is a noble pattern for us. Notice the character of it: (1)
It was the *work of faith*. (2) It was a *labour of love*. (3)
It was in *patience of hope*. (4) It was *in the Lord Jesus
Christ*. (5) It was *in the sight of God* (see chap. 1. 3). This
was no mere eye service. One is your master, even Christ.
Please Him.

V. **Waiting for the Son of God.** "They turned to
serve, . . . and to wait for His Son from Heaven" (chap.
1. 10). Jesus had said He would come again, and they
believed Him, and looked for the glorious appearing of
their great God and Saviour (Titus 2. 13). Active service
is most consistent with patient waiting. They serve in
waiting. Those whose expectation is *only* from the Lord
will wait on Him and for Him. Blessed are all they that
wait.

VI. **Learning of God.** "Ye yourselves are *taught* of
God" (chap. 4. 9). They never leave the high school who
sit at Jesus' feet. They are wise who are taught by the
great teacher come from God. Those who have the Holy
Ghost have the holy anointing, and need not that any man
teach them (1 John 2. 27). The chief lesson taught by our
Divine Master is to *love one another* (chap. 4. 9). "By this
shall all men know that ye are My disciples" (John 13. 35).
"Learn of Me" (Matt. 11. 29).

VII. **Walking Worthy of God** (chap. 2. 12). To this
holy occupation are we called. "Walk worthy of the Lord,

unto all pleasing" (Col. 1. 10). Are we walking as
becometh the sons of God—worthy of His love, of His
fulness, of His holiness, of His power? If our lives are
dissatisfied, powerless, and fruitless, they are not *worthy of
God*. All *worthiness* comes from Himself. It is by His
mighty indwelling Spirit alone that we are made to walk
worthy of the vocation wherewith we are called (Eph.
4. 1). Walk as He walked.

PROGRESSIVE EXPERIENCE,

AS SEEN IN THE "I AM'S" OF PAUL IN HIS EPISTLE TO THE ROMANS.

THESE "I am's" are glimpses given us of the inner workings
of the apostle's soul. They are, as it were, a spiritual
autobiography.

I. **I am Carnal** (chap. 7. 14). Being carnal he is sold
under sin. He realises that the law is spiritual, and deals
with his *spirit* rather than with his *actions*. His spirit being
carnal he cannot fulfil a spiritual law. So he is *sold*. He
finds himself enslaved by sin, a helpless enemy to the
righteous will of God. Such is our state by nature. There
is no *truth* in the *inward* part (Psa. 51. 6).

II. **I am Wretched** (chap. 7. 24). When by the light
of God's Word we discover our true state in His sight it is
enough to make us the most wretched creatures on earth.
It is only when we do become wretched that we cry out,
"Who shall deliver me?" Job's cry, "O for a daysman!"
came also out of the depths of his wretchedness.

III. **I am not Ashamed** (chap. 1. 16). This is the lan-
guage of one who has now experienced the saving power of
God as revealed in the Gospel of Christ. "Thanks be unto
God who giveth us the victory" (1 Cor. 15. 57). The

salvation of God in Christ is both a *victory* and a *transformation* (chap. 12. 2). It is a deliverance from the *power* of Satan and from the *love* of sin.

IV. I am Debtor (chap. 1. 14). Now that he has received salvation through the grace of God he becomes a debtor to the unsaved, whether they be Greeks or barbarians, wise or unwise. Every Christian is a *steward* of the manifold grace of God (1 Peter 4. 10). Have we paid our debt to those who know not Christ by giving them the Gospel? or, like unfaithful stewards, are we selfishly using our Master's goods?

V. I am Ready (chap. 1. 15). Paul was prepared to pay this debt, even to the Romans, and that at any cost. This ought to be the constant attitude of the heart toward the God of our salvation. "Ready!" Ready for whatever the King may appoint. Like soldiers, we should be always and entirely at the disposal of Him who hath chosen us. The way to get ready for great things is to be always ready for the little things.

VI. I am Persuaded (chap. 8. 38). Here the apostle unveils to us his deep, unalterable conviction concerning the unchanging love of God which is in Christ Jesus. This is a prime necessity for the joy and comfort of a Christian worker. Be always ready to please God, and you will all the more readily be persuaded of the abiding and inseparable love of God.

VII. I am the Apostle (chap. 11. 13). Ask Paul what he is, as regards his mission, and his answer is ready, "I am the apostle of the Gentiles." He received his work from the Lord, and he knew it. All are not apostles. No. What are you? What definite work has the Lord committed to you? Many a Christian life is frittered aimlessly away for the lack of this deep consciousness of having some definite, special work given by God. Ask Him, "Lord, what wilt Thou have me to do?" (Acts 9. 6).

VIII. **I am Sure** (chap. 15. 29). It is a great blessing to be assured that when we go in God's Name we go in God's power, and in the fulness of the Gospel of Christ. Although Paul went to Rome in chains he nevertheless went in the fulness of the blessing. Nothing can hinder our usefulness as Christians but sin. This blessed assurance ought to characterise every preacher of the Gospel.

IX. **I am Glad** (chap. 16. 19). This gladness sprang up in the heart of the apostle because of the obedience of others to the truth of God. The closeness of our fellowship with Jesus Christ may be tested by the depth and intensity of our sadness, or gladness, at the disobedience, or obedience of others to the call of God. Do you feel the evil treatment of Christ as keenly as you would that of your nearest earthly friend? Jesus said, "I am glad for your sakes" (John 11. 15). Are you sad or glad for His sake?

CHRISTIANS AS SENT ONES.

"As Thou has sent Me into the world, even so have I sent them into the world" (John 17. 18).

"As My Father hath sent Me, even so I send you" (John 20.21).

HAVE we ever realised that as Christians we take the place of Christ in the world? We are to occupy in His stead till He come (2 Cor. 5. 20). As the Father sent the Son, so has the Son sent you—after the same manner, and for the same purpose. If we would see our true relationship to the world as sent ones, let us see how the Father sent the Son.

I. **He was Sent as One who did not belong to the World.** He made the world, but the world knew Him not. He came as the Son of God. "That holy thing which shall be born of thee shall be called the Son of God." "This is My beloved Son." "As My Father sent Me, even so send I you." "Now are we the sons of God." Therefore doth the world hate you. Having been saved out of the world, separated from it by a new and divine life, imparted to us by the Holy Spirit, we are now sent into it as witnesses against it and as ambassadors for God.

II. **He was Sent in Love to the World.** "God so loved the world that He gave His only begotten Son" (John 3. 16). Love for the perishing constrained the Father to send His Son. "As My Father sent Me, even so send I you." The love of the Father still burns in the heart of His Son. "Go ye into all the world and preach the Gospel to every creature" (Mark 16. 15). Does this love constrain us? Is the love of God shed abroad in our hearts? Have we the same motives for serving God that Christ had? Would we be equally zealous in our Christian work if we received no wages nor any favour from man?

III. **He was Sent to Reveal the Character of God** (John 17. 6). "He that hath seen Me hath seen the Father." "I and My Father are One"—One in nature, likeness, and purpose. "As My Father sent Me, even so send I you." Does the world see Christ in us? Can we say, "He that hath seen me hath seen Christ Jesus?" Did Paul not mean this when he wrote, "To me to live is Christ?" "Be ye followers of me, even as I also am of Christ" (1 Cor. 11. 1). "I live, yet not I, but Christ liveth in me" (Gal. 2. 20).

IV. **He was Sent to Declare the Word of God** (John 17. 8-14). "I have given them the words which Thou hast given Me." Oh, how faithfully did Jesus deliver the words which the Father gave Him to speak! "As My Father sent Me, even so send I you." Are we declaring the whole counsel of God as Jesus Christ did? See how like their Lord in this respect Peter and John were: "We cannot but speak the things which we have seen and heard" (Acts 4. 20).

V. **He was Sent to Give His Life a Ransom** (Mark 10. 45). "He came not to be ministered unto, but to give His life." "As My Father sent Me, even so send I you." Are we willing and ready, as He was, to yield up our lives wholly for the glory of God the Father? Our Lord and Master girt Himself with the towel of lowly service, and was obedient unto death. Have we girt ourselves with that lowly mind which was in Him? What a privilege is ours to give our lives that we might minister the things of God to weary, perishing souls around us!

VI. **He was Sent Equipped with Power from on High** (Matt. 3. 16). The Lord anointed Him with the Holy Ghost that He might preach, heal, deliver, and recover (Luke 4. 19). He was empowered by Him who sent Him for the work given Him to do. "As My Father sent Me, even so send I you." Ye shall receive power by the Holy Ghost coming upon you. If the sinless Saviour, Jesus, could not accomplish all the will of God concerning us without this endowment, no more can ye. Are you sowing to the flesh or to the Spirit? Christ's way of service must be ours—through the eternal Spirit.

THE PROMISE OF THE FATHER.
Acts 1. 4.

JESUS CHRIST is the gift of God to the world; the Holy Spirit is the gift of Father and of Son to the Church. Both gifts should be thankfully accepted and equally enjoyed.

I. **What this Promise is.** It is the promise—

1. OF AN INDWELLER (John 14. 16).

2. OF A COMFORTER (John 16. 7).

3. OF A WITNESS (John 15. 16).

II. The Conditions of Receiving the Promise. This promise was not made to the world—only to those who had obeyed Him, and were desirous of following Him.

1. BELIEVING.

2. WAITING (Luke 24. 49).

3. THIRSTING (Isa. 44. 3).

III. The Results which follow—

1. POWER TO WILL ACCORDING TO GOD'S MIND (Phil. 2. 13).

2. POWER TO WALK ACCORDING TO GOD'S WAY (Ezek. 36. 27).

3. POWER TO WITNESS ACCORDING TO GOD'S WORD (Acts 1. 8; 4. 33).

THE TRIAL OF FAITH.
Genesis 22. 1-14.

FAITH is precious (2 Peter 1. 1). See what it has done (Heb. 11). The trial of it is more precious than gold (1 Peter 1. 7). Here we might notice—

I. The Sacrifice of Faith. "His only loved son" (v. 2). This simply meant his all. ALL must be given up to God (Matt. 19. 21; Rom. 12. 1, 2; 15. 3).

II. The Obedience of Faith. "He rose up early" (v. 3). By faith he obeyed (Heb. 11. 7). Love makes swift the feet of faith. He reasoned not (John 2. 5).

III. The Expectation of Faith. "I and the lad will come again" (v. 5); accounting that God was able to raise him up (Heb. 11. 19). His promise could not fail (Gen. 21. 12).

IV. **The Work of Faith.** "He laid the burden (wood) on the offering" (v. 6). Solemn work to faith. "He bore our sins in His own body on the tree" (1 Peter 2. 24).

V. **The Assurance of Faith.** "God will provide" (v. 8). On the path of obedience many a question will arise (v. 7) which only faith can answer (Acts 27. 25).

VI. **The Persistence of Faith.** "He bound Isaac, and took the knife" (v. 9). The faith that fails in the hour of trial is no faith (Mark 4. 40).

VII. **The Victory of Faith.** "Now I know," says God, and the lad is saved; yet an offering made (v. 12), and faith abundantly rewarded (Rom. 9. 33; Mark 9. 25; 1 John 5. 4). _____

JESUS AS KING.

WHILE our Lord was on earth He taught as a prophet; while He tarries in Heaven He intercedes as a priest; when He comes again it will be as a King in power and great glory. "In His times He will show who is the blessed and only Potentate, the King of kings, and Lord of lords" (1 Tim. 6, 15). These are not His times with regard to this weary, wicked earth; this is the "hour and power of darkness" (Luke 22. 53). The whole world lieth in the wicked one. During this day of salvation God is by the Holy Ghost, through the atoning death of His Son, rescuing all who believe from out of the kingdom of Satan and the guilt of sin. That Jesus will yet be King over all the earth is clearly taught in the infallible Scriptures of Truth.

I. **Look at the Prophecies.** In Psalm 72. 6-9 we read: "He shall come down; in His days shall the righteous flourish. He shall have dominion from sea to sea." If He rules on earth now, where is His authority? Again, in Isaiah 9. 6, 7, "Unto us a Child is born, and the government shall be upon His shoulder; . . . upon the throne of David." In His times the "wolf shall dwell with the lamb" (Isa. 11. 1-6) "Thou, Bethlehem, out of thee shall come a Governor that shall rule My people" (Matt. 2. 6). This Governor came, but they would not have Him to reign over them; they put the Prince of Peace to death, and so put an end to His government meanwhile. Christ was born a King. "Where is He that is born King of the Jews" (Matt. 2. 2), and was crucified as such. Pilate wrote the truth when he put over the cross, "This is the King of the Jews" (Matt. 27. 37).

II. **Look at the Angelic Announcement.** "Glory to God in the Highest, on earth peace, goodwill toward men!" (Luke 2. 14). This was sung at the birth of the King, and in prospect of a universal kingdom of peace. But that it has not yet come we are not ill to convince. The God of Glory does not get the highest place in the world's business; there is not peace on the earth; the goodwill of God is not being manifested among men. Wars, and rumours of wars, labour conflicts, social strifes, and restlessness all bear evidence that God's appointed Ruler has been rejected by man.

III. **Look at the Prayer Christ Taught His Disciples.** "When ye pray, say, Our Father which art in Heaven, hallowed be Thy Name. Thy kingdom come. Thy will be done in earth, as it is in Heaven" (Luke 11. 2)—all this before one request was offered. It is the purpose of God that His kingdom and rule should come among men, and that His will should be done on earth as it is done in Heaven. The will of God is perfectly done in Heaven, because the perfect Ruler is there. It will be done on earth as it is done in Heaven when the Divine Governor—the

King of kings—has His throne here over the earth; then
every knee shall bow to Him, confessing Him Lord. "He
shall sit upon the throne of His father David."

IV. Look at His Parables. Several of the parables
make mention of the "Coming of the King," notably that
one of the "nobleman" (Luke 19). Jesus Christ is the
Nobleman. He goes into the far country to receive a kingdom, and to return. In Daniel 7. 13, 14 the Son of Man
is seen receiving the kingdom, that "all people, nations,
and languages shall serve Him." When He returns He
reckons with His servants, rewarding them with earthly
privileges—"rulers over cities," they shall inherit the
earth. And punishing His enemies—those who would not
that He should reign over them.

V. Look at His Answer to Pilate. "Art Thou a
King then?" (John 18. 37). If ever there was a
moment when Christ might desire to deny His Kingship it
is now, as He stands a prisoner. Mocked and helpless,
crowned with thorns before Pilate, when this question was
put what is His answer? "To this end was I born, and for
this cause came I into the world" (John 18. 37). In giving
this answer our Lord looks right into the future, and for the
joy that is set before Him He endures the cross. Just now
His kingdom is not of this world (this present state of
things); it is within you. But He shall yet put down all
authority, and reign from sea to sea. "He shall see of the
travail of His soul, and be satisfied" (Isa. 53. 11). He
was "born a Saviour," but He was also "born King of the
Jews." He had not where to lay His head; but He shall
yet be King of kings. He appears as a "wayfaring man"
to put away sin; when He comes again it will be the
glorious appearing of our Great God and Saviour. He shall
come whose right it is to reign. "Even so, come, Lord
Jesus" (Rev. 22. 20).

THE PLEASURE OF THE LORD.

THERE is a difference between the "will of the Lord" and the "pleasure of the Lord." He may permit a thing, and yet take no pleasure therein. We ought to be exceedingly interested in whatever our Lord takes pleasure in; and if He has no pleasure in a thing neither should His people. We shall notice the pleasure of the Lord—

I. In Regard to the Wicked. "As I live, saith the Lord, I have no pleasure in the death of the wicked" (Ezek. 33. 11). That the wicked will die is certain if they repent not; but that God has no pleasure in their death is just as certain. Then why will they die? Because they choose death rather than life. By preferring the pleasures of sin they incur its wages. No sinner will find pleasure in hating God because God hates him. The knell of the sinner's doom affords no pleasure to the Lord.

II. With Regard to Christ. Here we see the pleasure of the Lord in a threefold aspect—

1. IN THE PERSON OF CHRIST. "This is My beloved Son, in whom I am well pleased" (Matt. 3. 17). Here we have the Lamb that was to take away the sin of the world brought before the holy eye of God for examination. Not only is He without spot and blemish, but with all that He did God was well pleased. There seems to be more here than bare satisfaction. There is a filling of the heart of God with pleasure.

2. IN THE SUFFERINGS OF CHRIST. "Yet it pleased the Lord to bruise Him. . . . And the pleasure of the Lord shall prosper in His (Christ's) hand" (Isa. 53. 10). In bruising Him (His beloved Son) He was bruised Himself. It is the pleasure of the Lord to bruise Him instead of us, to save man through Him, and this pleasure shall prosper

in the hand of the bruised One. "He is able to save to the uttermost" (Heb. 7. 25).

3. IN THE MEDIATION OF CHRIST. "It pleased the Father that in Him should all fulness dwell" (Col. 1. 19). He is the Mediator between God and men, and the Father hath pleasure in committing all into His hands, that we might receive of His fulness, and be filled with all the fulness of God.

III. **With Regard to His Word.** "My Word shall accomplish that which I please" (Isa. 55. 11). His Word went forth over the void creation in the beginning, and turned emptiness into fruitfulness. He says it shall not, even now, return unto Me void. We cannot tell what His Word is accomplishing when it is spoken, but we are assured that it will accomplish that which is pleasing unto God.

IV. **With Regard to a Preached Gospel.** "It pleased God by the foolishness of preaching to save them that believe" (1 Cor. 1. 21). So that God takes pleasure in saving them that believe through the foolishness of preaching. Not certainly through foolish preaching. There is much preaching in which God can have no pleasure, because man is lifted up and Christ hidden. Comforting thought, God is pleased to save them that believe, not them that work. So if you have nothing but faith it will please God to save you.

V. **With Regard to Fitness for Service.** "It pleased God to reveal His Son in me that I might preach Him" (Gal. 1. 15, 16). What a revelation this is! Christ in us, in all His love and grace, in all His wisdom and power. When this is seen it is impossible not to preach Him. Oh, that every preacher had this revelation, then Christ would be preached. And why not have it? It pleases God to reveal Him in you. He is in you if you are His, and if you have not seen Him in you in all His fulness, to give you all your fitness, it is because sin is blinding your eyes.

VI. **With Regard to the Believer's Privilege.** "The Lord will not forsake His people for His great Name's sake, because it hath pleased the Lord to make you His people" (1 Sam. 12. 22). We are His people because it hath pleased the Lord to make us so, and having made us His people it is His pleasure not to forsake us for His great Name's sake. "He hath said, I will never leave thee nor forsake thee, so that we may boldly say, The Lord is my Helper, and I will not fear" (Heb. 13. 5). This is the only answer we can give as to how the Lord hath made us His people; and being His, we can count on His guidance, protection, presence, and help.

VII. **With Regard to the Believer's Prospect.** "Fear not, for it is your Father's good pleasure to give you the kingdom" (Luke 12. 32). Then it must be His good pleasure to take us there and fit us for it. "My kingdom is not of this world," said Christ (John 18. 36). "In the world ye shall have tribulation" (John 16. 33). The fashion of this world passeth away, but the kingdom we are to receive "cannot be moved" (Heb. 12. 28). And our title to it cannot be disputed, for He hath made us kings unto God (Rev. 1. 6). And the promise is, "They shall reign for ever and ever" (Rev. 22. 5).

GOSPEL OUTLINES.

A SEARCH FOR ONE THING.
Psalm 27. 4.

ALL men are seekers. What seekest thou?

I. What this One Thing Was. Not any earthly object. It was *fellowship* with God. He sought this—

1. Because he was reconciled to God.

2. Because he loved the company of God.

3. Because he had a resemblance to God.

II. Why He Sought This. For two reasons.

1. To SEE HIS BEAUTY. He is altogether lovely. There is great beauty in His *Person*—divine and human; in His *character*—holy, pitiful, mighty; in His *work* as Prophet, Priest, King. This is a beauty that never fades. Human forms, pleasures, and possessions will wither. Thou remainest. Seek His beauty; He can put it on thee.

2. To INQUIRE IN HIS TEMPLE. He was an anxious inquirer, seeking the truth of God from God's own lips. Christ is the great Teacher come from God. He says, "Learn of Me" (Matt. 11. 29). They shall be all taught of God. His teaching gives rest—rest above all the problems of life—soul satisfaction.

III. How He Sought this One Thing.

1. HE SOUGHT IT EARNESTLY. All his desire centred in this *one thing*. He had the single eye.

2. HE SOUGHT IT DETERMINATELY. "That will I seek after." He will not cease till he finds.

3. HE SOUGHT IT SUCCESSFULLY. This we may be assured of, because he sought it *from the Lord.* "Seek and ye shall find" (Matt. 7. 7).

THE ENDURING SIGHT.

"By faith Moses forsook Egypt, not fearing the wrath of the king, for he endured, as seeing Him who is invisible" (Heb. 11. 27).

THERE may be much sight-seeing and yet few *enduring* sights. Peter, James, and John never forgot the sight of their transfigured Lord. Saul never forgot the sight he saw on the way to Damascus. A saving look at Jesus is always a memorable and enduring sight.

I. This is a Glorious Sight—seeing HIM. Moses saw this wondrous sight at the burning bush when the "God of glory appeared unto Him" (Exod. 3. 2), and said, "I am come down to deliver" (Exod. 3. 8). In the flame he beheld the King immortal and invisible. This is what we see in Jesus Christ. God came down to deliver, God in Christ seeking to save the lost. It is a glorious sight, though humbling and awful.

II. This is a Transforming Sight.

When Moses turned aside to see this great sight (Exod. 3. 3-10) it was the turning-point in his life. The purpose and attitude of his life toward God were now for ever changed. It is impossible to look upon God in Christ without being transformed. No man can see Jesus and remain the same as before. When Saul saw Him he fell to the earth.

III. This is a Separating Sight.

"He forsook Egypt" (Heb. 11. 27). It was after Isaiah had seen the Lord that he was made willing to cry, "Here am I, send me" (Isa. 6. 8). A sight of the glorified Jesus is a soul-blinding sight, as far as the world and the pleasures of sin are concerned. "Who is blind as My servant, or deaf as the messenger that I send?" (Isa. 42. 19).

IV. This is an Inspiring Sight.

"Not fearing the wrath of the king" (Heb. 11. 27). Moses had not yet seen God when he "fled from the face of Pharaoh." (Exod. 2. 15). Seeing God saves from the fear of man. Look at the faithful Micaiah (1 Kings 22. 14). Elijah, while standing before God, was above the fear of Ahab (1 Kings 17. 1). A sight of Jesus Christ saves not only from the fear of man, but also from the fear of death and of judgment.

V. This is a Sustaining Sight.

"He endured as seeing Him" (Heb. 11. 27). Think of how much Moses had to endure at the hands of his wife, of Pharaoh, and his unbelieving brethren. In this life there will be much to suffer. The secret of the Christian's enduring strength lies in looking unto Jesus. They looked unto Him and were lightened.

VI. This is a Satisfying Sight.

"He esteemed the reproach of Christ greater riches than the treasures in Egypt" (Heb. 11. 26). Paul gladly suffered the loss of all things seeing Him who is invisible. A Christian can suffer no real *loss* while in touch with the unsearchable riches of Christ. How much value do we set upon the riches of the *reproach of Christ?*

VII. This is a Spiritual Sight.

"By *faith* ... he endured" (Heb. 11. 27). It needs faith to see the *Invisible*, whom having *not seen* ye love. Moses *believed* the promise of God at the bush, "I came down to deliver" (Exod. 3. 8), and "Certainly I will be with you" (Exod. 3. 12). The *promise* of God must be trusted if the soul is to see Him and endure and conquer. Is it not written, "Believe, and thou shalt see?"

HEZEKIAH, or the Secret of Success.
2 Kings 18, 5, 6.

I. His Confidence in God. (1) He trusted. (2) He clave. (3) He kept.

II. What God did for Him. (1) Was with him. (2) Prospered him.

III. What He did for God. (1) Called things by their right names (v. 4). (2) Separated from the ungodly (v. 7). (3) Conquered His enemies (v. 8).

THE WINNING SIDE.
"Greater is He that is in you than he that is in the world"
(1 John 4. 4).

I. Who is He that is in the World? The spirit of antichrist (no Christ) manifested in those who: (1) Despise His Name. (2) Neglect His Word. (3) Avoid His people. (4) Delight in worldliness. (5) Make light of sin.

II. Who is He that is in Us? The Holy Spirit of God (vv. 12, 13). God dwelleth in us. (1) The Spirit of wisdom. (2) The Spirit of truth. (3) The Spirit of power. (4) The Spirit of holiness.

III. How is He Greater? (1) As light is greater than darkness. (2) As truth is greater than falsehood. (3) As the king is greater than the subject. (4) As the Creator is greater than the created.

NO CONDEMNATION.
Romans 8. 1.

I. A Happy Condition. "In Christ Jesus." This implies—

1. BEING IN HIS FAVOUR. Enjoying His grace.

2. BEING IN HIS NAME. Sharing His honour.

3. BEING IN HIS HEART. Filled with His love.

In Him *by faith*. As Noah entered the ark (John 6. 37).

In Him for *fruitfulness*. As the branch is in the vine (John 15).

In Him for *fellowship*. As the members in the body (Eph. 4. 16).

II. **A Blessed Privilege.** "No condemnation." This does not mean no affliction or temptation. These may all work together for good.

1. No CONDEMNATION BY THE LAW. "Ye are dead" (Col. 3. 3). The law is done with a dead man. "Christ is the end of the law for righteousness to those who believe" (Rom. 10. 4).

2. No CONDEMNATION BY GOD. He who justifies will not condemn. "It is God who justifieth" (Rom. 8. 33).

3. No CONDEMNATION BY CONSCIENCE. The conscience being purged from sin is void of offence.

III. **A Solemn Reflection.** If there is no condemnation to them which are *in* Christ, what is the condition and prospect of those who are *out* of Christ? A man may be in much that is good and yet be without hope before God. He that is without Christ is without hope (Eph. 2. 12). "He that believeth on Him is not condemned" (John 3. 18).

THE BACK OR THE FACE—WHICH?

"THEY have turned their back unto Me, and not their face; but in the time of trouble they will say, Arise, and save us" (Jer. 2. 27).

Man has both a back and face. He has power to frown or to favour, to accept or to reject. Israel had forsaken

God, the fountain of living water (v. 13). Yet in distress they would cry to Him for salvation. Common conduct.

I. What is the Attitude of God toward Men? His face, and not His back, is turned—

1. In Pity and Compassion (John 3. 16).

2. In Grace and Entreaty. "God in Christ reconciling the world unto Himself" (2 Cor. 5. 19). "All day long have I stretched out my hands" (Isa. 1. 18).

II. What is the Attitude of Man toward God? Either our face or our back is turned to Him. Some have their faces turned to God, and are—

1. Seeking Him. "Thy face, Lord, will I seek." "Sir, we would see Jesus" (John 12. 21).

2. Trusting Him. "Lord, I believe."

3. Serving Him. Looking unto Jesus, and following on to know the Lord.

Some have the back turned. Turning the back to a friend is the attitude—

1. Of Indifference. Heeding not the loving message.

2. Of Worldly Preference. Rebellion. "Turn ye, turn ye; why will ye die?" (Ezek. 8. 16).

III. The Cry of the Craven. They turn their back on God in prosperity and health, then cry, "Arise, and save," in the day of trouble. Serving the world, the flesh, and the devil, then seeking help from God (see Judges 10. 13, 14).

THE ARK OF SALVATION.
Genesis 7. 1-7.

Since Cain and Abel there have always been two classes in the world. The Cain posterity are mighty in their own eyes, while in the eyes of God they are only evil, and that continually. The Abel line, like Noah, find grace in the eyes of the Lord. The only hope for man is that he "finds grace." Christ, the Divine Ark, is God's open door of mercy for all who will enter.

I. **The Place of Refuge.** "Ark!" This was God's appointed way of salvation. The ark was—

1. A PLACE OF SAFETY. No condemnation here. God is our refuge. Hid with Christ in God.

2. A PLACE OF SEPARATION. Saved ones åre always set apart for God (Psa. 4. 3). Separated from sin and judgment to be witnesses for Him.

3. A PLACE OF SAFETY. Noah's wants were all met in his hiding-place (Isa. 32. 2; Phil. 4. 19).

II. **The Divine Invitation.** God said, "Come unto." It is with God's own invitation that men have to do (Matt. 11. 28). Instead of obeying and entering in—

1. SOME LOOK AT IT. Their interest only constrains them to take a passing glance at the great provision.

2. SOME TALK ABOUT IT. Their curiosity is awakened.

3. SOME SNEER AT IT. Laughing at those who accept.

III. **The Acceptance of the Offer. (v. 7).**

1. NOAH WENT IN. He believed for himself, and took the decided step.

2. HIS WIFE WENT IN. Sad when a house is divided on this momentous subject. What if the husband had not gone?

3. HIS SONS WENT IN. The promise is to *you*, and to your children,

4. HIS SONS' WIVES WENT IN. "Believe, . . . and thou shalt be saved, and *thy house*" (Acts 16. 31).

WAITING FOR THE DEAD.
Judges 5. 28.

IT is a very sad picture that we have before us here. Sisera's mother sitting wearily watching at the window for the coming of one who was already lying cold in death in the tent of Heber's wife. She was waiting for one who would never come. Vain waiting—waiting for the dead. The cause of her vain waiting is the cause why so many still wait in vain—want of a *knowledge of the truth*. You are waiting for the dead—

1. IF YOU ARE WAITING TO GET PEACE WITH GOD WITHOUT THE BLOOD OF JESUS (Col. 1. 20).

2. IF YOU ARE WAITING FOR SALVATION WITHOUT BELIEVING ON THE SON (John 3. 36; Eph. 2. 8)

3. IF YOU ARE WAITING TO FEEL SAVED BEFORE YOU COME TO CHRIST. The woman *touched* Him before she felt healed (Mark 5. 27).

4. IF YOU ARE WAITING FOR POWER WITHOUT RECEIVING THE FULNESS OF THE HOLY SPIRIT (Acts 1. 8). All power is in Him. He doeth the work.

5. IF YOU ARE WAITING FOR PROMOTION WITHOUT BEING FAITHFUL WHERE YOU ARE (1 Sam. 16. 12).

6. IF YOU ARE WAITING FOR THE CONVERSION OF THE WORLD BEFORE THE COMING OF THE KING (Luke 19. 12; Isa. 2. 2; Zech. 2. 10).

7. YOU ARE NOT WAITING FOR THE DEAD IF YOU ARE WAITING FOR THE SON FROM HEAVEN (1 Thess. 1. 10; Acts 1. 11). Though He tarry, wait.

FAITHFULNESS.

"THOU hast kept My Word, and hast not denied My Name" (Rev. 3. 8).

I. **The Word to be Kept.** Word of Jesus, Word of God (John 17. 8).

II. **How to Keep It.** Hide it in the heart (Psa. 119. 11).

III. **The Name.** The Name above every name.

1. WHAT IT MEANS. Saviour (Matt. 1. 21). Emmanuel, God with us.

2. HOW IT MAY BE DENIED. (1) By faithless silence. (2) By practical unbelief. (3) By a hasty temper. (4) By a grumbling disposition. (5) By a worldly life. (6) By a fruitless testimony. Those who keep His Word will not deny His Name. _____

THE POOR MAN'S MARKET.
Isaiah 55. 1, 2.

1. A COMMON NEED. "Bread." There is much we have that we might do without, but we cannot *live* without bread. Christ is the Bread of Life. Except we eat of this bread we shall die (John 6. 50).

2. A FOOLISH LIFE. "Spending for that which *is not* bread" (v. 2). You are spending needlessly when you are trying to *save yourself*; when you are hewing out cisterns that can hold no water; when trying to live without strength.

3. A POINTED QUESTION. "Wherefore do ye spend?" Will you answer this question, and *tell* God *why* you *go on* working and *giving* to *get* satisfaction, and yet never attaining it?

4. A GOOD ADVICE. "Hearken unto Me." Hear Him.
Take *His way*, and you will find what you need. "If any
man thirst, let him come *unto Me*, and drink." Salvation is
of the Lord. He only can reveal and impart eternal life.
Hear what God the Lord will speak.

5. A GRACIOUS INVITATION. "Ho, every one that
thirsteth, come." A fountain has been opened. Christ
has finished the work. Those who hearken unto Him will
surely get an invitation. Whosoever will, let him take
the 'water of life freely.

6. A SIMPLE CONDITION. "Without money." Your
emptiness and need is your best and only plea. I counsel
thee to *buy gold*. Your paltry pence is no use for this. "By
grace are ye saved through *faith*" (Eph. 2. 8).

7. A HAPPY PROSPECT. "Your soul shall delight itself
in fatness." This delightful satisfaction comes when you
drink of the *river of His pleasures* (Psa. 36. 8). The world
cannot give it. "Incline your ear, and come unto Me.
Hear, and your soul shall live" (v. 3).

SUBMIT YOURSELVES TO GOD.
James 4. 6, 7.

MAN, away from God, is represented as an enemy and a
rebel.

I. What is not Submission. A man has not submitted to God as long as he is—

1. IN A STATE OF INDIFFERENCE. Like Gallio, caring
for none of these things (Acts 18. 17).

2. LIVING ONLY FOR SELF. Desiring his own praise
and honour.

3. SEEKING TO PLEASE MEN. Satisfied with an outward
appearance.

4. LOVING THE WORLD. If the world is in the heart, it is still an enemy to God.

II. To Whom we Should Submit. To God.

1. Because *He hath made us.* Our Creator.

2. Because *He hath sent His Son to save us* (John 3. 16).

3. Because He hath given *His Spirit to quicken and comfort us.*

4. Because He hath given *His Word to guide and assure us.*

III. What is to be Submitted. "Yourselves." This implies—

(1) Your will and affections. (2) Your time and talents. (3) Your plans and purposes. (4) Your pleasures and possessions. (5) Your cares and anxieties.

IV. Why you Ought to Submit. "Submit *therefore*" (v. 7)—

1. Because God *resisteth the proud*—setteth Himself against those who rebel against Him. It is vain to hope to succeed in the face of a resisting God.

2. Because God *giveth grace to the humble.* Those who submit will receive grace sufficient to pardon, to reconcile, to keep, to satisfy, and to bring into the presence of His glory (Psa. 138. 6). ———

REJECTING THE LIGHT.

"This is the condemnation, that light is come into the world, and men loved darkness rather than light, because their deeds were evil" (John 3. 19).

As the Light of the world Jesus Christ was a great Teacher come from God.

I. A Joyful Announcement. "Light is come into the world," a light brighter than the sun.

1. WHAT THIS LIGHT IS. It is the Light of Life (chap. 1. 4). This is no mere cold, shining moonlight. It is the warm, living, compassionate light of the *life of Jesus* (2 Tim. 1. 10).

2. WHERE THIS LIGHT HAS COME. "Into the world." "In Him was life," and He was *in the world* (chap. 1. 10). Into the place of darkness and death, to shed abroad the light of life (John 3. 16).

3. WHAT THIS LIGHT REVEALS. The revelation is two-fold. The life of Christ, like the light of the sun, reveals *His own* hidden glory and power. The wisdom and love of the Father shine out in the Son. He is the image of the *invisible* God. It reveals, also, the true condition and destiny of man as an unclean and guilty sinner in His sight. The holiness of God and the awfulness of sin appear in eye-blinding brightness.

II. A Lamentable Condition. "Men *love* darkness rather than the light." What is the *darkness*? Just that place, or condition, where Christ is not. A Christless life; they love—

1. THE DARKNESS OF IGNORANCE rather than the light of the *knowledge of God* as seen in the face of Jesus (2 Cor. 4. 6).

2. THE DARKNESS OF SINFUL PLEASURE rather than the light of the glorious Gospel of Christ (2 Cor. 4. 4).

3. THE DARKNESS OF DEATH rather than the light of *life*. This miserable choice reveals the depravity and perversity of man—a mind *blinded* by the god of this world.

III. A Sorrowful Reason. "Because their deeds were evil." Evil deeds lead to shame and confusion when suddenly brought into the light. The Holy Spirit has

come to *reprove* the world of sin. At the shining of the
light some confess their sin and forsake it. Others hug to
their hearts their evil deeds, and deliberately hide their
face from Heaven's merciful light. The *Light* has come;
the responsibility *is now* with those who reject it (1 Kings
22. 8).

IV. **A Solemn Conclusion.** "This is the condemnation." The condemnation will be just, because they *loved*
the darkness. It is the *wilful* sinning for which there re-
maineth no more sacrifice (Heb. 10. 26). If a man turn
away from the sun, and refuse its light, then he can never
see any light more convincing. If the deep ocean of God's
mercy is reckoned too shallow to cover a man's sins, then
they can *never* be covered. The *presumptuous* soul shall be
cut off (Num. 15. 30). While ye have the Light, *believe*
in the Light. Yet a little while is the light with you.
Has not Jesus said, "I am the Light of the world; he that
followeth Me shall not walk in darkness, but shall have
the Light of life" (John 8. 12).

REPENT AND BELIEVE.

"The kingdom of God is at hand; repent ye, and believe the
Gospel" (Mark 1. 15).

I. **What is the Gospel?** It is the good news of—

1. THE LOVE OF GOD (John 3. 16). In giving His Son.

2. THE DEATH AND RESURRECTION OF CHRIST. His
atonement for sin, and acceptance by God.

3. THE GIFT OF THE HOLY SPIRIT. The witness and
the indweller.

4. THE COMING KINGDOM OF GLORY. He shall reign.

II. **What is Repentance?** It implies a change of
mind—

1. TOWARD GOD. Love, instead of slavish fear.

2. TOWARD CHRIST. Faith, instead of doubt.

3. TOWARD SIN. Hate, instead of delight.

4. TOWARD SELF. Loathing, instead of pride.

III. Why Should we Repent?

1. Because it is a great necessity (Luke 13. 3).

2. Because Christ commands it.

3. Because the kingdom of God is at hand.

4. Because He is exalted to give it (Acts 5. 31).

BUT WE SEE JESUS.
Hebrews 2. 9.

(1) SEE Him as *God's equal* (John 1. 3; Heb. 1. 3). (2) See Him in *great poverty* (2 Cor. 8. 9). (3) See Him in *deep sorrow* (Isa. 53). (4) See Him in *self-sacrificing love* (Matt. 20. 28). (5) See Him in *His unfailing obedience* (John 6. 38). (6) See Him in *His mighty power* (Eph. 1. 20, 21; Phil. 2. 9, 10). (7) See Him in *His infinite compassion* (Heb. 4. 15). (8) See Him in *great glory* (1 John 3. 2).

FOR OR AGAINST.
Luke 2. 23.

IN this chapter you may observe that (1) A *dumb* spirit makes a dumb man (v. 14). (2) An *unclean* spirit makes an unclean man (v. 24). (3) The *Holy Spirit* makes a *holy man* (v. 13).

I. What is Meant by being for Christ. This implies—
(1) Decision for Him. (2) Reconciliation to Him. (3) Companying with Him. (4) Working for Him.

II. What is Meant by being against Christ. We are
against Him when we (1) Reject His claim. (2) Neglect

His grace. (3) Refuse His company. (4) Despise His cause. (5) Persecute His people.

There is no neutral ground. FOR OR AGAINST.

COME TO THE REWARDER.

"He that cometh to God must believe that He is, and that He is a rewarder of them that diligently seek Him" (Heb. 11. 6).

I. **To Whom.** "To God." (1) To God *in Christ* (1 Cor. 5. 19). (2) To God *Almighty*. (3) To God as a *Father*.

II. **How to Come.** "Must believe." Must believe (1) That He is—His existence. (2) That He is a *rewarder*—His grace. (3) That He rewards them that *seek Him*—His faithfulness.

III. **What are His Rewards?** He rewards (1) The *seeking sinner* with salvation. (2) The *fighting saint* with ammunition. (3) The *suffering servant* with glorification (Rom. 8. 17, 18).

LOOK AND LIVE.
Isaiah 45. 22.

(1) A GREAT NEED—"Salvation." (2) AN EASY WAY—"Look." (3) A PERSONAL CLAIM—"Unto Me." (4) A WIDE INVITATION—"All the ends of the earth."

TRUST AND TESTIMONY.
Psalm 13. 5, 6.

I. **Mercy Accepted.** "I have trusted in Thy mercy." (1) God is *merciful*. (2) God requires *trust*.

II. **Salvation Enjoyed.** This salvation is: (1) Great—*Thy* salvation. (2) Joyful—"Rejoice." (3) Satisfying—"My *heart*."

III. Praise Rendered. "I will sing." (1) He only is worthy. (2) Praise becometh the saved.

IV. Testimony Given. "He hath dealt bountifully with me." This testimony is—(1) Needed. (2) Happy. (3) Helpful. ———

A GREAT WORK.

"We are His workmanship, created in Christ Jesus unto good works" (Eph. 2. 10).

I. The Work. "We are His workmanship, *created*." In saving man God has to do what He did at the beginning —create out of nothing. There is nothing good in man to begin with. "In me (that is, in my flesh) dwelleth *no good thing*" (Rom. 7. 18). "If any man be in Christ He is a *new creation*."

II. The Worker. "His workmanship." The worker is God. Like a skilful artist He selects His own material and implements. He asks no counsel. He doeth His own will. He speaks, and it is done; commands, and it stands fast. It is God that worketh in you. None can stay His hand from working.

III. The Workmanship. "*We* are." The character of the workman is seen in the workmanship. The beautiful sculpture or painting manifests the skill of the artist. *We* are the exhibitions of God's gracious handiwork. Every Christian is a monument of God's mercifulness, love, patience, and holiness. Are we a credit to Him who hath made and fashioned us after the image of His beloved Son? We are created *unto good works*. Fear not, He that hath begun a good work in you will carry it on (Phil. 1. 6; Rom. 8. 29).

IV. The Workshop. "Created *in* Christ Jesus." This article may be made in Germany, or anywhere else

wherever there is a soul abiding *in* Christ. *In* Christ Jesus
we are fashioned after the divine pattern. Abide in Him,
and you will abide in the workshop of Almighty grace.
"Ye are God's building" (1 Cor. 3. 9). Sinner, if you
want to be made a new creature, come into God's workshop. Come to Jesus, and He will work on you and in you
that which is pleasing in His sight.

THE MISSION OF CHRIST.

"Even the Son of Man came not to be ministered unto, but to
minister, and to give His life a ransom for many" (Matt. 20. 28).

EVERY twig on this golden branch is laden with the fruit
of Heaven. It is a great cluster of ripe grapes, full of the
new wine of the kingdom. Let us pluck them carefully
one by one.

1. HE CAME. Then He must have existed *before* He
came. Then He was not *driven* out of Heaven, but left
of His own good will. His pre-existence and infinite love
are herein revealed.

2. HE CAME AS THE SON OF MAN. He was the Son of
God, divine and eternal, but He appeared as the Son of
Humanity. He was in closest touch with God. He came
into closest touch with man, taking upon Him the likeness
of sinful flesh.

3. HE CAME NOT TO BE MINISTERED UNTO. He could
have had plenty of ministers had He desired them. All the
angels of Heaven, and all the laws and resources of Nature,
were at His call, but He came not to be served as a king.

4. HE CAME TO MINISTER. Man had nothing to give
Him. He had all the riches of the Godhead. He came to
minister to the need of poor, sinful humanity. Who else
could undertake such a mighty task? To this end He girt
Himself about with the towel of lowly service.

5. HE CAME TO GIVE HIS LIFE. Mark the words, HIS LIFE. Man had no *life* worth giving; in fact, no life to give. As a sinner against God all was already forfeited. Condemned already. What a life His was—pure, full, powerful! He yielded up all.

6. HE CAME TO GIVE HIS LIFE A RANSOM. Then a ransom was needed. Christ's death was substitutionary. He bore *our* sins in His own body on the tree. To whom was the ransom paid? Not to Satan, not to man, not to death, not to angels, but in answer to the inexorable holiness and justice of God. "It pleased the Lord to bruise Him. He hath put Him to grief" (Isa. 53. 10). "Behold the goodness and the severity of God" (Rom. 11. 22).

7. HE CAME TO GIVE HIS LIFE A RANSOM FOR MANY. His death was *"in the place of many."* This ransom is sufficient for the whole world (1 John 2. 2). It is a door as high as the throne of God, as low as man's deepest need, and as wide as "Whosoever will." Have you entered in?

THE GOSPEL OF CHRIST.

"I am not ashamed of the Gospel of Christ, for it is the power of God unto salvation to every one that believeth" (Rom. 1. 16).

THIS was Paul's bold and fearless testimony. The Gospel Christ preached to him on the way to Damascus revolutionised his whole life. Now he was neither ashamed of Him nor His words (Mark 8. 38). Those who are ashamed of the Gospel are utter strangers to its power.

I. **What Paul was not Ashamed of.** "The Gospel of Christ." There are some gospels that are not of Christ. "By their fruits ye shall know them" (Matt. 7. 16). The gospels of carnal reasoning and mere human effort can only lead to shame and confusion. The Gospel of Christ is the God-spell-binding news of—

1. DIVINE COMPASSION. The manifestation of infinite love toward guilty and perishing men—a love stronger than death.

2. ALMIGHTY REDEMPTION. The Redemption that is in Christ Jesus possesses infinite power, to satisfy all the holy demands of God's righteous character, and so to cover and cleanse every stain and sin of all who believe.

3. GLORIOUS RESURRECTION. Not only salvation from sin comes to us through Christ, but the sure hope of a glorified body—a body like unto *His own*—incorruptible.

4. ETERNAL SATISFACTION. "I shall be satisfied when I awake in His likeness" (Psa. 17. 15). The deeper yearnings of the inmost heart shall be fully met when we are made fit for His *everlasting* fellowship in the presence of the Father's glory. What a glorious Gospel this is!

II. Why he was not Ashamed of It.

1. BECAUSE IT IS THE POWER OF GOD. Oh, what a power seems pent up in the Gospel of Christ! There is in it the dynamic force of Almighty *love, mercy,* and *righteousness*—a love that melts the heart of stone; mercy in ocean fulness to cover every sin; righteousness, as pure as light, into which the trusting soul is brought; a threefold cord that is not easily broken.

2. BECAUSE IT IS THE POWER OF GOD UNTO SALVATION. The Gospel of Christ means the great strength of God concentrated and directed toward the *saving* of men. It takes the same power to save a soul as to create a world. Vain is the help of man. This salvation is twofold: The soul is saved from sin and wrath by being *reconciled* to God; the *life* is saved from fruitlessness and failure by being *yielded* up to Him. When a branch has been engrafted into a better stock, it is not only saved from its old life, but possessed and filled and used by the new life. It is a full salvation.

3. BECAUSE IT IS THE POWER OF GOD UNTO SALVATION TO EVERY ONE THAT BELIEVETH. Why is this salvation for *believers*? Because it is for the *heart*. "With the heart man believeth" (Rom. 10. 10). Sin has smitten man with heart disease; God, in mercy, has provided a heart cure. If the remedy is to touch the disease it must be received in the heart. A Chinese convert said, "I came first with my eyes, then with my ears, then with my heart." The provision is co-extensive with the need. "*To every one*" that believeth. "Ho, every one that thirsteth, *come ye* to the waters" (Isa. 55. 1).

SALVATION IMPOSSIBLE WITH MEN.
Matthew 19. 25, 26.

I. Salvation is Needed. "Who, then, can be saved?" All have sinned and come short of the glory of God, as seen in His holy law, so all alike need to be saved.

II. Salvation is Impossible with Man. It is impossible with man because—

1. HE CANNOT BLOT OUT HIS OWN SINS. They are written in the memory of God.

2. HE CANNOT ATONE FOR HIS OWN GUILT. The price is too great for one who is poor, and needy, and without strength.

3. HE CANNOT CHANGE HIS OWN HEART. It is deceitful, and desperately wicked. He cannot alter it any more than the Ethiopian can change his skin.

4. HE CANNOT PURCHASE SALVATION WITH HIS OWN WORKS. By the works of the law shall no flesh be justified in His sight.

III. Salvation is Possible with God.

1. BECAUSE THE OFFENCE IS AGAINST HIM. "Against Thee, Thee only, have I sinned" (Psa. 51. 4). "Father, I have sinned against Heaven and before Thee" (Luke 15. 18).

2. BECAUSE HE LOVES THE SINNER. "Herein is love, not that we loved God, but that He loved us" (1 John 4. 10).

3. BECAUSE HE LAID OUR SINS ON JESUS. "It pleased the Lord to bruise Him" (Isa. 53. 10). "Behold the Lamb of God, which taketh away the sin of the world" (John 1. 29).

4. BECAUSE HE IS MIGHTY TO SAVE. The things which are impossible with men are possible with God. "Look unto Me and be ye saved,.. FOR I AM GOD" (Isa. 45. 22).

QUICKENED FROM DEATH.

"You did He quicken when ye were dead through your trespasses and sins" (Eph. 2. 1, R.V.).

LIVING or dead, which? There is no middle state here. A man is either quickened or he is not. These two states include all.

I. **Their Past Condition.** "Ye were dead." Only those *alive* from the dead can realise that they *were dead*. It was—

1. A STATE OF SEPARATION. Every dead one has been cut off from the cause and power of life. Death separates a man from the bread and air so necessary for the living. Spiritual death means severance from the sustaining presence of God. No fitness to enjoy heavenly things.

2. A STATE OF INSENSIBILITY. The dead are neither charmed nor alarmed by anything said or done in their presence. They have neither tears nor fears concerning their sins or future state. Neither law nor Gospel moves them.

3. A STATE OF HELPLESSNESS. We never expect anything from the dead. Those dead in sins are *without* Christ, and so can do *nothing*—nothing by way of imparting divine life into their hearts. "While we were without strength, Christ died for us."

4. A STATE OF ABSOLUTE INCAPACITY. The dead have nothing in common with the living. They are repulsive, and altogether unfit for fellowship. While we were *in* our sins we were *out* of communion with God. Sin always has a *killing* effect. Death by sin!

II. **Their Present Enjoyment.** "You hath He quickened." LIFE is the only remedy for death. Man may come with his forms and garnishings, but they are worse than useless. God's method of saving from sins is QUICKENING. This implies—

1. IMPARTATION. It is the imparting of a new life by the direct energy of the Almighty Spirit of God. "You hath *He* quickened." Born from above. "The *gift* of God is eternal life" (Rom. 6. 23).

2. SEPARATION. When Lazarus got life he soon got out of the place of the dead. No one with Christ's healing touch on them will *dwell* among the tombs. When the light of life dawns we arise from the dead and come out from among them. Death separates from God; life separates from the things of death.

3. RESTORATION. A quickened one is not only restored to life, but to all the joys and responsibilities of the higher state—restored to God, to the fellowship of Christ, and the communion of the Holy Ghost.

4. CONSECRATION. This new life is to be all for God. "*Alive unto God*." Quickened *together with* Christ, that we might show the exceeding riches of His grace. Ye are not

your own. Your old life was a *dead one*, "alienated from the life of God." This new life is from God, that ye might glorify Him. "My life I give Thee."

TWO GREAT QUESTIONS.

1. To the Sinner. What hast thou done? (Gen. 3. 13).

2. To the Saviour. What hast Thou done? (John 18. 35).

A STRAIGHT QUESTION.

"How long wilt thou refuse to humble thyself before Me?'
(Exod. 10. 3).

Pharaoh, like many more in our own day, has frequently resisted the call of God.

I. **The Pride of Man.** Not to humble ourselves before Him is—

1. Foolish. It shows awful ignorance of God.

2. Presumptuous. A deliberate resisting of His will.

3. Vain. God will sooner or later break the pride of man. Haughtiness goes before destruction (Prov. 18. 12).

II. **The Question of God.** "How long wilt thou refuse?" This searching question is to us a revelation of—

1. The Grace of God. Why not smite at once with judgment? O the forbearance of God!

2. The Grief of God. "How long?" God asks as if His heart was pained to its very depths.

3. The Impatience of God. "How long?" as if His great patience and longsuffering were nearly exhausted. "My Spirit will not always strive with man" (Gen. 6. 3).

III. The Excuses Sometimes Offered. To God's "How long?" proud, self-satisfied man has many answers—

1. TILL A MORE CONVENIENT SEASON.

2. TILL I FEEL A LITTLE BETTER.

3. TILL I SETTLE DOWN IN LIFE.

4. TILL I RETIRE FROM BUSINESS.

5. TILL I COME TO DIE.

All this simply means: When my own time comes. Humble yourself, and God will lift you up (1 Peter 5. 6).

———

THE LOVE OF GOD.

"The love of God is shed abroad in our hearts by the Holy Ghost, which is given unto us" (Rom. 5 5).

I. The Character of this Love.

1 IT IS GOD'S LOVE. It is the nature of love to seek out the helpless and the needy, and to pour into the lap of poverty all the wealth of its possession. Love cannot remain inactive.

2. IT MANIFESTS ITSELF. "God commended His love toward us, in that, while we were yet sinners, Christ died for us" (Rom. 5. 8). Love will not hide; it overleaps every barrier and shows itself. "Herein is love; not that we loved God" (1 John 4. 10).

II. The Sphere of its Operation. It is not enough to see the evidences of God's love; His love is not satisfied with that. It is to be—

1. IN OUR HEARTS. In the citadel of the soul, watering the roots of our affections and purifying the springs of the life.

2. "SHED ABROAD." The love of God is to fill and flood our being, as the light of the sun is shed abroad on the earth, scattering darkness and turning barrenness into fruitfulness. If the love of God possesses us we shall take pleasure, like Him, in loving sinners and making sacrifice for their salvation. Love is the most practical thing on earth (see 1 Cor. 13).

III. **The Divine Operator.** This great work is done by—

1. THE HOLY GHOST. It is the Spirit's work to unveil the love of God to us in Christ Jesus, and to create that love within us. He sheds it abroad in our hearts by taking the things of Christ and showing them unto us.

2. THE HOLY GHOST GIVEN UNTO US. If our hearts are to be filled with the love of God, the Holy Spirit must have His abode within the heart. The fruit of the Spirit is love. "Because ye are sons, God hath sent forth the Spirit of His Son into your hearts" (Gal. 4. 6). Beloved, if God so loved us, then, in the power and after the manner of that love we ought also to love one another (1 John 4. 11).

THE LOVE OF CHRIST.
Ephesians 5. 1, 2.

I. **The Loving One.** "Christ loved us." "God is love." Christ is the Son of this living, loving God, and the very image of His Father. He is also the Son of Man made in the likeness of sinful flesh.

II. **The Objects of His Love.** "Loved us."

1. WHEN? While we were yet sinners. When dead in sin.

2. How? With a love that is divine, all-embracing, and stronger than death. He loved us more than the fallen angels; more than we loved ourselves; more than the angels of Heaven; more than He loved Himself. Behold, what love!

III. The Evidence of His Love. "He gave Himself for us." Man's love opens up gradually, and may manifest itself in gifts of ever-increasing value. The love of Christ gives all at the first. All the riches of God are embodied in "Himself." He gave Himself for us—

1. As a Voluntary Offering. The offering of Christ's life and work to God was an acceptable gift, well-pleasing in His sight. He offered Himself without spot. The heart of God was infinitely satisfied with the life and character of His beloved Son. He was obedient unto death.

2. As a Vicarious Sacrifice. "He gave Himself for us, an offering and a sacrifice to God." Here we have the thought of substitution. Christ died for us. He bore our sins in His own body on the tree.

3. As a Sweet-smelling Savour. There is a great difference between the savour of our carnal lives and the savour of the character of Jesus. "In me, that is, in my flesh, dwelleth no good." "In Him dwelleth all the fulness of God." "Ye are complete in Him."

IV. The Fruit of this Love in Us.

1. Followers of God. The love of Christ is to constrain us to be imitators of Him who loved us: imitators of His love, patience, purity, devotion, and self-constraining zeal. What poor imitations we are! May the Holy Spirit work in us His own good will, that we may be conformed unto the image of His Son!

2. WALKING IN LOVE. Following this new and divine pattern, our walk will be in a new and heavenly atmosphere. Abide in Him, and ye will walk in love.

TRANSFORMING GRACE.

"This grace wherein we stand', (Rom. 5. 2).

THE grace of God, which bringeth salvation, works a complete transformation in the character and relationship of all who believe. It changes our relationship—

1. TO GOD THE FATHER. No longer enemies, but sons; instead of being under the wrath of God, now under His special care.

2. TO CHRIST THE SON. We were without Him, and without hope, but now grace hath made us nigh—united to Him, cleansed by His blood, and kept by His power.

3. TO THE HOLY SPIRIT. Before He had no place in our hearts, which was like a cage full of unclean birds. Now He abides within as our Guide and Comforter.

4. TO THE LAW. Before grace came we were under the law, and, because of sin, under the curse. Now we are not under the law, but under grace, and the law is being fulfilled in us who walk after the Spirit.

5. TO THE POWER OF SIN. Sin used to have dominion over us; we were its slaves. Now its guilt has been cleansed and its power broken. Freed from sin.

6. TO THIS PRESENT WORLD. In times past we walked according to the course of this world. But now we have been chosen out of it, and sent into it to be witnesses for God against it (John 17). We used to love the world, but now we love not the world, and are hated by it.

7. To Good Works. Until grace came we trusted in our good works for salvation, but being saved by grace without them, we now become co-workers together with God.

8. To Trials and Afflictions. While unsaved all trials and afflictions were looked upon as enemies to our good. Now we know that "All things work together for our good" (Rom. 8. 28).

9. To Death. Before the grace of God was known death was clothed in robes of dreadful terror; its fear was ever and anon upon us. Now we know it to be a vanquished foe, and a gateway into glory. "O death, where is thy sting?" (1 Cor. 15. 55).

10. To the Judgment. When we wandered in the darkness of doubt and sin the prospect of judgment past an awful shadow over the soul. Now the judgment-seat for the faithful Christian means a place of reward.

"Grace, 'tis a charming sound!"

FORGIVENESS.
"To whom gave all the prophets witness that through His Name whosoever believeth in Him shall receive remission of sins."
(Act 10. 43).

I. Of Whom the Prophets Witnessed. "Him."

II. Their General Testimony. "*All* the prophets."

III. The Nature of their Testimony—

1. They testified to the *forgiveness of sins.*

2. That this forgiveness is only *through His Name.*

3. That this forgiveness is received through *faith.*

4. That *whosoever* believeth receiveth remission of sins

SEED THOUGHTS.

A CURE FOR THE UNCLEAN.
Matthew 8. 1-4.

I. **Who He Was.** "A leper." (1) Diseased, not sound; (2) Unclean, polluting; (3) Separated, shut out from fellowship and privilege; (4) Incurable, beyond all human skill and hope.

II. **What He Did.** (1) He came to Jesus, the fountain of living waters; (2) he came in the presence of the crowd, not ashamed; (3) he came worshipping Him, in deep, unfeigned reverence; (4) he came confessing his need, "Make me clean;" he acknowledged his real condition; (5) he came believing, "If Thou wilt, Thou canst."

III. **What He Received.** (1) The touch of Jesus, identification; (2) The word of Jesus, illumination; (3) The power of Jesus, salvation.

REPENTANCE.
Mark 6. 12.

THERE is no virtue in our repentance if it does not bring us to God. Mere sorrow for sin cannot lessen the guilt. There may be vexation, and yet no repentance. Bible repentance is a great necessity (Acts 17. 30). Here it is connected—(1) With turning from all iniquity (Ezek. 18. 30, 31). (2) With turning to God (Acts 26. 20). (3) With faith in Jesus Christ (Acts 20. 21). (4) With forgiveness of sins (Acts 3. 19). (5) With salvation (2 Cor. 7. 10). (6) With receiving the Holy Ghost (Acts 2. 38). (7) With joy in Heaven (Luke 15. 10). This is the repentance that needs not to be repented of.

SEEK AND FIND.
Matthew 7. 7-11.

I. A Threefold Attitude. (1) *Knock* at the door. (2) *Seek* the Master. (3) *Ask* what ye will.

II. A Threefold Promise. (1) It shall be opened. This means *acceptance*.

2. Ye shall find. This implies *fellowship*,

3. Ye shall receive. This is *satisfaction*.

III. A Threefold Encouragement—

1. Would a father give his son a stone for bread?

2. Would he give a serpent for a fish? Never.

3. Would your heavenly Father refuse to His children that which they cannot do without—Bread—Holy Spirit?

A LONGSUFFERING LORD.
2 Peter 3. 9.

1. The Character of the Lord—"Longsuffering, not willing that any should perish" (Isa. 30. 18).

2. The Objects of His Compassion "Usward"—"While we were yet sinners" (1 Tim. 2. 4).

3. The Purpose of His Patience—Salvation (1 Peter 3. 20).

4. The Great Need of Man—"All should come to repentance" (Ezek. 33. 11).

SAVED TO SERVICE.
Galatians 1. 15, 16.

1. A Divine Call—"Called by His grace."

2. A Divine Revelation—"Reveal His Son in Me."

3. A Divine Commission—"That I should *preach Him*."

REDEMPTION.
Ephesians 1. 7.

1. A Great Work Done—"Redemption through His blood."

2. A Great Blessing Secured—"Forgiveness of sins."

3. A Great Measure Used—"According to the riches of His grace."

4. A Great Necessity Implied—"*In* whom?" "If any man be in Christ he is a new creation."

"I AM THE LIGHT OF THE WORLD."
John 8. 12.

I. **Think of the Nature of this Saying.** What a revelation of Christ's character! What a consciousness of *unlimited* fulness!

II. **Think of the Light the World has had.** Light of science, philosophy, and of experience; yet, apart from Christ, it is a world rolling in spiritual darkness.

III. **Think of the Light Christ has Brought into the World.**

1. Light on the true character of God.

2. Light on the world's own character and need.

3. Light on the dark problems of human history.

4. Light on man's future and eternal destiny.

A DIVINE COMPLAINT.
"Hear, O heavens, . . my people do not consider" (Isa. 1. 2, 3).

THEY do not consider—(1) The cost of their purchase. (2) The all-sufficiency of their Saviour. (3) The claims of their Redeemer. (4) The purpose of their redemption. (5) The responsibility of their position. (6) The glory of their destiny.

THIS IS OUR GOD.
Isaiah 25. 9.

CONNECT this verse with "Behold the Lamb of God" (John 1. 29). In it there is the language of—

1. RECOGNITION. This is our God; my God.

2. ASTONISHMENT. "Lo, this is our God." "Behold the Man!" (John 19. 5).

3. EXPECTATION. "We have waited for Him." "Behold, He cometh with clouds" (Rev. 1. 7).

4. CONFIDENCE. "He will save us." He is the mighty to save.

5. APPROPRIATION. "We will be glad in His salvation."

6. EXULTATION. "We will rejoice."

HOW CAN A MAN BE JUST WITH GOD?
Job 9. 2.

1. THIS IS A COMMON QUESTION. It is being asked in every age, and belongs to every creature.

2. IT IS AN IMPORTANT QUESTION. Man's eternal destiny is connected with it.

3. IT IS A DIFFICULT QUESTION. No *man*, by mere human wisdom, can answer it. It is difficult (1) because of the character of God—holy, righteous, just; (2) because of the character of man—sinful, guilty, helpless.

4. IT IS A QUESTION MEN TRY TO ANSWER. They say— (1) God is merciful. (2) Man is not so very bad. (3) All will come right in the end.

5. IT IS A QUESTION GOD ALONE CAN ANSWER. (1) It is not of works (Rom. 3. 20). (2) It is by grace (Rom. 3. 24). (3) It is through the blood of Christ (Rom. 5. 9). (4) It is by faith (Rom. 4. 5).

A MIGHTY SAVIOUR.

"THEY shall call His Name Jesus, because He shall save His people"—(1) From sin. (2) From the fear of man. (3) From the bondage of self-consciousness. (4) From the burden of discontent. (5) From the tyranny of temper. (6) From drudgery in service. (7) From seeking the applause of Christians. (8) From doubting the providence of God.

Is this great salvation yours?

THE PEACE WHICH RULES.
Colossians 3. 15.

I. A Great Possession. "The Peace of God." (1) Peace through faith. (2) Peace that passeth understanding. (3) Peace the world cannot give.

II. A Gracious Calling. "To the which ye are called." Called of God. O hear Him!

III. A Blessed Rule. "Let the peace of God rule in your hearts." His yoke is easy. His burden is light. Submit to the reign of grace.

IV. A Simple Condition. "Let." The sun has arisen, open the window, let the light come in. Let the sceptre of His peace rule the heart and life.

V. A Grateful Result. "Be ye thankful." Be thankful that He is able, that His grace is sufficient, that He never fails.

A THREEFOLD PROVISION.
Psalm 104. 15.

1. *Bread* to Strengthen, ...   Christ.
2. *Oil* to Illumine, ...   Spirit.
3. *Wine* to Gladden, ...   Word.

ALL MEN SEEK THEE.
Mark 1. 37.

1. All men tired of sectarianism.
2. All men sick of mere theories.
3. All men who have found out their own helplessness.
4. All men who wish to be saved from sin.
5. All men who desire to have peace with God.
6. All men who want to be kept by Almighty grace.
7. All men who look for a kingdom of glory.

    To whom else can they go?

THE CHRISTIAN'S REWARD.
Revelation 2. 10.

1. The Condition—"Faithful unto death."
2. The Reward—"The Crown of Life" (R.V.).

CHRIST PASSED THE ANGELS.

1. When He sank far below them in His humiliation.
2. When He rose far above them in His exaltation. R.C.C.

THE GREAT SALVATION.
Hebrews 2. 3.

1. A Great Certainty, ... "Salvation."
2. A Great Possibility, ... "Neglect."
3. A Great Impossibility, ... "Escape."

JESUS SAVES.
Matthew 1. 21.

1, He came to save (Matt. 18. 11); 2, He came to save sinners (1 Tim. 1. 15); 3, He came to save by putting away sin (John 1. 29); 4, He came to save by His own blood (Col. 1. 14); 5, He came to save from all iniquity (Titus 2. 14); 6, He came to save because no one else can (Acts 4. 12).

ENMITY AGAINST GOD.
Romans 8. 7.

THE carnal mind shows its enmity—

1. By Trifling with the Name of God.
2. By Neglecting the Word of God.
3. By Sneering at the Work of God.
4. By Scoffing at the People of God.
5. By Unthankfulness for the Mercies of God.
6. By Resisting the Holy Spirit of God.
7. By Rejecting the Saving Son of God.

ALL MY SPRINGS ARE IN THEE.
Psalm 87. 7.

1. The Spring of Spiritual Life (Eph. 2. 1).
2. The Spring of Spiritual Power (Acts 1. 8).
3. The Spring of Spiritual Nourishment (Luke 4. 4).
4. The Spring of Spiritual Enjoyment (Rom. 5. 11).
5. The Spring of Spiritual Expectation (1 John 3. 2).

THE MIND OF CHRIST.
Philippians 2. 5.

HIS mind was—

1. A lowly mind (Matt. 11. 29; John 13. 4, 5).
2. A pure mind (Luke 22. 61; 1 Peter 2. 22).
3. A strong mind (Heb. 12. 3; Matt. 4. 10).
4. A fruitful mind (Matt. 4. 7; John 8. 29; 1 Peter 2. 23).
5. An unselfish mind (Rom. 15. 8; John 11. 35; 1 Peter 2.23).
6. A prayerful mind (Luke 6. 12; John 17).
7. A loving mind (Luke 23. 34; Eph. 5. 2).

Let *this mind* be in you.

"Ever gazing, loving, praising,
With the angel hosts above;
One eternal 'Hallelujah!'
One eternal song of love."

ILLUSTRATIONS.

PURITY.

EVERYBODY knows that certain fabrics, when exposed to the *open air*, will be bleached, or made whiter. But to get this cleansing there must be *complete exposure* to the purifying elements. So with the Christian life. There must be the entire surrendering up of all, and the continual and unreserved exposure of the whole sinner's heart and life to the purifying influence of the Holy Ghost.

THE GOSPEL.

IT is supposed that the *flavour* of every spice is to be found in Jamaica pepper. Not only the flavour, but the ingredient of every earthly and heavenly blessing is found in the glorious Gospel. It is a blessed compound of all the sweet spices of Jehovah's character. They are rich and satisfied who possess it. May it perfume all our hearts and lives!

TESTIMONY AND AFFLICTION.

FROM the *inner parts* of a certain tree in tropical Asia there is taken what is called "Aloes-wood." This wood is most fragrant when in the fire. There will be no fragrant testimony for God in the fires of affliction unless the *inner* man is kept sweet and thankful in fellowship with Jesus Christ.

THE NAME OF JESUS.

THE amulet carried about by the heathen is supposed to possess a *charm* against evil. The savour of His precious Name charms the heart *from* evil. Take the Name of Jesus with you.

WORD OF GOD.

THE slender, climbing, woody night-shade, with its red berries, has been called the "bitter-sweet," because when you chew its root it is first bitter, then sweet to the taste. The *convicting* Word of God may be very bitter to the soul at first, but afterwards it is sweeter than the honeycomb. To feel the sweetness of this divine root we must keep eating at it. "Thy Word was found, and I did eat it."

WATCH.

WHEN an army is on a campaign the soldiers have to "bivouac." That is, they spend the night in the open-air, and *every one* remains on guard. Ought not this to be the position of the Church of Christ, now at war against the world, the flesh, and the devil? The night is setting in. Let the Church bivouac—every one become a watchman. "What I say unto you, I say unto all, Watch!" (Mark 13. 37).

THE BLOOD OF JESUS.

THERE is a plant called "adder's wort," because it is supposed to cure the bite of the serpent. The divine adder's wort is the blood of Jesus Christ, which cleanses from all sin—every bite of the old serpent the devil. Wort means plant. Jesus is the plant of renown. Mighty to save!

THE GREAT COMMISSION.

WHEN a ship has been commissioned by one Government to make reprisals on the vessels of another Government it is said to carry a "letter of marque"—the mark of Royal authority. Every ship or subject belonging to the kingdom of God carries such a letter, and ought to make reprisals upon the souls and interests of those who are still the enemies of God, serving in the kingdom of Satan. Board them for God.

UNITY OF THE SPIRIT.

In the human body there is a muscle called the "adductor," because it draws one part of the body towards another. This is the work of the Holy Spirit in connection with the mystical body of Christ. The moving of this great "adductor" is much needed in these days.

REDEEM THE TIME.

In the year 1360, on Easter Monday, the army of Edward III. suffered terribly from the severity of the winter. That day is now known as "Black Monday." But is that the only black Monday? Does not a misspent Sunday always bring a black Monday? Bright days of privilege neglected are sure to bring dark days of remorse. Redeem the time.

THE HOLY SPIRIT.

Long ago, in Scotland, many people believed in the "kelpie," that was a spirit which was supposed to give those who were to be drowned an intimation of it, and assisted them in the drowning when the time came. There are many still who believe in the heavenly *kelpie*, a Spirit which intimates to men their need of salvation, and which assists them in being saved.

COMPROMISING.

In the North of Scotland, and in the time of Rob Roy, wealthy farmers used to pay regularly what was known as "black-mail"—so much corn or money given annually to powerful robbers for their goodwill and protection. If Christians are to maintain friendship with the world and ungodliness, it will only be on the "black-mail" principle, that is by sacrificing so much of their good for the encouragement of the others' evil. He that is the friend of the world is the enemy of God.

THE GOSPEL OF CHRIST.

THE mistletoe was called by the Druids "the all-heal," because wonderful cures were supposed to be wrought by it. The Gospel is not only "*the all-heal*" from Heaven, but also the *heal all*. It heals *all* who believe, as well as *perfectly heals* those who do believe.

PREJUDICE.

THE moral disease of prejudice, like the physical disease of jaundice, is characterised by the colouring of the eyes. If thine eye be single (pure), then thy whole body shall be full of light. If thine eye (jaundiced) offend thee, pluck it out. Prejudice bars the door against many a friend. It is the *open face* that is transformed into His likeness.

SECRET SINS.

THERE is a terrible disease called marasmus; it is a wasting of the flesh, without any apparent cause. The withering goes on, yet no disease is visible. Spiritual marasmus is a common malady. The life and testimony of the Christian may be slowly decaying, yet no outward fault or failure may be visible. There is secret sin, and the Holy Spirit has been grieved, so that the spiritual life and power is only the dried skeleton of what it once was. "Cleanse Thou me from secret faults" (Psa. 19. 12).

BEAUTIFUL INDIFFERENCE.

WHEN a man is callous and insensible he is said to be "marble-hearted." Yet everybody knows that marble can take on a most beautiful polish. It is possible to have a life highly polished, and to wear a great shine, and yet have a heart as dead and insensibile to the love of God as a bit of limestone. "With the heart, man believeth unto righteousness" (Rom. 10. 10).

DIVINE FORGETFULNESS.

POLITICAL offenders are sometimes granted what is called "an amnesty"—that means a *not remembering*. This is what God grants to all who submit to Him through His Son Jesus. No matter how many the offences, the God who is ready to pardon says, "Their sins and iniquities will I *remember no more*" (Heb. 10. 17).

SINS FORGOTTEN.

IN Greek mythology we read of a river in hell called *lethe*. Its waters were said to cause *forgetfulness* of the past to all who drank. The rich man in Luke 16 would have been glad to have drank such water. The river of forgetfulness is not in hell, but in Heaven. It comes from the very heart of God. "Their sins and iniquities will I *remember no more*" (Heb. 10. 17). Blessed lethe!

DIVINE LIFE.

THE finest variety of asbestos is the "Amianthus." It is so called because it is unpollutable and undestructible. Such is the divine life in the soul. That which is born of God cannot sin—cannot be touched with evil. It is also indestructible—it cannot perish.

THE FETTERS OF FEAR.

THE game of blind-man's-buff is a very old one, and, metaphorically, a very common one. The game was first to bind the eyes of one, then say, "Catch me." Of course it is easy to escape from the hands of one who is blindfolded. If men can only get the preacher afraid to offend them they have succeeded in binding up his eyes, and can afford to smile at his vain attempt to catch them. It is sad to see ministers in the pulpit every Sunday playing at blind-man's-buff. "The fear of man bringeth a snare" (Prov. 29. 25).

TESTIMONY.

THERE is a class of coal called "blind coal," because it burns without showing any flame. But although it shows no flame it may yield a good heat. If it cannot be *seen* it may be *felt*. Is it not possible to have a flaming lip testimony and yet the life to lack warmth? There are blind coal Christians, very useful ones, who are not to be *seen* so much as *felt*. Still it is better to have both flame and heat, both lip and life testimony.

SUPPORTING PROMISES.

IN some nurseries there are what are called "leading-strings." They are used to support children when beginning to walk. The children of God in these days have much need to keep by the divine leading-strings of God's sure promises, especially the babes in Christ, if they would learn to walk worthily. "Pride goeth before a fall" (Prov. 16. 18).

THE LIVING BREAD.

IN mythology we read of the food of the gods called "Ambrosia." This food was supposed to confer immortality upon all who partook of it. What the heathen so much felt the need of we have now offered to us in Christ Jesus. He is the Bread of Life. "He that eateth of this bread shall live for ever" (John 6. 58).

INSTABILITY.

A THING is said to be amorphous when it is without any determinate shape or form. Are there no professing Christians who might be designated so, who seem to be neither the shape of a true worldling nor the form of a true believer? Characterless; neither cold nor hot; savourless salt; good for nothing.

TREASURE IN HEAVEN.

THOSE who fawn and court the wealthy with the object of gaining a legacy are called "legacy-hunters." Those money-grubs will do anything to please if only they can get their name secured in the will. The Christian does not need to hunt for a legacy; he has got enough left him through the death of the Son of God. But he may well fawn and court the continual favour of Christ, doing all to please Him, and so laying up treasure in Heaven.

DEVOTEDNESS.

IT is said of the Amazonians—a race of female warriors— that they cut off their right breast that they might use their weapons more efficiently. Why should the soldiers of Christ not cut off everything that hinders them in their holy warfare? "If thy right hand offend thee (hinder thee), cut it off" (Matt. 5. 30). "Lay aside every weight" (Heb. 12. 1).

COWARDLINESS.

THERE is a certain moral disease peculiar to soldiers called "malingery." It means to feign sickness when there is some fighting to do. There are many malingerers in the religious camp when the trumpet of battle is sounded. They have no gifts; they can do nothing but talk about their leanness.

IN CHRIST'S STEAD.

EVERY Christian is, in a most real sense, a lieutenant for Christ. A lieutenant is one who *holds the place of another* in his absence. In the absence of Christ, the great Captain of Salvation, we are to act in His stead. Paul said, "We pray you, *in Christ's stead*, be ye reconciled to God" (2 Cor. 5. 20). What a responsibility! We shall need to give an account of our lieutenantship.

THE NEVER-WITHERING WORD.

THE richly-coloured amaranth is supposed to be a flower that never withers. They last long, but by and by they do fade away. They have a name to live, but they die. The promises of God are the true amaranths. They are *never*-withering flowers. "The words that I speak unto you they are spirit and life" (John 6. 23).

A BUSYBODY.

IN the common acceptance of the term a "busybody" is one to be shunned, because they are always busy about the *affairs of others*. By way of intermeddling with other people's affairs be not busybodies. But if we are to be followers of Jesus Christ we must, in another sense, be indeed "busybodies," minding the spiritual affairs and the temporal interests of others. In the way of looking after the affairs of Jesus Christ and His cause may we be busybodies. A busyless body is a useless body.

UNREALITY.

PERHAPS you have seen a man who had just got a snuff of "nitrous oxide" (laughing gas); how it excited his laughter. He was neither richer nor happier, yet he laughed loud and long. It was only gas. Covet not the laughter of the ungodly, nor the mirth of the worldling--it is only gas. The devil's bottle may seem to bring gladness, but it is only the mirth of fools—the hollow mockery of laughing gas. Judge not by the outward appearance.

HUMAN LIFE.

WHAT is a "*breve*?" In *writing* it is a *short* note; in *music* it is a *long* note. What is your life? Is it a short, hurried scrawl? or is it a long, musical note of sweetness? In any case it is a breve—a note that, if it is short, may be by the grace of God made sweet.

THE MARKET CROSS.

IN ancient times a cross used to be set up at the place where the market was to be held. If strangers asked where they could get such and such things they were told to go to the cross for them. The Cross of Christ is God's market-place for the world. Stranger, if you want pardon, life, and rest, go to the Cross. But you must buy *without money*.

HOLY FIRE.

LONG ago certain wonderful virtues were superstitiously attached to what was called "need-fire." This was generated by friction. By rubbing two sticks together this wonder-working flame was supposed to come from God. The Holy Spirit is the "need-fire" of this present time. He will come into the heart as a living flame, in answer to the continued pleading of the soul. Then great and marvellous things will be done.

HYPOCRISY.

SOCIETY, so-called, often has its times of masquerade. They love to disguise themselves that they may participate in some new pleasure which they could not have without the mask. In matters of religion how many are only masquerading—putting on the disguise for some selfish pleasure—deceiving and being deceived. The time is coming when every mask must be torn off, and every hidden thing revealed. "Be not deceived; God is not mocked" (Gal. 6. 7).

CHOOSE THE BEST.

THE ancient Romans doubtless thought themselves wise in choosing the biggest star in the heavens as their god—Jupiter (*the father of heaven*). Let Jesus—the brightest and best—be our choice. He is "the chiefest among ten thousand" (S. of S. 5. 10), and the "altogether lovely" (S. of S. 5. 16)—the Star which brightens into eternal day.

POWER NEEDED.

WHO has not seen the Volunteers at drill? They have good guns, they *aim* well, they shoot, you see the fire, and hear the noise, but it is only a blank cartridge. It is powerless. Is it not possible for preachers to use the bulletless cartridge? We may have a good sermon, mean well, and have a grand *delivery*—both loud and fiery—yet entirely powerless to slay the enmity of the human heart against God. Without the power of the Holy Ghost the sermon is only a blank cartridge (1 Cor. 4. 19, 20).

PLEASURES OF SIN.

THIEVES and robbers have what they call their "junkering times;" times when they feast in secret on stolen goods, banqueting on forbidden fare. Their hardness of heart is seen in the fact that they really enjoy such devilish delights. What shall we say of those Christians who can find *pleasure* in those things which are displeasing to God? Delighting at times in a stolen entertainment, it may be a book, a friendship, or a lust.

CLEANSED BY FIRE.

To *bream* a ship meant to cleanse off all the seaweed, shells, stones, etc., by the process of *burning*. It was cleansed by fire. Every fiery trial is for the purging of the soul. There are little things that lodge in our hearts. They grow and multiply till they become *weights* and hinder our progress in the Christian life. When the fire of the Holy Ghost comes upon us, or fills us, those habits or lusts, which are but excrescences on the new life, are soon burnt off.

> " Come as the fire and purge our hearts
>   Like sacrificial flame;
> Let our whole soul an offering be
>   To our Redeemer's name."

ROOTED IN CHRIST.

A NEOPHYTE is *one newly planted*. This is the name given by the Romish Church to one newly admitted to a monastery. They are to be pitied who get planted in such barren soil. Those planted in Christ have their roots where all the fulness of the Godhead dwells. "Every plant which My heavenly Father hath not planted shall be rooted up" (Matt. 15. 13).

SIN AND GUILT.

THE ancients used to make drinking-cups of the amethyst, supposing that they prevented drunkenness. But the blue amethyst could not prevent the *blues*. The cup of sinful pleasure, no matter how beautiful, will not save from guilt and judgment. "Be sure your sin will find you out" (Numb. 32. 23).

SECRET CHRISTIANS.

THE microscope has revealed to man an unknown world of living animals, but God knew that they were there, and had them all numbered. There may be many Christians living unseen and unknown to men, although the microscoptic eye of God discerns their living form; but how very small they are! "Ye are the light of the world" (Matt. 5.14).

REST AND PROGRESS.

REST does not mean inactivity or uselessness. We are being whirled through space while we rest on the earth. While we rest in the train or steamboat we are being rapidly carried along; so while we rest in Christ we grow in grace, and are being filled with His fulness, as the branch grows and is fruitful through its absorbing of or resting in the vine. Of course much depends on where we rest. "Come unto *Me*, and I will give your rest. Take My yoke upon you, and learn of Me" (Matt. 11. 28).

MY SHEEP.

SHEEP have no means of defence; they have neither wings nor swiftness of foot; they flock together, but their numbers do not increase their strength. Their only safety lies in the power and carefulness of the shepherd. We are the sheep of His pasture, and can be fed and defended by no one else. "Live by faith on the Son of God" (Gal. 11. 20). "The Lord is my Shepherd" (Psa. 23. 1).

POISONOUS SELF.

THE rattlesnake is well known and justly dreaded as the most venomous and deadly of all reptiles. Dr. Bell has proved that its poison is even secreted *after* death. Sinful self is the rattlesnake which every Christian has to fear. While we reckon ourselves dead, and have crucified the flesh with its lusts, even while we are *dissecting self*, we are in danger of being poisoned by it. "Cease from man" (Isa. 2. 22).

SPIRITUAL BREATHLESSNESS.

A MAN is said to be breathless when he is out of breath or much exhausted and unfit for work. What a fuss some people make when they do a little work for the cause of Christ. They are out of breath for a week after it, and can talk about nothing else. It is wonderful how long-winded some professing Christians are when talking about the things of the world, and yet they pant and puff and seem utterly breathless when spiritual things are being dealt with. This spiritual asthma is the result of diseased respiratory organs, brought on by breathing the foul air of worldliness, and neglecting the fresh and healthful air of secret prayer and holy fellowship with God. A man not filled with the Holy Ghost will always be a *breathless* man. Breathless men make poor workmen. "Be filled with the Spirit" (Eph. 5. 18).

THE CHURCH.

THE Church has been called the "Bride of the Lamb" (Rev. 21. 9). The name *bride* literally means one owned or purchased. Christ's bride is *owned* by Him, because she was *purchased* by His own precious blood. Every believer in Jesus is a purchased one; every purchased one will be owned by Him. "The Lord knoweth them that are His" (2 Tim. 2. 19).

LIFE INSURANCE.

EVERYBODY is familiar with the Life Insurance Society. But, after all, no society can insure life for a single moment. It may insure money at *death*, but that is not insuring life. The only *life insurance* for man is in the Gospel of the grace of God—union with the ever living Son of God. "He that believeth in ME shall *never die*" (John 11. 26). Is your life insured?

A BEAUTIFUL NAME.

IT is said that the "angel fish" is remarkable for its voraciousness and ugliness, being allied to the shark family. You would expect a different character from such a heavenly name. The name does not make it angelic in nature. We may put on angelic looks, even when we have a sharky heart. We may have the Name of Christ, while the heart is at enmity with God.

PRIDE.

PRIDE and ambition are twin brothers. The word "ambition" had its origin in Rome, from candidates going about seeking votes. Seeking the honour that comes from men is an unholy ambition, and betrays a pride of heart which is opposed to the Spirit of Jesus Christ. If God be for us, then we have the majority, and should not canvass for the favour of men.

THE PURE WORD.

THE reddish dye of the "anotta tree" (South America) is largely used in colouring butter and cheese. Some like them all the better because of the colouring. In any case, the pure Word of God needs no colouring. Man has nothing to add to it to make it any better. But the colouring process does go on. The Word is mixed with human wisdom to make it more palatable to the unregenerate mind. So much do men love the colouring that they will not have the pure milk and butter without it. Some even seem to swallow the colouring, and nothing else.

THE BREAKWATER PROMISE.

A BARRIER is frequently erected outside the harbour to break the force of the waves, and so protect the ships lying in port. "All things work together for good to them that love God" (Rom. 8. 28). This precious promise surrounds the Christian in every circumstance, and breaks the force of every wave of trouble that would dash in and disturb the ship of peace resting in the harbour of the heart.

WHAT IS MAN?

MAN has been very aptly designated a "microcosm," that is, "a little world"—a little world full of great possibilities, a little world wrapt up in the darkness of sin and death or rolling in the light of eternal day, a little world of chaos, confusion, and disorder because of rebellion against God, or of harmony, fruitfulness, and beauty because of obedience to God; a world loved by God, and for which Christ died, and in which the Spirit of God desires to brood and dwell; a world that may be saved and transformed into a paradise of God, or lost and burned up in the flames of eternal wrath. "What is man that Thou visitest him?" (Heb. 2. 6).

AMBASSADORS FOR CHRIST.

SAILORS have sometimes to use what they call a "jury-mast." This is a temporary mast which takes the place and does the work of the one which has been carried away with the storm. Christ was carried away with the storm of human indignation and hate. We as Christians are now in "Christ's stead" (2 Cor. 5. 20)—doing His work in His place. Our work is also like the "jury-mast"—very temporary, only for a little while.

AFFLICTION.

To *temper* metals they must be subjected to great heat and cooled slowly, otherwise they would become brittle and easily broken. Paul had been well tempered in the furnace of trial when able to say, "I have *learned* in whatsoever state I am, therewith to be content" (Phil. 4. 11). Those easily discouraged have not been well tempered. "It was good for me that I was afflicted" (Psa. 119. 71).

NONCONFORMISTS.

THERE are more Nonconformists than those who refused to conform to the Established Church at the Restoration of Charles II. Every Christian is called of God to be conformed to the image of His Son (Rom. 8. 29). We talk about the "noble Nonconformist conscience." May it be noble, indeed, in not conforming to the world. If our lives are not being conformed to the likeness of Him who hath called us, then are we Nonconformists indeed.

VOLUNTEERS OR REGULARS.

WHEN a man joins the Volunteers he offers himself for military training, but only for home service; but when a man joins the Regulars he offers himself for service anywhere. Are you a volunteer or a regular in the service of Christ? Are you willing to go anywhere for Jesus?

LOVING THE DARKNESS.

"Nyctalopia" is a peculiar disease causing such a defect of vision that objects can only be seen *by night*. The brighter the day the more blind do such become. Are there not many Christians who seem afflicted with a kind of spiritual nyctalopia? They like just a little light. The bright sunshine of a wholly consecrated life pains their weak and diseased eyes. They love the *darkness* rather than the light, because there is some hidden evil within.

THE HOLY SPIRIT.

There is a certain key called the "master-key," because it is so constructed that it can open many locks. The master-key to the Scriptures is the Holy Spirit. He can unlock every hidden truth. He has come to guide us into all truth. He takes the unsearchable riches of Christ and shows them unto us. They are always getting fresh visions of secret things who possess this master-key. Have you got it?

DOUBLE-MINDEDNESS.

Bunyan speaks about Mr. Face-both-ways. He is the image of indecision, like the amphipod, whose feet are directed both ways; as the sand-hoppers, which do not pledge themselves to go either way, and who can go as easily backwards as forwards. Such are the double-minded—unstable in all their ways.

POISONOUS THOUGHTS.

It is said that the hair of Medusa—one of the Gorgons—was turned into snakes. What a venomous head he must have had! When the thoughts and imaginations of men are evil, and only evil continually, what a headful of moral snakes he possesses! Unclean thoughts are venomous vipers. Shake them off into the fire.

SPIRITUAL LUNG POWER.

WHEN a man is afflicted with asthma it cannot be hid; every breath he draws is a confession of it. Are there not many Christians troubled with a breathing difficulty. Every time they pray they seem more like being choked. They do not breathe freely in the presence of God. Their spiritual lung-power is very low. They have need to pray, "Come, O breath!" (Ezek. 37. 9).

SIN IN THE HEART.

THAT little lump in front of the throat has been called "Adam's apple," from the idea that the forbidden fruit stuck in Adam's throat. The sin did not stick in his throat; it went deeper down into the very springs of his being. The heart is deceitful. It is still the belief of many that a man may have a good heart and a bad life. "Out of the heart are the issues of life" (Prov. 4. 23).

CHRIST, THE MIDDLEMAN.

A MIDDLEMAN in Ireland is one who rents large tracts of land and lets it out in portions to the peasantry. Jesus Christ has rented large tracts in the heavenly kingdom. He portions it out to the peasantry of the skies—to the poor in this world who are rich in faith. "In My Father's house are many mansions; I go to prepare a place for you" (John 14. 2).

INCONSISTENCY.

THE fabled mermaid had the upper part like a woman and the lower like a fish. Beautiful in the distance, but repulsive when near. The mermaid Christian is no fable. They put on the form, but deny the power. The visible part of their character is attractive, but the hidden part is brutish. "As a man thinketh in his heart, so is he" before God (Prov. 23. 7).

LITTLE DEEDS.

WE gaze with admiration on the wide-spreading branches of the great oak which has braved the storms of centuries. How came it there? Who planted it? A little squirrel dropped a little acorn into that spot hundreds of years ago. "Behold, how great a matter a little fire kindleth!" (James 3. 5). What will be the outcome in the ages of eternity of the seeds of Divine Truth and kindness sown now in the Name of Jesus? Even a cup of cold water shall not lose its reward. The rewards in the world to come last for ever. Be fruitful.

RIGHTLY DIVIDING THE WORD.

TEA-BLENDING has become quite an art in these latter days. The great object is to make it palatable to all. The flavour is the chief thing. It is also quite an art in these days to mix up the thoughts of men with the Word of God, and so blend (corrupt) them that itching ears are highly pleased with it. Law and Gospel, works and faith, are so artfully blended that unrenewed hearts receive it gladly. But we are not told to rightly blend the Word, but to rightly divide it.

FASCINATION OF SIN.

THE rattlesnake is justly dreaded. Mr. Murray says: "When the piercing eye of the rattlesnake is fixed upon them (birds), terror and amazement render them incapable of escaping, and while involuntarily keeping their eyes fixed on those of the reptile, birds have been seen to drop into its mouth as if paralysed, squirrels descend from the trees, and leverets run into the jaws of the expecting devourers." Many young men, in like manner, fall helplessly into the destructive jaws of sin, because they keep looking at it until its fascinating eye overcomes them. "Turn ye, turn ye, why will ye die?" (Ezek. 33. 11).

OUT AND OUT.

AMPHIBIOUS animals, which have a double life, and can live equally well in sea or land, are no use for man. The amphibious religious professor, who feels equally at home in the world or the Church, who finds pleasure both in sins and sermons, is useless for God. "I would thou wert cold or hot" (Rev. 3. 15).

PLEASURES OF SIN.

CONNECTED with the lotus tree, in North Africa, is the fable that if strangers eat of its fruit it will make them forget their home. The fruit of the lotus tree of sin has made many forget their heavenly home. As pilgrims and strangers on the earth, beware of this lotus tree. Moses refused to eat of its fruit (Heb. 11. 25). Abraham looked for a city.

ONE THING I DO.

"MONOMANIA" has been defined as "madness to one subject." One subject is about enough for any one man who wishes to fathom and master it. Paul was a monomaniac when he said, "This one thing I do" (Phil. 3. 13). The Christian who wishes to know nothing among men, save Jesus Christ, will be reckoned by the many-sided worldling as a madman. But such madmen have a blessed asylum in their Father's house above.

TEMPTATIONS.

THE "fishing-frog" has been named the "sea-devil," because it is supposed to allure and catch little fishes by means of worm-like appendages at its mouth. How many delusive appendages has the drink-devil dangling at its mouth? Burns' clubs, fishing clubs, free suppers, etc. Silly men catch at these, and get devoured. The attractions of sin are but the tempting worms hanging on the lips of the old serpent the devil. Be not deceived.

SING OF HIS LOVE.

SOME of the ancient lyric poets of Germany were called "love-singers," because the subjects of their productions were generally love and beauty. Is there not room for more love-singers among the patriots of the heavenly fatherland? If the love of God is shed abroad in our hearts, and our eyes feasted on Him who is altogether lovely, surely we ought to take rank among the royal "love-singers." Oh, sing of His love!

PARALYSING FEAR.

THERE is a "fear which is the beginning of wisdom" (Psa. 111. 10)—the filial fear of God—but why should a son of God be paralysed and stupified at the sight of the enemy, like a partridge struck with stupor and so overcome with fear at the sight of a vulture, or sparrow-hawk, that it loses all power of self-control until its enemy has disappeared? Our enemies are great and deadly, but greater is He that is with us. The threatening attitude of present-day evil should in no way hinder the faith and activities of the servant of Jesus Christ.

PRIVILEGE AND SUPPLY.

A MILITARY officer sometimes receives what is called a "brevet," that is, a commission to take rank above that for which he receives pay. His place of honour is exalted, but his *income* is not increased. His responsibility is greater, but the supply is not enlarged. Thank God, there are no *brevets* in the Lord's service, although the devil has been preaching it for centuries, and many Christians seem to believe him. For every *enlarged* privilege in the service of Jesus Christ there is given an increase of supply. *According* to your day, so shall your strength be. "My grace is sufficient for you" (2 Cor. 12. 9).

AFFLICTION.

BEAUTIFUL figures and statuettes are made of a fine species of unglazed porcelain called "bisque." It is so called because it has twice passed through the furnace. A double portion of the fiery trial may only be fitting as the more perfectly to bear the image of Him who is the image of the invisible God. "Perfect through sufferings" (Heb. 2. 10).

BORN AGAIN.

SPENSER uses the word "misborn" in connection with those whose lives are full of evil and misfortune. Sooner or later every life will turn out an evil and a misfortune that has been born in a wrong direction—born of the flesh. The only true and effectual remedy is to be "born again"— born of God. "Ye must be born again" (John 3. 7).

THE GOOSE NATURE.

THE goose has always been a name of reproach. Darwin says, "This bird deserves some notice, as hardly any other anciently domesticated bird has varied so little." It seems that centuries have not improved the goose. In this it resembles the "carnal mind"—unchanged, and unchangeable in midst of all the advances of the ages. The unrenewed nature of man has proved inflexible—apart from regeneration—to all the higher influences of the spiritual kingdom.

WORD OF GOD.

THE kaleidoscope is an ingenious optical instrument in which you may see an endless variety of colours and forms. It is to be feared that many use the Bible after the same fashion and pretty much for the same purpose— they turn it about merely to gratify their curiosity. The Word of God is a sword, a hammer, and a fire—something to be felt more than admired.

REVIVING NEEDED.

THE Rev. J. G. Wood, in his "Homes without Hands, tells of an artificial colony of ants prepared for experiment, that when the ants got languid and ceased to work for lack of moisture a slight shower of spray would set them all in activity with renewed energy. Many a Church is inactive and dormant in aggressive work for God for lack of the heavenly refreshing. A *shower* of blessing would do more to stir up its drowsy members to work than miles of barren sermons. "I will be as the dew unto Israel" (Hosea 14. 5).

PRAYER.

IT is one of the greatest wonders of this inventive age that two little instruments in tune with each other, although a thousand miles apart, can respond to each other. The roaring sea, or towering mountains, cannot interrupt, as long as the instruments are true to each other. In tune with the will of God, what can hinder prayer? It is said that the only danger of disturbance in wireless communication lies in too *much sunshine*. Let not prosperity disturb your fellowship with Him. Get right with God.